Learn, From an Unknown
Author, The Art of Forging Unknown Facts into Fabulous Fables

Some Unknown Facts of American History
The Saga of Governor Pierpont

Col. Julian G. Hearne, Jr.
Army of the United States

McClain Printing Company
Parsons, West Virginia

1987

International Standard Book No. 0-9618158-0-9
Library of Congress Catalog Card No. 87-90754
Printed in the United States of America
Copyright © 1987 by Julian G. Hearne, Jr. (Retired)
Wheeling, West Virginia
All Rights Reserved

Photo, by courtesy of the late Delf Norona

Statue of Francis Harrison Pierpont
in Statuary Hall in the National Capitol

It was executed by Franklin Simmons, an American sculptor residing in Rome, Italy, under a contract entered into 11 August, 1902, with the Pierpont Statue Commission, which was created by the West Virginia Legislature by an act passed 22 January, 1901. It was unveiled 30 April, 1910.

Contemporary photo, by courtesy of the late Delf Norona

The Capitol of Virginia in Wheeling
Noon 20 June, 1861 — Noon 20 June, 1863

Known locally as "The Old Custom House." this building was the Custom House, Federal Court Rooms, Post Office, and offices of various federal Government officials. Thomas Hornbrook, Surveyor of Customs, was generous to the Restored Government of Virginia, and provided space for numerous state government officers and for legislative and convention sessions as well.

Photo by Jack Robey, 1973

The Capitol of Virginia in Alexandria
26 August, 1863 — 23 May, 1865, by proclamations
of Governor Pierpont

Located at 413-415 Prince Street, this building became the
seat of the Restored Government of Virginia and the Governor's
mansion; it had been the business office of the Potomac Bank
Company, chartered by Congress in 1806. It is now a privately
owned apartment house, not open to the public or sightseers. It
bears a plaque on a side-wall not visible from the sidewalk.

Courtesy of the Virginia State Library, Richmond, Virginia

Richmond Capitol, Richmond, Virginia
May 1865

TABLE OF CONTENTS

Foreword by a Virginian.....................................i

Foreword by a West Virginian...............................iii

Preface..v

Acknowledgements...xiv

The Saga Of Governor Pierpont And The Restored
    Government Of Virginia..................................1
        Part I — Paucity Of Publicity........................1
        Part II — The Saga Surges...........................3
        Part III — Epilogue — Spelling Of Surname..........21
        Part IV — Notes — Citations Explained..............22
        Part V — Aftermath Of The War — The
           American Union..................................27

APPENDIX

Chapter I — The Molding Of Mythology From
    Molehills Into Mountains...............................33

Chapter II — How Prevalent Is Mythology In
    Other Historical Writings?.............................51

Chapter III — The University Press Of Va. And
    Its Book *The Governors Of Virginia*
    The Party Line: Conflict Of Interests?................54

Chapter IV — Sectionalism In West Virginia................59

Chapter V — The Courts Looked The Other Way..............64

Chapter VI — Fables, Facts & A Miracle Too...............68
    Additional Comment By Hearne..........................71

Chapter VII — Virginia's Old Capitol In Wheeling —
Another Independence Hall?............................73
    The Building Itself.................................80

Chapter VIII — The West Virginia Debt Case...............82

Chapter IX — West Virginia Political Chronology
1860-1863 86
    1860...86
    1861...87
    1862...90
    1863...91

Chapter X — Virginia Bill Of Rights......................93

Chapter XI — Virginia's Consent To Transfer
Of Counties..96

Chapter XII — President Johnson's Executive
Order, 9 May 1865, Recognizing Pierpont As
Governor Of Virginia.................................98

Chapter XIII — President Johnson's Proclamation
Appointing A Provisional Governor Of
North Carolina......................................100

Chapter XIV — First (Congressional) Reconstruction
Act, 2 March 1867...................................103

Chapter XV — Resolutions of First Post-War General
Assembly in Richmond, under Alexandria
Constitution 106

Chapter XVI — Orders Terminating Governor
Pierpont's Administration And Appointing Henry H.
Wells Governor Of Virginia..........................109

Chapter XVII — Reports Of Cases In Supreme Court
Of Appeals Of Virginia, Richmond....................110

Chapter XVIII — Virginia vs. West Virginia, 78
U.S. 39, Dec. Term, 1870 (Abstract),
Relating To Berkeley And Jefferson Counties.........125

Chapter XIX — Historical Synopsis Of The Changes
In Virginia Law And Constitution 1860-1872
By George W. Munford................................135

Chapter XX — Sketch Of The Formation Of West
  Virginia From The Territory Of Virginia
    By John Marshall Hagans.............................168

Biographical Sketch Of The Author.......................210

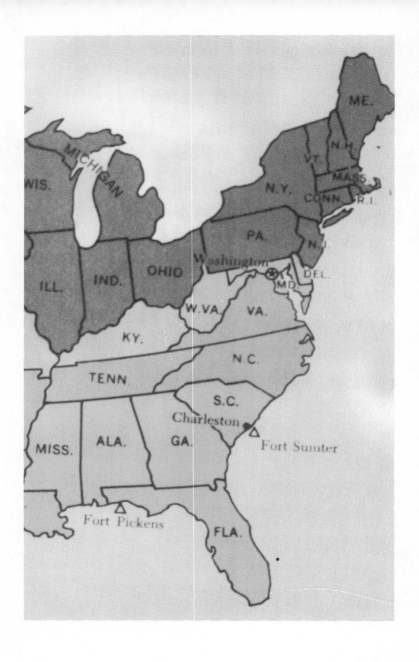

Foreword by a Virginian

It is difficult for a Virginian to accept the fact that any son or daughter of the Old Dominion could secede from their beloved Commonwealth in the time of her greatest need; and I am also sure that it must have been equally difficult for most western Virginians of that era to forgive those who favored secession from the Union for which Virginia's hero, George Washington, had played such a large and gallant role in establishing. On both sides of the Alleghenies each person searched in his own soul and made the judgment he believed to be both right and just. Those who chose to don the blue felt just as righteous as those who opted for the grey. For every Robert E. Lee adherent, there must have been an equal number of less known devotees of the Union cause.

Col. "Jule" Hearne has produced a carefully researched book which should delight historians, for it gives insight into the western Virginian (and, later, the West Virginian) mind of the period and explains why the "mountaineers" chose to remain in the Union and to fight for the Union, albeit nearly ten thousand men from west of the Appalachian Mountains joined the Confederate forces. Maryland, Kentucky, Tennessee and Missouri furnished many men for both sides, but Virginia was the only state to suffer dismemberment because of the War Between the States, Col. Hearne gives the reasons for this divorce and candidly states that the constitutionality of the procedure by which it was obtained had to be confirmed by the result of the war itself.

Col. Hearne has pinpointed and corrected numerous errors which have accumulated in historical writings throughout the many decades since Appomattox and he has brought to light a number of facts and points of law which have remained unpublished, some of which appear to be have been (deliberately?) withheld. And from the text as a whole Francis Harrison Pierpont emerges with a greatly enhanced stature as a citizen and a chief executive of Virginia who deserves recognition as belonging among those who are considered "great."

This book deserves careful reading since it explains in detail what actually happened during the divorce of western Virginia and thereafter throughout the duration of the Pierpont administration.

i

It is in fact an unpublicized chapter of Virginia history.

Elie Weeks

Mr. Weeks is well-known among Virginia historians, having written many articles for various publications circulating within the Commonwealth. He was a past president of the Goochland County Historical Society and served as chairman of the Military Map Committee of the Virginia Bicentennial Commission. Mr. Weeks graduated from this life during the winter of 1984.

Foreword by a West Virginian

West Virginians who know little else about their history know about Francis H. Pierpont. He was the Founding Father, wasn't he? The proud, independent mountaineer who stood firm with the Union when Virginia sought sovereignty in secession?

Well, yes and no.

Initially, at least, Pierpont did not think of himself as a West Virginian. "Western," surely, from Marion County, but not "West, by Gawd."

He did not set out to create a second state where one, stretching from the Tidewater to the Ohio, had been enough.

Thus let us move to the question which still obscures what happened at the First Wheeling Convention, which convened on May 13, 1861, before the Virginia electorate voted on the Ordinance of Secession, and the Second Wheeling Convention of June 11, 1861, after Virginia had taken itself out of the Union and joined with the Confederacy:

Was it as Pierpont had hoped it would be, the "restored" government of Virginia, or only the rash misdeed of some "rump" parliament of hotheads wandering in the wilderness west of the mountains?

Was it legitimate or illegitimate, the misbegotten off-spring of some wayward parentage with scant regard for the legal niceties?

Was it *de jure,* as lawyers like to phrase it, or merely *de facto* another phrase whereby lawyers can acknowledge a fact without giving their professional blessing?

In the larger, historical view, none of this matters greatly now. Events write history; historians spend decades thereafter trying to figure out what happened and why.

When the fury unleashed at Fort Sumter had spent itself and subsided at last in the stillness at Appomattox, West Virginia was a state, and there was no one left to challenge the reality. The sword had accomplished what the pen might not have written, and the pen acquiesced.

But before history buffs in general and West Virginians in particular there remain those absorbing technicialities on a common theme: did fact follow form?

The answers are the subject of Col. Hearne's thesis in another

iii

assessment of the separation, and he brings to his task a refreshing look at Francis Pierpont's life and its impact upon the founding, a skilled forensic touch in his agrument and, withal, a nice regard for sensibilities on both sides of the Appalachian Mountains.

Col. Hearne is not interested in the revival of hostilities. Peace with honor and union is better.

Clarification, rectification and a broader canvas are his objects, and Virginians of either persuasion — east or west — will find in his narrative a chapter in their history too little and often garbled and glossed over.

Indeed, Americans generally, with an eye for their origins and their experiments in freedom, will find in it a further dimension to their understanding. As Col. Hearne writes, it reveals "a sequence of events and a leadership which, though but regional in scope, are as much a part of their country's history as, for example, the Bear Flag Republic in California, and is no less thrilling."

J. D. Maurce

J. D. Maurice won a Pulitzer Prize in 1975 for his series of editorials on the Kanawha County (W. Va.) textbook controversy. Maurice is currently a contributing editor for the Charleston (W. Va.) Daily Mail.

Preface

The purpose of this book is to present to the American people generally, and to Virginians and West Virginians especially, a portrait of a man who became a governor of Virginia; who, like Governor Sam Houston of Texas, stood by the Union when his state purported to secede from the Union. But, unlike Houston, he was overlooked by the late John F. Kennedy for inclusion in his best-selling book of a generation or so ago, entitled *Profiles in Courage*.

An additional purpose of equal priority is to make known to the world a unique saga of the Civil War and reconstruction period which has been withheld from publication for, lo, a century and many moons more! As this saga — of Governor Pierpont and the Restored Government of Virginia — unfolds, it will become apparent that the Restored Government was *de jure* from its very inception, and that the consent of its legislature to the transfer of certain counties of Virginia to become the new state of West Virginia was in accord with the Constitution of the United States.

If this book concerned the Alamo, you would likely "remember the Alamo" and Davy Crockett, Jim Bowie and other heroes of that episode in American history; but it's dollars to doughnuts (in pre-inflation United States currency) that you never heard of Pierpont or the Restored Government of Virginia. Therefore, I now offer in capsule form just enough background information so that you may follow the text without having to "peek" ahead. So here goes:

(1) In April of 1861 a convention of Virginia citizens meeting in Richmond adopted an "ordinance of secession" whereby they intended to take Virginia out of the federal Union; they placed the state's armed forces — principally militia — under the supreme command of "President" Jefferson Davis; they entered into an agreement to join the so-called "Confederate States of America;" and they suffered the Confederate flag to be flown from the staff of the state's capitol after suffering Old Glory to be torn down and desecrated;

(2) In June of that year a convention of Virginia citizens from the areas west of the Appalachian Mountains met in Wheeling (then a city of Virginia) and declared that the Richmond convention's action trying to take the state out of the Union was null and

void; that all state offices held by Confederates had thereby become vacant; that a new government would be formed to replace the Richmond state government; that the new government would be called "The Restored Government of Virginia;" and they then proceeded to elect Pierpont governor of the whole state of Virginia;

(3) The Wheeling Convention met again in August and set up the machinery whereby West Virginia would become a state;

(4) The legislature of the Restored Government gave Virginia's consent to this transfer of western Virginia counties to the new state; Congress ratified the transaction; and so it was that West Virginia entered the Union on 20 June 1863; and

(5) The Confederate government of Virgina denounced the deal as not having had the consent of "the real" Virginia, in that the Confederate Virginians had had no voice in the matter.

There you have it in the proverbial nutshell!

This saga will, I feel sure, come as *news* to the great majority of readers everywhere, despite its antiquity. To most native Virginians I daresay it may come as something of a shock, for they will find that it contradicts portions of history taught them in their public schools and that it is at odds with many current beliefs held and taken for granted by Virginians generally throughout the Commonwealth. Indeed, it will reveal to most of them an entirely new (and probably astonishing) chapter of Virginia history heretofore not taught and scarcely ever hinted. And many West Virginians will likewise be astonished to learn that Mr. Pierpont was neither a governor of West Virginia nor did he even become a citizen of their state until he left Virginia and returned to Fairmont from Richmond sometime after April, 1868. They will also learn that the Restored Government of Virginia did not instantly meld into the new government of West Virginia when that state entered the Union on 20 June 1863.

In accomplishing its stated purposes, this book now becomes the *only* book that presents an historical sketch of the high spots of the Restored Government of Virginia and Governor Pierpont's administration from start to finish. Nothing of significance has been omitted. Errors appearing in past writings have been identified and corrected, and new material uncovered in my own research is included; and I believe it to be a fair statement that the saga herein presented does in fact present unpublicized chapters of the history of Virginia and West Virginia and portrays Mr. Pierpont as a great governor of Virginia. Now, at long last, this book should set the record straight in both states!

A book having purposes such as this one has must be read and understood by the *general public* — not just by historians, teachers, and lawyers, but also the butchers, bakers, and candle-stick makers as well; or, as precinct workers and political pros are wont to say, it must be read "at the grassroots level" to accomplish its missions. Now *this particular* book consists mainly of appendix of such length to be appropriate for scholarly research and is not likely to entice one to read it; in fact, it is more likely to turn off the would-be reader UNLESS he is assured at the very beginning — in the preface — that the *saga* is the main thing, the very thrust, so to speak, of the entire tome. I have purposely written the saga in everyday, "grassroots" language and have limited it in length so as to be entirely readable by anyone of average eyesight in not much more than an hour. If the reader's interest is then aroused to the point of wanting documentation for statements in the text, the notes following the saga can be read in no more than an additional fifteen minutes. And, as I sincerely hope, if the historians, teachers, newscasters, and lawyers — plus a large component of "grassrooters" — want even more on the subject, the appendix is supplied to provide the additional information they desire. Indeed, as shown in the appendix itself, there is a vast accumulation of misinformation which has been building up for more than a century, and much — if not most — of it has been and is now accepted as gospel, even by prestigious writers whose honor and veracity have not been questioned. They, in turn, have passed and are passing it on — albeit unwittingly — to an unknowledgeable public. Therefore, this book may be equated to the pouch of ammunition pebbles carried by an unheard of David, with enough such pellets to shoot holes in the hundreds of supposedly authoritative tomes written by a host of Goliaths in the fields of literature and history during the past twelve decades. It follows that hundreds of pebbles must be readily at hand, making the appendix essential. Furthermore, as Mark Twain wrote in *A Tramp Aboard*: "Nothing gives such weight and dignity to a book as an Appendix." — *Herodotus*.

Who am I to argue a point against the Father of History?

In the following pages I propose to demonstrate that, under the actual circumstances then existing, the Restored Government of Virginia was *de jure* from its inception. I also propose to show that the consent given by its Legislature to the transfer of counties from the territory of the Old Dominion to form a new state was strictly in accord with the applicable provisions of the United States Constitution, regardless of anyone's opinion as to the "righteousness" of such transfer, and notwithstanding anyone's opinion that the consent so given was a "legal fiction" or some form of "technicality." On the other hand, I do not deny the right of others to disagree with me on any point IF in so doing they recognize and accept all applicable and established facts *and* points of *law*. Then, IF they frankly concede that their disagreement with established facts or points of law is given as "dissenting opinion," they may hold forth for as many pages as they believe the reader can digest. From the foregoing it is as natural as mint is to julep that no person having the degree of doctor of history should regard his diploma as a license to doctor history, not for anyone at all knowingly to give out gossip the guise of gospel!

This book relates primarily to the Restored Government of Virginia and to Governor Pierpont's impact thereon. Granted that the Legislature of that government gave Virginia's consent to the formation of West Virginia from her territory, neither the governor nor the Legislature as such or acting in their respective official capacities played any other major on-stage role in the dismemberment of the Old Dominion. Instead, it was the Virginia Convention that met in Wheeling in June 1861 and reassembled there in August of that year that played in the center ring under the big top insofar as the formation of West Virginia was concerned. Therefore, the formation of West Virginia is scarcely touched in the saga which follows. However, the formation of West Virginia is set out sufficiently in the appendix by Messrs. Munford and Hagans.

I have made a sincere effort to refrain from moralizing in this saga and to express no opinion of approbation or censure for any decision made or action taken by any governmental body or officer, whether Confederate or Union. How well I may have succeeded is for you to determine.

Due to the frequency with which these terms are employed in this book, I believe it well define them in the beginning.

De jure: Of right; legitimate; lawful; by right and just title.

De facto: A phrase used to characterize an officer or government, a past action, or a state of affairs which actually exists and must be accepted for all practical purposes, even though it be illegal or illegitimate.

Inasmuch as this book relates to the manner in which new states may be admitted to the Union, Clause 1, Section 3 of Article IV of the Constitution of the Unites States is set out verbatim:

New States may be admitted by the Congress into this Union; but no new State shall be formed or erected within the Jurisdiction of any other State, nor any State be formed by the Junction of two or more States, or Parts of States; without the consent of the Legislatures of the States concerned as well as the Congress.

Col. Julian G. Hearne, Jr.
Army of the U.S. (Retired)

20 May 1982

ADDENDA TO ORIGINAL PREFACE OF MAY, 1982
Updating to time of going to press.
Evolution of the Manuscript

The manuscript for this book began early in 1964, and has had several titles and has increased in length from the five or six pages appropriate for a state magazine such as "Virginia Cavalcade," to the book as now finally in print.

The primary purpose in the beginning was to introduce to the 99% of Virginians who had never heard of Governor Pierpont, as well as to those who had heard of him, but knew only the "party line." The original title was "Governor Pierpont in Proper Perspective."

But simply because no one had ever heard of any relevant court decision, and were constantly disputing my writing in whatever its state simply because some other writer had offered a book purporting to contradict me on some supposed fact or point of law, I finally had to include an appendix to provide nuts and bolts to hold the saga together. By the time Washington's birthday of 1982 rolled around, when my friend Elie Weeks (the Virginia historian who wrote a foreword hereto) went with me to see the senior editor of the University Press of Virginia in Charlottesville, the manuscript was nearly as it now stands. That publisher rejected my offering; whether or not a conflict of interest occurred, I know not. Others will have to decide that point, if indeed there is such a point.

By March of 1986, I had found a publisher in West Virginia, and when the manuscript was ready to go to press, he had gone into bankruptcy. This was not due to any fault with his publications but to some ill-advised adventures aside from publishing. He was and is an honorable man, and a good publisher. I regret his failure.

Jim Comstock of "West Virginia Hillbilly" Fame Takes Over Publication Duties

In August of 1986, Jim Comstock came to the rescue of this manuscript. He recommended a change in title — one that would not appear to limit its interest to readers inhabiting a certain region only, but to indicate that the Saga of Governor Pierpont is ideal as an example of how history books of any state or even nation can be distorted 180 degrees off-course, whether intentionally, neglegantly by failure to do the proper homework (including visits to law libraries), or by short cuts in order to make a fast buck — such as by transient writers offering to some society to write its history or to some chamber of commerce to write a picture story book boosting the town's reputation, or what-have you.

Having given much thought to this, I realized that my example (in the appendix) of a 1908 Texas school history book is probably the most honest one even today; and that a Canadian provincial school board threw out their texts on Russian history simply because they taught that the USSR frequently violated treaties they had made; and that the book "Blood Over Texas" (also in the appendix) brought out facts that may well be considered conclusive that Mexico taunted the United States so much that our country simply had to take up arms.

All of which reminded me that as recently as 1985, a publication apparently promulgated by a federal agency at taxpayers expense which disclosed what may well be considered a deliberate misstatement on an important fact of history. This will be shown in the following subtitle.

"Social Security" — A Newspaper Supplement Which Conveyed Misinformation To The Public At Taxpayers' Expense

On Tuesday, August 13, 1985, there appeared in many, if not most daily newspapers in the United States a special supplement entitled "Social Security." It appeared to have been written by some bureaucrat at the federal Social Security Administration, and undoubtedly it presented that agency's official position on the subject. I now shall quote therefrom a few extracts which appeared in both of the Wheeling journals on that date:

"In August 1985, this country will mark the 50th anniversary of the Social Security program. President Franklin Delano Roosevelt's message to congress in support of the proposal stated: 'Security for the individual and for the family concerns primarily with three factors. People want decent homes to live in; they want to locate them where they can engage in productive work; and they want some safeguards against misfortunes which cannot be wholly eliminated.' "

"The passage of this legislation and the role the government assumed was certainly not unique in world history. In fact, some modern industrial nations of Europe had social insurance systems in place nearly 50 years prior to our system.

"But over the years one thing has remained constant — the concept that the social security system is an orderly transfer of income from current workers to retirees . . ."

Succeeding sections or paragraphs of the same item go on to relate the many extensions of the social security system, from the basic provisions down through medicare and the numerous benefits thereof; and it goes on to state that many workers [now] find that the taxes they pay no longer bring the higher returns of prior years. *But this is simply because the program has matured, and this maturing has always been expected by the original planners of the program.*" [Emphasis added]

And finally, in this same newspaper supplement item, it goes on to state that "In the years to come, aspects of the program will be reassessed, and adjustments may be made to payroll taxes, benefits, [and so forth]. *Whatever modifications may lie ahead, some form of massive transfer from workers to retirees will continue to be a major part of the system in the foreseeable future.*" [Emphasis added]

"SS Remains Strong
After 50 Years"

Now it must be conceded that it is certainly true that this system does indeed transfer funds from each younger generation to the elders, although the headline as to the system being strong after 50 years may be open to question. But certainly this was not the original intention of the 1935 act as passed by congress.

The original concept was that upon reaching a certain age the beneficiary would be entitled to benefits to *supplement* his retirement pay from sources other than Uncle Sam. Remember President Roosevelt's statement that the beneficiaries wanted to have home near their work. It was to be based on acturial statistics just how much taxes would be required from both employee and employer to pay for the benefits, and such taxes were to go into a social security trust fund for the sole purpose of having funds drawing interest and assuring availability for the retirees as they become eligible. It was a sound basis and there was no understanding then that one generation would pay for its elders; it was a system wherein each retiree felt — correctly — that he had paid for the benefits, and his dignity was not impaired. It amounted to insurance as known commercially, but administered by Uncle Sam isntead of private enterprise. Which system is better suited is not material here, and this book takes no stand on that point.

It is fortunate for posterity that there remain a very few of

x

those in congress who voted to pass the 1935 first social security act who are still living and in good health. One of those representatives was Honorable Jennings Randolph, of Randolph County, West Virginia. He went on to become a United States senator and voted on various additions to the social security system. He has read the foregoing paragraphs of the social security system as presented in the newspaper supplement, and has authorized this author and the publisher of this book to quote his concurrence that the original system, as enacted in 1935, was indeed based on actuarial statistics and that the taxes derived therefrom were to be placed in a special trust fund for beneficiaries as they became eligible, and meanwhile to draw interest thereon.

Let there be no doubt that this book does not pass judgement on the merits of any of the numerous additions to the social security system enacted by both Democrat and Republican administrations over the last fifty years. But it does seem to be the prevailing opinion of the beneficiaries that, "I paid taxes for these benefits; I am not taking a hand-out which I do not deserve."

It is this author's belief that the newspaper supplement discussed was a deliberate attempt to mold fables from facts; and to editorialize on the government's policies rather than to report facts.

This is but one example of the doctoring of history that some very few present day writers who hold doctor diplomas seem to regard as license to peddle gossip in the guise of gospel.

HISTORY TEXTBOOKS IN PUBLIC SCHOOLS
Failure To Teach The Role Of Religion
And Morals In The Birth And
Development Of Our Country

The Intelligencer, Wheeling, W.Va., in its issue of Friday, 17 October 1986, carried a column by Mr. David E. Anderson, religious writer for United Press International; and another column by Mr. Gary Baker, Under-Secretary of the United States Department of Education, whose column was taken from the Fall, 1986 issue of *Policy Review*, quarterly journal of The Heritage Foundation.

These items emphasized the importance of religion and morals in the founding and development of our country, and the "dumbing down" of these roles in school history books. Mr. Anderson states that "there is substantial evidence available from recent studies that many textbooks used in the nation's schools virtually ignore religion, thereby distorting the historical record, denigrating religion, and depriving students of knowledge of America's religious heritage." Mr. Bower concludes that "our children are not taught those basic principles on which there is little disagreement: honesty, loyalty, patriotism, courtesy, responsibility." He then goes on to state "a recent department of education study finds that there is a shocking bias against religion in textbooks. The Pilgrims, for example, are identified as 'people who make long trips,' and Christmas is defined as "a warm time for special foods.' "

I respectfully submit that these shortcomings in school history textbooks give an extremely biased and distorted concept of the birth and development of our country; but it did not shock me to read *The Intelligencer* on that October morning; I have been a subscriber to *AIM Report* for more than ten years. (Accuracy in Media, Inc., 1275 K Street, N.W., Suite 1150, Washington, D.C. 20005, Mr. Reed Irvine, Editor.) There is proof abundant that The Art of Forging Forsaken Facts into Fabulous Fables has been well known and profusely applied by many — too many — journalists, columnists, newscasters and authors of books constantly working at it; although a goodly portion of those engaged in forging fabulous fables from forsaken facts are not aware that in downgrading religion, morals and family training they are but spreading the communist-atheistic doctrine, which is to a large extent orchestrated from Moscow.

Our country was very literally — repeat "literally" — born unashamedly as a Christian nation. The late Justice Joseph Story of the United States Supreme Court, in an appendix to his renowned "Story on the Constitution" (1872) quotes the preamble to the Treaty of Paris, 3 September 1783, by which His Britannic Majesty acknowledged the independence and sovereignty of our United States of America; and I now quote verbatim the one line preamble to that treaty:

"In The Name Of The Most Holy And Undivided Trinity"

Now it so happens that one John Jay was a draftsman and signer of that treaty on behalf of the United States. And who was that Mr. Jay? Well, he later became the first Chief Justice of the United States Supreme Court, that's who! Furthermore, he was a member — along with George Washington — of the constitutional convention of 1787 in Philadelphia. And I submit that President George Washington and Chief Justice John Jay knew a whole lot more about the intent and construction of the constitution and the first amendment than do executives, jurists and legislators of today. And it is interesting to note that President Washington, in his "Farewell Address," refers to them as "mere" politicians and who, along with the "pious" man, should observe the necessity of complying with the dictates of religion and morals in the conduct of government.

The full text from which the foregoing extracted quote from the *Farewell Address* is so important that it ought to be set out in full:

"Of all the dispositions and habits which lead to political prosperity, religion and morality are indispensible supports. In vain would that man claim the tribute of patriotism, who should labor to subvert these great pillars of human happiness, these firmest props of the duties of men and citizens. The mere politician, equally with the pious man, ought to respect and cherish them. A volume could not trace all their connections with private and public felicity. Let it be asked the security of property, for reputation, for life, if the sense

xii

of religious obligation *desert* the oaths which are the instruments of investigation in the courts of justice? And let us with caution indulge the supposition that morality can be maintained without religion . . . It is substantially true, then that virtue or morality is a necessary spring of popular government. The rule, indeed, extends with more or less force to every species of free government. Who, that is a sincere friend of it, can look with indifference upon attempts to shake the foundation of the fabric?''

Having read the admonition of the Father of our Country, what do you think he would have thought of the Art of Forging Forsaken Facts into Fabulous Fables? Especially if the cost of such forging were to be at the expense of the taxpayers?

It occurs to me that no true history of California can be complete without recording the role played by the Franciscan monks who were the mainspring of the early settlements of the Golden State. Working for no compensation other than the satisfaction of serving God and fellow men; frequently walking from San Diego to San Francisco — and sometimes to Mexico City — these brave and Holy men are as important to history as are, for example, Lewis and Clark, Kit Carson, and Zebulon Pike. Roger Williams, founder of the State of Rhode Island and the Providence Plantations, left Massachusetts to settle where he could find more religious freedom. And the Mormon founders of Utah instilled into the citizens of that state the doctrine of sanctity of obligations under contracts and morality in business dealings. Limitation of space prevents any further examples. But think for a moment; there is hardly an area of congressional district size in the United States which does not have some religious background. Numerous citations are readily at hand. Providence, a city with a name of religious origin, abuts the Atlantic Ocean, and San Francisco abuts the Pacific; St. Paul is way up north and Corpus Christi is way down south, with St. Louis in between. Our two earliest cities, St. Augustine and Santa Fe, have religious names. The National Anthem's fourth (but little known) verse written during the War of 1812, praises "the Power that hath made and preserved us a nation;" and "this be our motto, 'in God is our trust!' "

The Saga of Governor Pierpont, which is the primary subject of this book, relates exactly how a sequence of events which led to the forging of West Virginia from Virginia territory, and how that sequence was and still is being told without regard to facts and points of law. Religion and morals were not at issue, but doctoring of history — mostly unwittingly — occurred and is occurring just as much as religion and morals are distorted in school history books. And the appendix to this book is rife with examples of the art of forging forsaken facts into fabulous fables. The school book distortions, however, are nearly always concocted at taxpayer expense.

Col. Julian G. Hearne, Jr.
Army of the United States (Ret.)

12 November 1986

xiii

Acknowledgements

In the spring of 1963, the West Virginia centennial year (remember when first class postage was only five cents and the Post Office Department — not Postal Service — issued a commemorative stamp for the occasion on June 20th with Wheeling as the first place of issuance?), I began writing a manuscript for an article entitled *"Some Unpublicized History of West Virginia and the Restored Government of Virginia,"* which was published in the *West Virginia Law Review* in December 1963 by the College of Law, West Virginia University, Morgantown. It was not written in lawyer lingo, but for the general public. Nevertheless, as is the case with many if not nearly all law review items, it was read by practically no laymen, and I venture to guess by very few attorneys, although one circuit court judge who was a history buff sent me by registered mail the file of a case which I had mentioned in the article. I had stated that I did not know what happened on appeal because I could not locate the record, and this judge sent the record to me with a plea not to lose it and to return it soon by registered mail. I guess he is one of the persons to whom I am really indebted, but I shall not give his name because he could be sent to the hoosegow for such an act if the statute of limitations has not run out by now.

Well, that subject captured my interest to such an extent that during the next ten years — until the graduation of my wife from this life — I devoted so much of my off-duty time to library research, writing and so forth that she began calling herself the "widow Pierpont." To her memory I am indebted beyond comparison with any other person! Since then, until this book is published, I have been so continually engaged in "Pierponting and Restored Governmenting" that I have had no time for anything else, except now and then to practice an art at which I have become an expert since my retirement in 1975. that being the art of doing NOTHING!

All of which means that ever since the spring of 1963 until right now I have been helped by so many persons that I cannot remember as many as half of their number — which could run as high as several hundred. To name some and neglect the others does not strike me as the way to play cricket (even if I knew how to play that game of "sticky wickets," which MI 5 personnel in Her Majesty's service are want to say.) They know who they are, however, and they know that I am aware of my deep gratitude for their help, without which this book could not have seen the light of day. Some people might say, however, that such a fate might well have been a boon to mankind — or is it "personkind" these days?

So I say sincerely to all those to whom I am beholden, "Whenever you come my way, please drop in for a drink and a chat!"

The Saga of Governor Pierpont and the Restored Government of Virginia

"I was born in Virginia. I desire to live in Virginia when this rebellion is subdued. I hope to see the old flag shortly unfurled in every county in the State, and the people acknowledging its majesty, and acknowledging with uplifted hands, the Constitution it represents to be the supreme law of the land. I never expect to have the *love* and *sympathy* of the rebels; but by the grace of God by doing *right*, I intend to command their respect. My ardent desire and sincere prayer is, that this rebellion may be speedily crushed, that freedom may be enjoyed, not only in the State, but in all the broad limits of the nation, and that when the impartial historian comes to make up the record, he may be able truthfully to publish, that in accomplishing this great result the Government never sanctioned a *wrong* that was done to any man, however humble." — *Concluding paragraph of Governor Pierpont's fifty-five page letter to the President and the Congress of the United States on the subject of abuse of military power in the command of Gen. Butler in Virginia and North Carolina, dated 18 April 1864.*

PART I
PAUCITY OF PUBLICITY

The general neglect of historians and other writers in the Old Dominion to publicize Governor Pierpont and the Restored Government of Virginia in any way[1], and their practice of characterizing them as "pretenders" or "usurpers" when necessary to refer to them at all[2] seems to have created a consensus within the state that they deserve no place in the heart of any loyal Virginian. That feeling came upon this author while doing research in the Alexandria Library in 1963 and finding that the pages were uncut in the chapter on Pierpont in Volume XI of *Calendar of Virginia State Papers,* although that tome had been published several decades before and bore evidence of much use.

Following Appomattox, the General Assembly of Virginia ex-

1

pressed its approval of the Johnson Administration's policy toward their Commonwealth in Joint Resolution No. 1, passed 6 February 1866; but it was about that time that the Radical Republicans, both in the Congress and throughout the country began to take a dim view of the president's handling of ex-Confederate affairs and became hell-bent on revenge. The bitterness thereby generated in the hearts and minds of Virginians, plus the ingrained feeling that Virginia had lost her western counties by means which they considered the equivalent of downright fraud, waned only at a snail's pace thereafter for as long as any ex-Confederate veteran remained alive. Thus, when Governor Pierpont's statue was unveiled in the nation's capitol in 1910, the Virginia congressional delegation was conspicuous by its absence, although this proceeding had been made the order of business for both the House and Senate.[3]

Fifty-three years later, 20 June 1963 to be precise, it is doubtful to the n*th* power that any ex-Confederate was yet living, and Mother Virginia deigned to recognize the centennial observance of the birth of her youngest daughter, West Virginia; but she sent her attorney general instead of the governor to represent her in Charleston, although the president of the United States was there in person![4] And a year later on 28 October 1964 the managing editor of a magazine published by the Virginia State Library in Richmond rejected an article written in support of the proposition that the Restored Government had been the *de jure* government throughout the Civil War.[5] In doing so, he gave as his reasons:

> "Articles for the magazine should not argue to a point. We cannot accept the premises of your article. We consider that the Richmond government was the *de facto* and *de jure* government of Virginia, while the Wheeling Assembly was an unconsitutional rump."

And so it was that the audience of an official state publication was denied the opportunity to read a presentation of the case against the dogma espoused by its editorial staff. It may be wondered, then, whether that magazine still regarded Governor Pierpont and other western Virginians who had met in Wheeling in 1861 as "evil disposed and traitorous" citizens, as they had been dubbed in a resolution of the Confederate Legislature of Virginia in 1863[6]. And once that same Virginia State Library purveyed a book entitled *A Hornbook of Virginia History,* which tells its readers (on page 90): "Soon after Lee's surrender, Pierpont was named Provisional Governor and sent to Richmond to re-establish civil government for the state." As this book will disclose, that statement is incorrect; but it seems to follow a pattern established many years ago, and there is no doubt that it expresses the belief of Virginians in general, even though many of them may not have read the *Hornbook*. This is what was taught in the public schools from at least 1954 until 1974 when a new method of teaching was introduced.[7]

Nearly twelve decades have now elasped since Appomattox, yet very little, if any, effort has been made to dispel the ever-prevailing notions that West Virginia is the "bastard child of a political rape''; that the Confederate Richmond government was *de jure* until Appomattox; and that thereafter Mr. Pierpont was designated by President Johnson as "provisional" governor and "sent to Richmond" to start from scratch to set up a brand-new government (presumably to do the bidding of the president) for the war-weary but proud and self-reliant Commonwealth!

Thus, and again it must be said, however unwittingly, there remains untold a saga of which all Virginians may be justly proud and which in no way casts reflection on the honor or glory of Confederate Virginian or any of her illustrious sons or daughters. While at the same time this saga brings to attention another great Virginian, from the west, who deserves to be honored with the other great governors of the Commonwealth, but who so far has been denied that recognition because of misinformation concerning him, much of which originated during the heat of a fratricidal war.

But this saga concerns more than the two Virginias, for the American people countrywide have been and are being denied knowledge of a sequence of events and leadership which, though but regional in scope, are as much a part of their country's history as, for example, the Bear Flag Republic in California and is no less thrilling!

PART II
The Saga Surges

Some eminent-*ologist* (or maybe he was a *-trician* or a *-tician*) in some prestigious field of academia once propounded a principle which could well bear his name:

"For every action there is an equal and opposite reaction.''

And sure enough, Virginia's action in adopting her Ordinance of Secession on 17 April 1861, just a few days after South Carolina artillery had bombarded Fort Sumter, was followed closely by her transfer of allegiance to the so-called "Confederate States of America" (Old Glory was torn from the capitol flagstaff in Richmond on 19 April and immediately replaced by the Confederate flag). Command of the Virginia military forces, both offensive and defensive, was given to Jefferson Davis — all these actions occurred well before 23 May (the date set for a referedum on the question of ratification or rejection of the secession ordinance) there promptly came an "equal and opposite reaction," at which point in time (the 1980s way of saying "when") the saga of Governor Pierpont and the Restored Government of Virginia began. As a contemporary writer put it:

No government existed in Virginia recognized by the Constitution of the United States; therefore it was the duty of the people to erect one. It was an absolute duty not confined to the impositions of responsibility resting on civilized men, but impelled by the discharge of a high patriotic trust, in the interest of constitutional government.[8]

3

On 11 June 1861 a convention assembled in Wheeling, Virginia which consisted of citizens from counties west of the Alleghenies. This had occurred as a natural result of the Ordinance of Secession because those counties had voted against secession at the 23 May election by figures revealing anything from a "landslide" on down to a "comfortable majority," depending on whose figures any given writer chose to quote. (For example, Virginius Dabney, on page 244 of his excellent *Virginia, The New Dominion* cites the statewide vote as 128,884 for secession and 32,134 against, but the school books on page 408 cite the figures as 125,000 for and 20,000 against.) It was a "natural result" for another reason as well, in that, as stated by a contemporary writer:

> "For thirty years before the rebellion the people of the eastern and western parts of the state had been in a condition of absolute hostility; and from the writer's earliest recollection the candidate for the legislature from the western part of the state, in order to secure the suffrage of the people of his district, was compelled to pledge his influence, if elected, to the principle of a division of the state, and this pledge had to be given, no matter of what political faith he was."[9]

That much, at least, is the subject of brief comment in school books used prior to 1975.[10] For many years there had been discontent in western Virginia, growing out of unequal taxation coupled with the ever-present question of human slavery. The slaves of the eastern plantations were by law assessed and taxed on one basis while the cattle and other personal property of the westerners were assessed and taxed upon another and greater basis. Similarly, the basis of legislative representation was fixed not alone upon the free white voting population but upon the slave population as well, and most of the slave owners were the Cavaliers of the East.[11] The immediate outcome of this assemblage, however, was not a separate state; it was, instead, a continuation of the Old Dominion under new management.

The convention spent several days in debate concerning its proper course of action, and on 17 June Mr. Francis Harrison Pierpont, a prominent lawyer of Fairmont in Marion County and chief architect of the Restored Government, delivered a speech which enunciated what was to become the guideline for the ensuing proceedings. In response to those who had advocated immediate action to form a new state, Mr. Pierpont contended that even if an immediate division of the state were practicable under the Constitution of the United States, it would not meet the existing emergency; that the proper course was to institute a new, loyal, government for the whole state of Virginia; that the convention represented the loyal people of Virginia, entitled by law to the control of its military and civic power as soon as they could get it; that control of a large portion of the state could be obtained at once; and that the federal government must succeed in putting down the rebellion in the eastern part of the state so that as fast as the rebels were driven out, the new state government would take over. He went on to say

4

he had no doubt that the state would "ultimately" be divided — and that he would, at the proper time, favor such division. But putting down the rebellion and assisting the United States to maintain constitutional liberty from the St. Lawrence to the Rio Grande was of vastly more importance to the convention and to the world than the formation of a new state out of Virginia's territory.[12]

The convention acting under an appropriate provision of the Virginia Bill of Rights then proceeded to declare that the Richmond Secession Convention "has attempted to transfer the allegiance of the people to an illegal confederacy of rebellious States, and required their submission to its pretended edicts and decrees." Therefore:

> All acts of said Convention and Executive, tending to separate this Commonwealth from the United States, or to levy and carry on war against them, are without authority and void; and that the offices of all who adhere to the said Convention and Executive, whether legislative, executive, judicial, are vacated."

An ordinance to reorganize the state government was adopted that provided for an oath of loyalty be taken by all officers in support of the United States and the "Restored Government of Virginia;" furthermore, it provided for the filling of all vacancies in office and for the election of a governor and other state officers.[13]

It is important to note that no significant change whatsoever was made in the Constitution or Code of the Commonwealth. The primary objective had been to keep Virginia within the Union by officers who professed to be loyal to The Stars and Stripes rather than to The Stars and Bars. On 20 June Mr. Pierpont was inaugurated governor, having been chosen by the convention to serve until an election could be held, at which time he was elected by the people who serve for the remainder of the unexpired term of the Governor Letcher.[14] On 1 July the General Assembly — consisting of all regularly elected members who would take the prescribed oath of office — met in special session in Wheeling, which of necessity had become the new capital, and a few days later the assembly proceeded to elect certain state officers and two United States senators to succeed Messrs. R. M. T. Hunter and James N. Mason, who had cast their lot with the Confederacy. Members of the House of Representatives who had been regularly elected were in due course seated in that body.[15]

It might be argued that this Legislature lacked a quorum; however, it must be remembered that a shooting war had started and a skirmish had been fought at Philippi — western Virginia soil. More than a majority of *loyal* legislators of the state were present, and at no time in history has a parliamentary body intentionally extended membership to persons known to be hostile or who refused to take the required oath. Nor has such a parliament when victorious in war ever been held illegitimate. The United States Senate seated Messrs. John S. Carlile and Waitman T. Willey as senators from Virginia, thus recognizing and confirming their election by

5

the General Assembly. And President Lincoln recognized Governor Pierpont and the Restored Government in a telegram from his Secretary of War that promised "all constitutional aid."[16]

There was an unimpeachable Virginia precedent for these actions which, in principle, were a re-enactment of the proceedings taken by colonial Virginianas some eighty-six years prior thereto. Virginia had then disavowed her constituted government and installed a loyal governor in place of the royal governor and had sent representatives to a continential congress, despite the lack of any constitutional authority to do so. She then proceeded to make good her renouncement of the Crown by force of her own and allied arms, and the legitimacy of that government has remained unquestioned ever since. In Wheeling, though but a sizeable minority of both population and area of Virginia were represented, the same principles applied and were on a more solid constitutional basis: the colonists has actually *revolted*, whereas the Wheeling proceedings were designed to *nagate a revolution* which had occurred in the eastern part of the state against the Constitution of the United States, the supreme law of the land, of which The War itself later proved to be superior to the constitution of any of the states. The Restored Government was recognized as *de jure* by President Lincoln[17] and Andrew Johnson,[18] by the Congress[19] and by the United States Supreme Court.[20] It neither needed nor could have had any more *authoritative* recognition! Furthermore, the Supreme Court of Appeals of the Commonwealth of Virginia gave its own "amen" in *Commonwealth v. Chalkley* and in *DeRothschilds v. The Auditor;* both cases are set out in the appendix.

Despite the *de jure* status of the Restored Government throughout the whole of Virginia, a *de facto* government in Richmond claimed such status also and in actuality it continued to wield authority in as much of the state as was within the grasp of Confederate military forces. Indeed, considerable portions of the area which became West Virginia were from time to time governed from Richmond instead of Wheeling; and in Grattan's (Virginia) *Reports,* on (WVI, 443) there is reported a case from Monroe County in 1864, after Monroe had become a county of West Virginia, the new state. The decision of the Confederate Virginia Supreme Court of Appeals in that case was based upon the construction of an act of the Confederate Congress. (Incidentally, Col. George S. Patton, who was ancestor to Gen. George S. Patton, of World War II fame, played a role in that case as commanding officer of the Gauley Military District.) The opinion was written by Judge Richard C. L. Moncure, who will be mentioned again in this saga. Until the fall of Richmond in 1865 this *de facto* government exercised jurisdiction throughout most of eastern Virginia except in the areas of Alexandria, Norfolk and Eastern Shore. It was, in fact, the "popular government" almost everywhere in the areas that remained in the state.

Nevertheless, for exactly two years, to the day, Mr. Pierpont governed a full-fledged state, comprising more than thirty counties and approximately one-third the territory of prewar Virginia in size.[21] All branches of government functioned effectively wherever

6

the Union army could maintain control and while the transmountain counties predominated, neither the Eastern Shore nor the areas of Norfolk and Alexandria were neglected. For example, the General Assembly remitted fines in Accomack County that had been imposed upon loyal citizens by secession military courts, amended the Alexandria city charter, chartered corporations in eastern Virginia and established election districts therein.[22] An act of great significance nationally is that of 13 February 1862. This act is Chap. 74 of the Wheeling Acts of 1861-62, whereby Virginia authorized the transfer to the United States of "not exceeding twenty acres of land in the county of Alexandria or Fairfax, for a place of interment of persons dying in the service of the United States;" *and so it was that Virginia has the honor of having played an important role in the establishment of Arlington National Cemetery!*

Governor Pierpont raised many troops for the Union,[23] and prior to West Virginia statehood the mere fact that a regiment bore a Virginia designation did not necessarily mean that it was Confederate. Thus, a blue-uniformed Seventh Virginia Infantry Regiment opposed a gray-clad Seventh Virginia Infantry Regiment at Sharpsburg, and Virginia units engaged each other on the Peninsula and in western Virginia.[24] But the governor tried in vain to raise troops in the east. He did succeed in organizing the Sixteenth Va. Infantry regiment, composed mainly of volunteers from around Norfolk, but it never saw action. The *Alexandria Gazette* of 2 June 1863 tells what happened to this outfit. "In the camp of the 16th Va. Regiment, near this place, a riding horse, saddle, and equipments complete, were presented by the officers under the command of Col. James T. Close to Mrs. Close." On 3 June 1863 the *Gazette* reported: "Col. James T. Close has resigned his office as Colonel, Sixteenth Virginia Volunteer Infantry, in order that he may accept the commission of U.S. Marshal of Virginia." And the final taps for the 16th is sounded with this item of 5 June 1863: "The 16th Virginia Regiment, U.S. V., formerly commanded by Col. J. T. Close, have been mustered out of service, the regiment never having reached the minimum in numbers required by regulations." (Col. Close, by the way, had represented Unionists of Fairfax County at the Wheeling Convention of June 1861.[25] He was a state senator who attended all sessions of the General Assembly in Wheeling.)

The General Assembly on 31 January 1863 enacted that all Virginia units in federal service at the time of West Virginia's admission as a state would thereafter be West Virginia troops[26] and so ended Virginia's *armed* participation in the Civil War as a Union state.

By Act of 13 May 1862 the General Assembly gave Virginia's consent to the creation of West Virginia from her territory. The subsequent birth of that state, pursuant to proceedings taken under Art. Four, Sect. Three of the Constitution of the United States, evoked from the *de facto* legislature in Richmond a disclaimer of Virginia's consent.[27] This disclaimer completely ignored the fact that Richmond had repudiated the Constitution, was waging war

7

against it and, therefore, was in no position either in law or in equity to nullify any action of a *de jure* state government which supported the Constitution, nor to challenge the congressional approval of West Virginia's statehood. Under those circumstances the disclaimer could have been valid only if enforceable by arms; but when hostilities terminated, the so-called "Confederate States of America" and the Confederate government of Virginia, and all legislation of both became void *ab initio*.[28] This result, and the loss of the western counties to West Virginia, were but two of the clearly foreseeable risks inherent in the course charted by the people of eastern Virginia when they freely chose to abandon the Constitution of the United States to join the Confederacy. Nevertheless, a notion persists even unto this day among Virginians that the Confederate regime was *de jure* and that West Virginia's birth was illegitimate or, at best, "highly technical."

The new state emerged on 20 June 1863, just before Gettysburg, when the Confederacy was at its height and its permanent separation from the Union seemed entirely possible. In Richmond Governor Pierpont stood condemnded as a tratior;[29] and even if the Union were to prevail, his political future in Virginia was at best uncertain. Furthermore, West Virginia was now a fact; and Wheeling could no longer be Virginia's capital. General Lee's army of northern Virginia was in firm control of most of the old state, which, in turn, reduced the territory over which the Pierpont government was able to exercise jurisdiction to Alexandria, Norfolk and the Eastern Shore; few, if any, Northern politicians other than President Lincoln could see any reason for keeping the Restored Government in existence. On the other hand, 5Mr. Pierpont could likely have been West Virginia's first governor, or a United States senator;[30] indeed, all but two members of his administration resigned to accept high offices under the new state.[31] But the governor considered that his first duty was to Virginia.[32] Already he was visualizing the postwar period and he foresaw the need for a government comprised of *bona fide* Virginians who, nonetheless, would be acceptable to the authorities in Washington. He therefore continued in his determination to remain in office as governor of Virginia (having been elected in May for a full term)[33] and shortly thereafter moved the capital to Alexandria. Had he determined otherwise, the Restored Government most certainly would have gone by default and stern military rule would have followed, for there was no other man on the horizon who would or could have filled his shoes. Therefore, in making and executing this decision, Mr. Pierpont surely attained the stature of a great Virginian and a great governor of Virginia!

Upon leaving Wheeling, the governor visited the Eastern Shore and Norfolk and then settled down in Alexandria sometime in August. During this period of itinerancy Secretary of State Seward is reputed to have said: "Governor Pierpont is carrying the capital of Virginia around in his pants pocket."[34] But, by a proclamation dated 26 August 1863 that was published the next day in *The Alexandria Gazette*,[35] he designated Alexandria as the new capital and reaffirmed his "ardent desire to restore peace and security to each

8

county and neighborhood in the commonwealth, assuring all that I have no other object in view than the present welfare and future prosperity of my native state." His first, though temporary, residence was the city hotel, which is a tourist attraction today, not because it once accommodated a governor of Virginia, but because it had been frequented by the Father of Our Country. In Washington's time, as now, it was known as "Gadsby's Tavern" and is located on the corner of Cameron and Royal Streets. The capitol building, which also became the official residence of the governor until his family joined him early in 1865,[36] was and still is a 3½-story brick building located at 413-415 Prince Street. In 1960 a plaque was placed thereon by the owner, on a side wall not visible from the street. The structure is now an apartment building, not open to tourists or sightseers.

Shortly after his arrival in Alexandria the governor received a personal note from Maj. (later Col.) John Singleton Mosby that warned: "I'll get you some night, mighty easy!"[37] Although a subsequent attempt to capture the governor by the famed guerrilla leader went awry, he did take the governor's military aide, Col. Daniel F. Dulaney, on 27 September 1863 and sent him off to Richmond as a prisoner of war.[38] As will be shown in the pages which follow, Maj. Mosby served his fellow Virginians by failing to take the governor than if he had removed Pierpont from this position from which he would later serve the Virginians so well.

Personal safety, however, was not the governor's primary concern, for he now performed the additional duties of a number of former officers who had resigned their posts to assume positions under the new state of West Virginia. Whereas the people of Wheeling were overwhelmingly pro-Union in sentiment, the governor now found himself in the unfavorable environment of a population even more overwhelmingly sympathetic to the Richmond government and the Confederacy. Finding Virginians who were both loyal to the Union and competent to perform the duties of public office must have been a chore of the first magnitude. He also had a major federal relations problem which a less dedicated governor might well have shunned as political dynamite. This, of course, was Maj. Gen. Benjamin F. "The Beast" Butler — the military district commander who had made Norfolk his headquarters. Butler actually exercised civil authority in the Norfolk area, and the Alexandria Constitutional Convention in February 1864 passed a resolution asking the president to define the powers of the Restored Government between its civil and military functions; this was followed by Governor Pierpont's 55-page printed letter to President Lincoln and the members of Congress, the subject of which was the abuse of power in Gen. Butler's command. Although both President Lincoln and Attorney General Bates supported Governor Pierpont's protest, they had even larger problems with which to cope, and Gen. Butler's harassment was never completely abated until his removal from command.[39] Within the Alexandria "bridgehead," however, civil government continued much as usual, and the *Alexandria Gazette* regularly reported city council meetings, sessions of the county court, elections to various local offices, *et cetera*, just as though times were altogether normal. (That one *et cetera* could be stretched considerably more ets and ceteras, but some of the items are of little interest and are thus omitted.) In this connection the issue for 1 June 1863 reported activity in the county court, and the 2 June edition carried a story of council's enactment of the annual revenue bill, which taxed real property sixty cents on one hundred dollars of valuation, and the "general personalty" tax was at the rate of fifty cents per hundred dollars. Except for the ability of the Restored Government to exert its influence in Alexandria even before the arrival of Governor Pierpont, there is little room for doubt that civil government in Alexandria would have gone the way of Norfolk. Upon his arrival he at once became, in effect, the advocate of all citizens of his tiny state who were oppressed by the federal authorities or imposed upon by Yankee profiteers. In fact, an anonymous reporter in the *Alexanderia Gazette* of 24 August 1863 prophesied that Mr. Pierpont "would see justice done to the people." This prediction was confirmed in numerous ways. The governor interceded successfully on Virginian's behalf with President Lincoln at least twice during his sojourn in Alexandria, once to obtain the lifting of the commercial blockade of that port[40] — which must have been a great boon to business — and again to procure the release of a young Fairfax County farm boy from a federal penitentiary. This lad, while sitting upon a roadside fence in front of his home, had seen a Union cavalry unit gallop past and, a few moments later, had pointed out its direction of flight to a pursuing detachment of Mosby's men. For this he had been sentenced to twenty years.[41]

The General Assembly held two sessions at Alexandria: the first from 7 December 1863 to 8 February 1864, and the second from 5 December 1864 to 27 March 1865. The senate consisted of six members under the presidency of Lieutenant Governor Leopold C. P. Cowper. Honorable James Madison Downey, Loudon County, was speaker of the House of Delegates, which consisted of thirteen members.[42] Incidentally, this was paribly the smallest legislature any of these United States of America has ever had. The counties of Accomac, Northampton, Alexandria, Fairfax, Loudon, Norfolk and Princess Anne, along with the city of Norfolk and Hampton district were represented in the Senate; and the counties of Accomac, Northampton, Prince William, Norfolk, Alexandria, Loudon and Fairfax along with the cities of Elizabeth, Norfolk, and Portsmouth were represented in the House. On 5 February 1864 this body reelected Lucian A. Hagans secretary of the commonwealth and reelected Lewis H. Webb auditor; it also elected John J. Henshaw to the post of treasurer.[43] The number of constituents any legislator actually represented at any given time is difficult to determine; it is even harder to ascertain the number of qualified voters in any election constituency. An item in the *Alexandria Gazette* of 1 June 1863, however, sheds some light on this point: "Enoch Haislip is elected to the House of Delegates from Prince William, having received 24 votes."

Probably the most noteworthy legislation of the General Assembly in Alexandria was ratification of the Thirteenth Amendment (abolition of slavery) to the federal Constitution on 9 February 1865. This amendment is still recorded in the office of the United States secretary of state as an act of the Commonwealth of Virginia.[44] This was followed up on 6 March (Acts 1864-65, Chap. 47) by an act which repealed Sect. 35 of Chp. 198 of the Code of Virginia, 1860, which then provided: "Every assembly of negroes for the purpose of religious worship, when such worship is conducted by a negro, and every assembly of negroes for the purpose of instruction in reading or writing, or in the night time for any purpose, shall be unlawful." Violators were to be "punished with stripes," that is, by flogging. Another act of the Alexandria General Assembly of the 1863-64 session passed 5 February 1964 (Chap. 21) reads: "Be it enacted that the donation of public lands proffered to the Commonwealth of Virginia by the act of Congress of July second, 1862, with the conditions and provisions therein prescribed, be and the same is hereby accepted." The congressional act herein referred to is better known as the Morrill Act or the Federal Land Grant Act. It required that states desiring to take advantage of its terms must first agree thereto by act of their respective legislatures. This was a *bona fide* try by the assembly, but it was of no effect due to a ruling by the United States attorney general having to do with the exact date Virginia (*de facto* regime) was declared no longer to be in rebellion, so it remained for the assembly of 1869-1870 to re-enact this legislation. The grant thereafter received was applied by the commonwealth to the benefit of the institutions at Hampton and Blacksburg.

Alexandria was the locale of the convention which brought forth the Virginia Constitution of 1864. Its primary purpose had been to facilitate Confederate Virginia's transition back into the Union after the Civil War (when the *de facto* Richmond government would have been replaced by the Restored government) by placing a constitutional ban on involuntary servitude except as punishment for crime. This was, of course, a first-time provision which has continued in effect ever since. Another first-time provision which has continued in effect reduced Virginia's two-year residence requirement for voting eligibility to one year. Still another first-time measure abolished voice voting and replaced it by the secret ballot, but this was repealed before it became effective. However, it was reinserted into the next Constitution (1869) and has remained in effect ever since. There is still another provision in current effect, although it was not a first-time matter when adopted at Alexandria: From 1851 until then judges of courts of record had been elected by popular vote. This was changed to appointment by the General Assembly — initially upon nomination by the governor, but some years later this procedure was limited to times when the assembly was on vacation and was subject to confirmation at the next legislative session. Another provision prohibited voting-and-holding-office eligibility to those who had held office or performed military service under the Confederacy, but this provision was repealed a year later upon Governor Pierpont's recommendation. Other provisions were dictated by the necessities of the times, such as prohibiting payment of debts incurred by the *de fac-*

11

to Richmond government. The Alexandria Constitution was recognized as valid by the Virginia Supreme Court of Appeals[45] and by mention in the preamble to the "Underwood" Constitution of 1869.

According to the Virginia Supreme Court of Appeals, the Restored Government continued in existence until the adoption of the Alexandria Constitution 12 February 1864; and the government organized under the Alexandria constitution (with Pierpont as governor), continued in existence until superseded by the Reconstruction laws under which the 1869 constitution was framed and adopted.[46] The Alexandria General Assembly, however, expired on 1 July 1865; its last session was held in Richmond at the call of the governor in the latter part of June of that year. The next General Assembly was elected under the Alexandria Constitution in October; it held two sessions: one in 1865-66 and one in 1866-67. After that the Reconstruction Act took over and there was no assembly until 1869-70, the first session under the 1869 Constitution.

A bitter controversy with the military decreased the popularity and imparied the usefulness of the Alexandria government, which was at no time popular with the people, not even with those of their number who remained loyal to the union. It continued, however, to function and to be recognized by president Lincoln and by Congress. Another factor contributing to its unpopularity was the alien origin of many of its personnel. Except Pierpont and Hagans (secretary of the commonwealth), who were from western Virginia, most of the officials were Northerners. As stated before, it was indeed a chore for the governor to find Virginians who were both capable to perform the duties of office and who would take the required oath of allegiance.[47]

Nevertheless, the Alexandria era of the Restored Government is historically important, for it preserved the federally recognized state government through the critical period which began when West Virginia became a state and ended with the restoration of the capital to Richmond; furthermore, it paved the way for Governor Pierpont and the government officers, offices and agencies under the Alexandria Constitution to resume the state's business at the historical seat of the government and in its capitol, all with the blessing of the president of the United States.

The General Assembly, by a joint resolution adopted 3 March 1865, authorized the governor to restore the capital to Richmond when safe to do so. On 9 May President Johnson issued an executive order which (1) nullfied all acts of Confederate national, state and local bodies or officers throughout Virginia; (2) directed members of his cabinet to re-establish the organization and functions of their respective departments within the state so as to resume their normal business under the laws of the United States; and (3) provided:

That to carry into effect the guaranty by the Federal Constitution of a republican form of State government and afford the advantage and security of domestic laws, as well as

12

to complete the re-establishment of the authority and laws of the United States and the full and complete restoration of peace within the limits [of the state] Francis H. Pierpont, governor of the State of Virginia, will be aided by the Federal Government so far as may be necessary in the lawful measures which he may take for the extension and administration of the State government throughout the geographical limits of said State.

Note these points well, for they contradict various history books as well as beliefs held by a great many people: the President did *not* *"appoint"* Pierpont; he *recognized* him as being *the governor* of Virginia. The word *provisional* does not appear in the executive order and the President did *not* give Governor Pierpont any directions or instructions of any kind — instead, he directed federal officers to assist the governor in his efforts to *extend the existing* state government throughout the state. The President did *not* "send" the governor to Richmond or anywhere else! *The Governor acted pursuant to a resolution of the General Assembly!* Primarily, however, he acted in accord with his statement to the Wheeling Convention on 17 June 1861: "When the federal government has succeeded in putting down the rebellion in the eastern part of the state — the new state government would take over!"

Restoring the capital to Richmond by his proclamation of 23 May, the governor and state officers moved to that city "to serve liberally and wisely under circumstances of peculiar difficulty."[48] Again there was a change in personnel. Among the newcomers were Francis J. Smith as treasurer and Charles H. Lewis as secretary of the Commonwealth. Mr. Lewis was a brother of John F. Lewis, who later became a United States senator from Virginia.[49] Thus, Virginia was unique among other ex-Confederate states in that her lawful government had continued in existence throughout the Civil War. Furthermore, it was headed by an executive who was resolute in his determination to work solely for the good of Virginia and to resist pressure from all sides. As stated contemporaneously in the *Richmond Republic:*

> [The Restored Government] is, in fact, the only link that connects the Commonwealth with the Federal Government and Union. If that fails we fall at once into the helpless and degraded condition of a conquered province. But for the existence of this government, which has been preserved through a long period of adversity and trial by the indefatigable exertions and rare skill and prudence of Governor Pierpont, Virginia would now be under the rule of a military governor, in the person, most likely, of some such man as Benjamin F. Butler.[50]

Upon arrival in Richmond the governor proceeded at once to ascertain conditions throughout the state from such men as John B. Baldwin, Hugh W. Sheffey, M. W. Harmon and William H. Tate, all prominent Virginians who had supported the lost cause.[51] The situation was bleak indeed. Much of Richmond was rubble, and destitution was widespread. Prompt action had to be taken, and the governor was equal to the task. He called the Alexandria General Assembly into special session just in the nick of time, for its tenure was to expire on 1 July. This legislature met in Richmond for five eventful days beginning Monday 19 June and ending Friday 23 June.[52] In recommending action to bring about repeal of the disenfranchisement and ban-on-office-holding amendment to the State Constitution, the Governor addressed the members as follows: "It is folly to suppose that a state can be governed under a republican form of government when, in a large portion of the state, nineteen-twentieths of the people are disfranchised and cannot hold office."[53] The Legislature responded favorably to this appeal and enacted legislation to authorize the next session of the General Assembly, subject to approval of the electorate, to amend the Constitution by striking out these provisions. This approval was given at the October election and the 1865-66 session of the assembly acted accordingly. As historian Robert Selph Henry wrote on page 112 of his book *The Story of Reconstruction* (Bobbs-Merrill, 1938):

> This action, taken under the wise leadership of Governor Pierpont, angered the small group which was growing into the Republican party in Virginia. Lewis McKenzie, defeated candidate for Congress in the Alexandria district declared that the "loyal men of the state were to be totally sacrificed and turned over to the power of the secessionists." The wholesome results of Governor Pierpont's leadership toward complete reconciliation were thus to be used when Congress met, as one more of the many arguments against allowing the South to governor itself.

Other enactments of the June 1865 special session included provisions for the immediate holding of local elections, and for a moritorium on collection of debts. The ensuing election in the city of Richmond resulted in ex-Confederates being elected to city offices, and the commanding general declared the election null and void. Bowing to obvious necessity, Pierpont then issued an order which prohibited ex-Confederates to hold office.[54] This tends to exmphasize a passage from George W. Munford's *Historical Synopsis* contained in the *Code of Virginia 1873* beginning on page 24 of that code that is, that from the time of Governor Pierpont's arrival in Richmond until the adoption of the 1896 Constitution:

> "A succession of commanding generals had established headquarters at Richmond with a supervising power over the state government, to keep not only the state in subjection, but to act as a watch over Governor Pierpont."

All this displeased many Virginians, who were already discontented with having for their governor a man who had been on the opposite side during the Civil War (and especially the man for whom they blamed the loss of the western counties), and his message to the assembly must have made him unpopular with the political majority in Washington. He had become caught in a squeeze between the Radical Republicans, the Union League, the Freedman's Bureau, die-hard conservatives, carpetbaggers and political opportunists who had descended on Virginia in droves. In view of these circumstances his accomplishments were truly remarkable.

Dr. R. A. Brock, the distinguished Virginia historian and ex-Confederate soldier, writing in 1882 said of the administration of Governor Pierpont in Richmond:

Another example is now presented of an honorable and successful career attendant upon probity and persistent purpose. He also found, upon his arrival in Richmond, the United States marshal busy libeling the property of the late Confederates for confiscation. A few days afterwards President Johnson issued a proclamation confiscating the estates of certain classes unless pardoned. It was stipulated that all petitions should be recommended by the governor. He soon perceived that the President was temporizing, and was led to apprehend that the "pardon mill" was a farce at least, if not worse. He accordingly determined to recommend all petitions offered him. He next protested to the Attorney General against the further iniquity of libeling property which it was never designed to confiscate, and which only entailed grievous expense on the owners. His protest was effective. He next interposed for the suppression of the class of pardon-broker harpies who obstructed the due course of executive clemency as provided. He refused to recommend any petition which would pass into the hands of any broker, and this disarmed these rapacious thieves. He next interposed for the relief of citizens who were under civil indictment for offenses which were within the province of military authority and recommended leniency and conciliation to the courts.[55]

With funds appropriated for the purpose, Governor Pierpont rehabilitated the Western Lunatic Asylum, the Institution for the Deaf, Dumb and Blind, and the Eastern Lunatic Asylum, all of which were then in extreme destitution. He appointed, upon the recommendation of those interested, efficient regents for the University of Virginia and for the Virginia Military Institute without reference to party affiliation, though, as is well known, the V.M.I. cadets had valiantly fought against Union troops at New Market.[56]

Exercising authority under an Alexandria constitutional provision, the Governor nominated and the General Assembly appointed a new Supreme Court of Appeals of three members, headed by the Honorable Richard C. L.Moncure, previously mentioned in this saga.[57] That so choice a plum should be given a "rebel" did Mr. Pierpont no political good in Washington but Judge Moncure served until 1882, the year of his death. A contemporary comment on the judiciary appointed by Governor Pierpont is contained in the *Richmond Whig:* "He [the governor] has secured for himself [by his appointments] a hold on the good will of the people of Virginia that neither the defamation of malice nor the intrigues of knavery can dislodge."[58] Indeed, three members of the present state Supreme Court are direct lineal successors of judges appointed by him; and its quality was attested by the federal military district commander, Maj. Gen. John M. Schofield, who stated: "No case arose in Virginia in which it was found necessary, in my opinion, to supersede the civil authorities in the administration of justice. not a single citizen of that state was tried by military commission."[59] And, speaking of justice, Governor Pierpont refused West Virginia's request for the extradition of Charles T. O'Ferrall, ex-Confederate army officer and later governor, on murder charges based upon his activities there in the lawful discharge of his duties as a soldier under the rules of land warfare. Governor O'Ferrall later said of Mr. Pierpont, "His heart was as warm as ever beat in a human breast."[60]

In October 1865 a new General Assembly was elected, comprised of capable, representative citizens. But there was skepticism in Washington, and some time thereafter Congress undertook to "investigate" affairs in Virginia. The Radical Republicans were riding high with little regard for reconciliation. In effect, this investigation put Governor Pierpont on trial, and many of his former colleagues deserted him.[61] As stated by the historian Eckenroad:

> Pierpont's policy, wise and conciliatory as it was, soon brought him into opposition with his former associates in Alexandria. They thought Pierpont had abandoned them. And, indeed, he had ceased to be the governor of a single town and had become, in a larger sense, the Governor of Virginia.[62]

The Congressional Committee on Reconstruction heard testimony by Radicals under the leadership of Judge John C. Underwood to the effect that the existing government under Pierpont was "unsafe" for the protection of loyal persons and were urged to begin the establishment of a territorial government. The committee, while strongly adverse to the president's plan, did not go so far as to make that recommendation to Congress. But it did, nevertheless, bring the governor into further disfavor with the Radicals and other varieties of politicians — pardon brokers, carpetbaggers, and opportunists — who were seeking to destroy what personal influence remained as Pierpont's command.[63]

The governor transmitted to the General Assembly in 1866 a copy of the proposed Fourteenth Amendment to the Constitution of the United States with a recommendation that it be ratified. His recommendation went unheeded. A year later, after some nine or ten other ex-Confederate states had likewise taken no action for ratification of that amendment Congress really cracked the whip by enactment of the Reconstruction Act of 2 March 1867.[64] The complete text of it is in the appendix, but a synopsis is of importance here:

Preamble recites that Virginia and nine other ex-Confederate states lack "legal State governments," "which are necessary for peace and good order";

Sec. 1. Divides those states into military districts; Virginia designated as District No. 1.

Sec. 2. Each district to be commanded by a general officer of the Army, appointed by the President.

Sec. 3. Powers and duties of commanders spelled out.

Sec. 4. Relates to trial of offenders by military commissions.

Sec. 5. Conditions and procedures for states to gain representation in Congress and to regain all rights of statehood.

Sec. 6. "and be it further enacted, That, until the people of said rebel States shall be by law admitted to representation in the Congress of the United States, ANY CIVIL GOVERNMENTS WHICH MAY EXIST THEREIN SHALL BE PROVISIONAL ONLY, and in all respects subject to the paramount authority of the United States at any time to abolish, control of supersede the same. (Capitalization supplied for emphasis).

Note well that this statute placed the entire governmental structure of the state — executive, legislative and judicial — under the complete domination and control of the military district commander, and observe further that the word provisional is made applicable to "civil *governments* which may exist" and does not purport to deal with trivialities such as the titles of officers in any civil government. Thus, the entire legislative body was discontinued by the district commander in that he permitted no election to be held in 1867 for members of the General Assembly. Instead, he set the machinery in operation to bring about a constitutional convention to frame a new basic law for the Commonwealth in order to hasten Virginia's restoration to its former status of a state in the Union, as provided in the statute. The executive and judicial departments were left intact. Fortunately for Virginia, both Maj. Gen. John M. Schofield — President Johnson's appointee as military district commander — and Governor Pierpont were "honest and understanding" men.[65]

Having noted "well" the foregoing paragraph, now please note "weller" what follows in this paragraph. (If it were proper, as undoubtedly it was, for Alice to have said on an appropriate occasion in Wonderland that something was "curiouser," then it is equally proper on this occasion to say "weller" in this wonderland jungle of underbrush verbage which originated some five-score and ten years ago from such seedlings as "provisional," "pretender," etc. And that little *et cetera* could be lengthened by another dozen or so of ets and ceteras by wordsmen with, no doubt, the best of intentions. The present day crop of verbage is accepted as the real McCoy by writers dealing with the subject matter of this saga — which prompts this author to cry out "O wordsmen, spare this treatise!") It is understood that diehard unreconstructed rebels might say "Nuts!" to all this and continue to refer to Mr. Pierpont as having been a "provisional governor;" if so, however, they should at least state correctly the date of the beginning of the "provisional" status as 2 March 1867 instead of in 1865, for in Virginia there is no other basis than the Reconstruction Act of 2 March 1867 for the use of that word at all. They would still be incorrect, however, for the official *Code of Virginia, 1873*, on page 198 lists both Pierpont and his successor, Henry H. Wells, as "governor" under the Restored Government!

That the Reconstruction Act of 2 March 1867 was enacted into law over the veto of President Johnson — whose conciliatory policy towards Virginia was appreciated and approved by the General Assembly in February 1866 — emphasizes the 180° change in direction the Congress had taken in just one year. Having formerly been supportive of the Restored Government of Virginia, now both Gen. Schofield and Governor Pierpont were made to feel its hot breath on their necks more and more, and, as stated by the Virginia historian Virginius Dabney, "the good offices of both of those officials were soon to be largely nullified."[66] The Radical Republicans, rabble-rousers, fanatics and carpetbaggers were "politicking" to win votes of the newly freed slaves to gain control of the forthcoming conventions so that a new constitution could be drafted and candidates for office be nominated; pressure was mounting in Congress to impeach the president; and the tenture of Mr. Pierpont as governor of Virginia was fast drawing to a close. Sometime during the trial of the president, Gen Schofield must have received the word that Pierpont had to go. On 4 April 1868 he issued an order which recited that inasmuch as Governor Pierpont's term of office had expired and he was ineligible under the Constitution of the state to succeed himself in office, he was relieved of office, and Gen. Wells was appointed governor (not "provisional" governor) as of that date.[67] The State Supreme Court of Appeals had already held that Governor Pierpont had been duly elected for a term expiring 1 January 1868 but lawfully continued in office thereafter until such time as his lawful successor in office had duly qualified.[68] It should be noted in passing that Gen. Schofield considered Mr. Pierpont to have been the *de jure* governor of Virginia and regarded neither Pierpont nor his successor, Gen. Wells, as "provisional," thus substantiating what has already been related herein on that subject.

The degree of regret engenered by Pierpont's removal from office may have varied from person to person. But there is reason to believe that most Virginians were sorry to see him go and recognized that he had indeed had their interests at heart — numerous politicians excepted, of course: For instance, a Richmond historian, the late W. Asbury Christian, D. D. relates that in

January of 1874 when the General Assembly elected Col. R. E. Withers to the United States Senate, "at the time ex-Governor Pierpont visited Richmond and was welcomed by the people, who remembered his liberal and considerate administration under most trying circumstances." Shortly after Mr. Pierpont left office Mr. Franklin J. Sterns, a Richmond business man, wrote to Pierpont saying that his administration had been "unselfish and wise" and that he had kept the state out of the "hands of thieves" as long as he was in control.[69] Be that as it may, it is appropriate to mention here what the governor had written while in Alexandria: "I never expect to have the *love* and *sympathy* of the rebels; but by doing *right* I intend to command their *respect*!" It is, therefore, respectfully submitted in retrospect that Mr. Pierpont — on his record — was entitled to the respect of his constituents, as well as some measure of love and sympathy. And this author is strongly inclined to believe that when this theretofore distorted chapter of Virginia history is published and read at the "grassroots" level, the governor will indeed be accorded the respect of twentieth century Virginians and some love and sympathy as well. Furthermore, it is worthy of note in those days of ever-accelerating inflation and habitual budget deficits that Mr. Pierpont retired from office leaving a handsome (for those days) cash balance in the treasury![70]

Finally, it should be noted in passing that the government of Virginia today is the direct, continuous and lineal successor of the one founded at Jamestown. The line of succession runs from Jamestown to Williamsburg to Richmond to Wheeling and Alexandria and back to Richmond. If this be not true, the only alternative on which such unbroken succession could be found would be through the line which in the spring of 1865 branched out from Richmond to Danville. While that line ran back to Jamestown, it did not run forward. It came to an end at Danville, and the government which it supported expired then and there, without executors, administrators, heirs, issue, legatees, successors or assigns — as did the government of the Confederacy. And the statutes and constitutions thereunto appertaining became just as defunct as Julius Caesar's ox.[71] When the Pierpont government moved from Alexandria to Richmond, it took with it the Alexandria Constitution of 1864 and the Code of 1860 as amended in Wheeling and Alexandria. The present Constitution and Code are successors thereto.[72] To state these facts, however, does no disservice to Confederate Virginia; but these facts are a *sine qua non* to link today with Jamestown.

And so concludes the saga of a great Virginian and the government which he headed. He was not to "blame" for the loss of West Virginia, a loss which became inevitable once the Civil War began. But the Restored Government of Virginia, though logical, was not *inevitable*. It was largely the product of Governor Pierpont. And its continued existence *after* West Virginia's admission to minister unto the needs of war-ravaged Virginia was due *solely* to him.

This saga is based on solid historical facts that do not affect — neither brightening nor tarnishing — the honor or glory of Confederate Virginia or any of her illustrious sons or daughters. To

19

recognize, publish and teach it is not to expose a skeleton in the closet; it is, rather, to disclose a heretofore chapter of Virginia and West Virginia history and to honor another great but little-known Virginian, who heretofore has been stigmatized. He deserves to be placed in proper perspective. This is, perhaps best stated by an unbiased Virginia historian of the nineteenth century who in writing of Governor Pierpont's administration in Richmond says in her book *The Governors of Virginia,* "He clearly had the good of the people at heart, and, by every effort and influence, he struggled, and not in vain, to mitigate the trials of those by whom he was surrounded."[73]

SUMMARY OF THE SAGA AS WRITTEN IN JUST TWO PARAGRAPHS BACK IN MAY 1877

From the *Intelligencer* (Wheeling, W. Va.), May 26, 1877: *"Governor Pierpont as a bogus Governor"* — The *Richmond Dispatch* replies to the *Intelligencer* on this subject by saying that Gov. Pierpont will never appear in history as the genuine governor of Virginia: "There was never a moment from the time he went into office until he went out when he could have maintained his position as governor if he had been left unsupported by federal bayonets. Mr. Pierpont and the rest of his disloyal sons of Virginia whom the federal government used as instruments to aid in the work of undermining the new Union which the old state had attached herself were more tools."

"The *Dispatch* begs the whole question by such a presentation of the case. We placed the genuineness of Gov. Pierpont's governorship upon the fact that he had adhered to the federal government as the representative of the loyal element in Virginia, and not on the ground that he represented a popular majority in the state. A man can be a rightful governor and yet be in a small minority, as, for instance, where several persons are condidates in any state. The United States government recognized Francis H. Pierpont as the governor of Virginia, and he stands on the records at Washington as the genuine governor of that state during the war, and no other person will ever appear on the records as the governor of Virginia during that period. John Leicher and Wm. Smith were governors *de facto* of the rebelious portion of Virginia during the war, and the latter's term of office ceased after the fall of Richmond over any portion of Virginia. On the other hand, as soon as the rebellion collapsed Governor Pierpont's governorship covered the whole area of the state *de jure* and *de facto.*"

Author's note: The foregoing is from Joe Hoffmann's column, "The News That Was," which appeared in the Wheeling *News-Register* in its edition of 11 November 1981; he garnered it from the microfilms of the Ohio County Public Library.

PART III
EPILOGUE — SPELLING OF SURNAME

Upon relinquishing the chair of governor of Virginia Mr. Pierpont found himself no longer in any position to be of service to the people of his native Commonwealth. Accordingly, he returned to his old home in Fairmont, and not until then did he become a citizen of West Virginia. Some forty-two years later it was West Virginia that presented his statue for placement in Statuary Hall in the national capitol. "The Old Governor," as he was now affectionately called, settled down again to the practice of law and he resumed his several business activities as well. In 1869 he was elected to the House of Delegates from Marion County, and some years later President Garfield appointed him to the post of collector of internal revenue for West Virginia.

Following the demise of his beloved wife on 26 March 1886, Mr. Pierpont went to Pittsburgh, Pennsylvania to reside with his daughter, Mrs. William H. (Anna Pierpont) Siviter, whose husband was a journalist. The Old Governor died there on 24 March 1899. His body rests in Fairmont's Woodlawn Cemetery.

There, it may be supposed a mere epilogue should terminate. In this case, however, a few more biographical notes seem appropriate to make better known this little-known but great Virginian.

Francis Harrison Pierpont — "Frank" to his friends — was born in Middleton, Monongalia County, Virginia on 25 January 1814. Middleton was chartered as Fairmont in 1843, and in 1842 Marion County was carved from Monongalia and Harrison Counties with Fairmont as the county seat.

Mr. Pierpont graduated from Allegheny College, Meadville, Pennsylvania in 1839. He taught school for some years while studying law and thereafter became a successful lawyer in Fairmont. He also engaged profitably in the mining of coal and the manufacture of firebrick. He was a leader of laymen of the Methodist Protestant Church and served as trustee of an educational institution.

On 16 December 1854 Mr. Pierpont married Julia Augusta Robertson of Gloversville, New York. Their daughter Anna was born 14 April 1858 and lived until 22 March 1932. Mamie and Willie Pierpont — twins — were born several years after Anna, but Mamie lived only a few years. The author has been unable to find any further reference to Willie.

Readers who seek further biographical information may find these books to be of interest: *Recollections of War and Peace* by Anna Pierpont Siviter (published posthumously by G. P. Putnam's Sons, 1938); *Francis H. Pierpont* by C. H. Ambler (University of North Carolina Press, 1937); *Virginia and Virginians, Eminent Virginians edited by Dr. R. A. Brock (H. H. Hardesty, Richmond and Toledo, 1888);* and *West Virginia Heritage Encyclopedia,* Vol. XVII, edited and published by Jim Comstock (Richwood, W. Va. 1876).

*　　　　　*　　　　　*

Pierpont's biographer, the above-mentioned Dr. Ambler, on page 3 of his book states that "after using 'Peirpoint' until 1881

[he] changed to 'Pierpont' because he believed that his grand-father's name had been incorrectly spelled on a land patent; and that the Governor believed his family to have been of New England origin." Dr. Ambler's statement appears to be correct as of 3 December 1866 in that governor's message of that date to the Virginia General Assembly bears the signature "F. H. Peirpoint." On the other hand, *Calendar of Virginia State Papers,* (the chapter relating to the Restored Government), contains entries made by Governor "Pierpoint" and a number of history books use that spelling (XI, 317). This might have been due to the governor's handwriting, of which this author has two samples: a letter written in Wheeling in 1863 and another from Alexandria in 1864. In those writings, after the capital "P" appears two straight up-and-down lines, not looped, with a dot over the next following letter "r" so that both of those up-and-down lines could be either an "e" or an "i." It's simply a matter of paying your money and taking your choice, as some astute/*ologist* (whose name doesn't come readily to mind) once said. Dr. Ambler's estimated date of change to "Pierpont," 1881, seems erroneous, however, because there is a book, *Partisan Life with Col. John S. Mosby,* by John Scott (Harper & Bros., New York, 1867), which on page 144 spells the governor's name "Pierpont." It may well be that Maj. Scott check-ed with the governor during the course of preparing his manuscript. What seems to be certain, however, is that the change was made, prior to 1870, for in the Supreme Court case Virginia v. West Virginia (78 U.S. 39 — see appendix) 1870, the name is spelled "Pierpont."

This book uses "Pierpont" throughout, as do most books, in-cluding Ambler's.

PART IV
NOTES
CITATIONS EXPLAINED

"Ambler" refers to Ambler, Charles H. *Francis H. Pierpont.* Chapel Hill: Univ. of North Carolina, 1937.

"Calendar" refers to the chapter on the Restored Government in Volume XI of *Calendar of Virginia State papers,* the volumes of which are published from time to time by authority of the Com-monwealth of Virginia.

"Dabney" refers to Dabney, Virginius. *Virginia: The New Dominion.* Garden City, N. Y. Doubleday, 1971.

"Hornbook" refers to *A Hornbook of Virginia History,* 2nd ed. Richmond: Virginia State Library, 1965.

"M&M" refers to Miller, Thomas C. and Hu Maxwell. *History of West Virginia and its People,* Vol. I, New York: Lewis Historical Publishing Co., 1913.

"Munford" refers to Munford, George W. *Historical Synop-sis of the Changes In The Laws and Constitution of the State of Virginia,* which includes the preface to, and is included in the *Code of Richmond 1873,* Richmond.

"Siviter" refer to Siviter, Anna Pierpont (the governor's

daughter). *Recollections of War and Peace.* New York, G. P. Putnam's Sons, 1938.

"School Books" refers to *Virginia: History-Government-Geography.* New York: Charles Scribner's Son, 1954 and 1964. These were "written and published under the supervision of the Virginia History and Government Textbook Commission, working in close consultation with the state Board of Education."

"Statuary Hall" refers to *Proceedings in Statuary Hall, etc., April 30, 1910.* Washington, D. C.: Government Printing Office. This work was published pursuant to the Concurrent Resolution of the Congress passed 6 June 1910. This book is a collection of historical and biographical speeches about Governor Pierpont and the Restored Government of Virginia delivered at unveiling the Pierpont statue in the national capitol.

NOTES

[1]For example, Professor Fishwick, in his *Virginia: A New Look at the Old Dominion,* published in 1959, makes no reference whatever to Governor Pierpont or the Restored Government of Virginia, though he assets that the fall of Richmond left the state without a government. While this was temporarily true at local levels of government due to the fact that judges and other officers were at that time Confederate, the Restored Government promptly took action to replace them, and the interruption of business was of short duration. Somewhat similarly, Mr. Dabney in his 1971 book refers to Mr. Pierpont as the "provisional governor" whose "capital" was Alexandria. He makes no mention of the period beginning in June 1861 and ending in June 1863 when the *de jure* capital of Virginia was Wheeling, thus omitting a two-year period of history relating to that area of Virginia west of the Alleghenies which adhered to the Union rather than the Confederacy. All together, Mr. Dabney devotes exactly seventeen lines of print to Governor Pierpont in a book 581 pages of text.

[2]School Books, p. 409, contain such statements as Pierpont "pretended to head the legal government of Virginia" and "a government calling itself the government of Virginia was organized in Wheeling."

[3]Ambler, pp. 361, 362.

[4]*Charleston* (W. Va.) *Daily Mail,* 20 June 1963, p. 14, col. 1.

[5]That article was a highly abridged version of the saga set out in this book, tailored to the space limitations of the magazine to which it has been submitted.

[6]See resolution passed 8 October 1863 by the *de facto* legislature in Richmond, wherein those Virginians who had remained loyal to the Union were classed as "evil disposed and traitorous citizens of this state."

[7]School Books, p. 610. In the list of governors of Virginia John Letcher is listed as serving "1860-1864" and William Smith is listed as serving "1864-1865." Then follows the name of Mr. Pierpont, who is stated to have been "provisional governor" from "1865-1868." See also *Hornbook,* page 110. These citations are erroneous. Pierpont was *de jure* governor (not provisional) from 20

23

June 1861 until 4 April 1868; Mr. Letcher was governor from 1 January 1860 until 17 April 1861 and *de facto* governor from 17 April 1861 until 1 January 1864; Mr. Smith was *de facto* governor from 1 January 1864 until 9 April 1865.

[8]John Marshall Hagans — see appendix.

[9]The contemporary writer was Brevet Col. Theodore F. Lang. *Loyal West Virginians 1861-1865,* (Baltimore: Deutsch Publishing Co., 1895.), p. 3.

[10]School Books, pp. 388 and 390.

[11]Statuary Hall, p. 44.

[12]Ambler, p. 374.

[13]Acts of Assembly, Wheeling, 1 July 1861, pp. 40, 41.

[14]Calendar, p. 355; M&M pp. 327, 328; Statuary Hall p. 5.

[15]M&M p. 329.

[16]*Ibid.*

[17]*Ibid;* see also *Luther v. Borden,* 7 How. 1: 12 L. Ed. 581 (1849).

[18]See Presidential Executive Order 9 May 1865 in *Messages and papers of the Presidents (in appendix),* Vol. 6, p. 338; see also Siviter, p. 154. See Appendix.

[19]M&M, p. 329.

[20]Virginia v. West Virginia, 78 U.S. (11 Wall.) 39 (1870). In this case the Supreme Court with unanimous voice took judicial notice that the Restored Government had been the lawful government of Virginia. The suit was brought by Virginia to recover Berkeley and Jefferson counties from West Virginia because the required referenda elections had not been held therein, wherefore Virginia had repealed her consent to transfer those counties while no action was taken by Congress to approve the transfer. The court held for West Virginia by a four-to-three vote. This author concurs with the dissenting opinions. The validity of the formation of West Virginia was not in issue. (See appendix).

[21]School Books, p. 409, state that Governor Pierpont "had control of only a small part of the state."

[22]See Acts of Assembly (*de jure*) Wheeling 1861 through 1863.

[23]Horace Greely asserted in September of 1861 that western Virginia "has, with her less proportionate means, mustered more troops into the service of the United States, in the ratio of her population, than has the State of New York." See Ambler, p. 122. See also Siviter, p. xix.

[24]*Report of General McClellan Upon Operations of the Army of the Potomac from July 1861 to November 1862,* Senate Executive Document, 38th Congress, 1st Session, p. 204. The Union designation of that battle is Antietam.

[25]M&M, p. 331.

[26]Acts of Assembly, Wheeling, Extra Session, 1862-63, ch. 52.

[27]Resolution of 8 October 1863, which affirmed a similar resolution passed 17 January 1862.

[28]See President Johnson's Executive Order of 9 May 1865 *Messages and Papers of the Presidents,* Vol. VI, 338. Post-war General Assemblies recognized this fact. See, for example, the act

of 2 March 1866 (Acts 1865-66, chap. 77, sec. 2, p. 191), which provided in pertinent part:

> "All rights and remedies saved or intended to be saved by an act passed March 14, 1862, by the body then sitting in Richmond and claiming to be the general assembly of Virginia are hereby confirmed and declared to be as valid and effectual as if the lawful authority of the body by which said act [was] passed had never been questioned."

See also another act of that date (Acts 1865-66, chap. 9, p. 79), which recognized as valid those bonds of the Commonwealth issued prior to 17 April 1861 (the date of the Ordinance of Secession) and those issued by the Restored Government of Virgina. Amendments to the 1860 Code of Virginia which were made by the Wheeling and Alexandria general assemblies were included in the next subsequent Code, that of 1873, as is illustrated by these examples: (1) On page 381 the historical citation for sec. 7 of chap. 38 shows that the section is set out as amended by the acts "1864-65. (Alexandria), chap. 25, p. 35"; and (2) on page 126 the historical citation for sec. 2 of chap. 2 shows that the section is set out as amended by acts "1862-3, Wheeling, chap. 71, p. 67, sec. 1." The Wheeling amendment referred to contains some language which is verbatim that of some portions of the present day Code of Virginia (Code 1950, as amended), sec. 1-19. On the other hand, the codifiers of the 1873 Code of Virginia rejected amendments to the 1860 Code that had supposedly been made by the so-called General Assembly of Virginia which supported the Confederacy, as is illustrated on p. 271 in the historical citation for sec. 2 of chap. 31, which reads: "Amended, Acts 1862 (Richmond), chap. 25, p. 60; amendment ommitted as not valid."

[29]See resolution of the *de facto* General Assembly cited in note 6.

[30]Siviter, p. 106. See also Ambler, p. 208.

[31]M&M, p. 361.

[32]Siviter, pp. 106, 107.

[33]Statuary Hall, p. 5. See also Calendar, p. 355.

[34]Siviter, p. 109.

[35]The 26 August 1963 issue of the *Alexandria Gazette* carries a centennial story of this event on p. 1.

[36]When the governor first moved to Alexandria, he sent his wife and children to Laurel, Md. to be further away from the theatre of war. The *Alexandria Gazette* reported on 5 January 1865 that the governor's family had joined him and that they were living at a small hotel at what was then the "upper end of Duke Street;" the hotel was "Magnolia House."

[37]Siviter, p. 128.

[38]John Scott, *Partisan Life With Col. John S. Mosby* (New York: Harper & Bros., 1867), p. 144.

[39]Ambler, p. 237 *et. seq.*

[40]Siviter, p. 109.

[41]Siviter, p. 251.

[42]M&M, pp. 361, 362, wherein the names of senators and delegates are given for a total of six senators and thirteen delegates. But see *Hornbook,* p. 90, which states that there were but three senators and nine delegates, none of whom are named.

[43]Statuary Hall, p. 32.

[44]See *The Constitution of the United States of America,* (Richmond: Virginia Commission on Constitutional Government, 1961), p. 42.

[45]*Commonwealth v. Chalkly,* 20 Grat. 404, (1871); *DeRothschilds v. The Auditor,* 22 Grat. 41 (1872); See also *Oneal v. Commonwealth* 17 Grat. 582, (1867); *Clarkson et al v. Booth,* 17 Grat. 49 (1867).

[46]*DeRothschilds v. The Auditor,* 22 Grat. 41, p. 44 (1872).

[47]Ambler, pp. 222, 223.

[48]Quote by Robert Selph Henry, *the Story of Reconstruction* (New York: Bobbs-Merril, 1938), p. 39. See also W. Asbury Christian, *Richmond — Her Past & Present* (1912; rpt. Spartansburg, N. C.: Reprint, 1973), p. 270. This book favorably refers to Pierpont as governor while in Richmond and states further that "General Schofield was considerate and kind, but others over him had urged him on, and he removed Governor Pierpont, who had made a good governor" and replaced him with Henry H. Wells of Michigan.

[49]Statuary Hall, p. 34.

[50]Ambler, p. 267.

[51]Statuary Hall, p 36

[52]*Ibid.* See also Ambler, pp. 272-274.

[53]Dabney, p. 360. See also Siviter, p. 174.

[54]Ambler, p. 275.

[55]*Virginia and Virginians, Eminent Virginians,* rev. ed. (Richmond and Toledo: H. H. Hardesty, 1888), p. 235. This is an excellent biography of Pierpont. See also Statuary Hall, p. 37: M&M, p. 364.

[56]Statuary Hall, p. 37.

[57]Calendar, pp. 462-464. Another Pierpont appointee, Alexander Rives, is referred to as a man "of distinction and large experience in public affairs" by John Goode of Virginia in his book *Recollections of a Lifetime,* (New York and Washington, D.C.: Neale Publishing Co., 1906), p. 29. Mr. Goode had been a member of the Bar of Virginia and a member of the Confederate Congress and other offices of distinction.

[58]Siviter, pp. 175, 176.

[59]Siviter, p. 185.

[60]Ambler, p. 361.

[61]Ambler, p. 284.

[62]Eckenroad, *The Political History of Virginia during the Reconstruction,* (Baltimore: Johns Hopkins Univ., 1904), p. 37.

[63]Dabney, p. 363; Ambler, p. 284.

[64]Dabney, p. 363.

[65]*Ibid.*

[66]*Ibid.*

[67]Calendar, p. 500.

[68]Ex Parte Lawhorne, 18 Grattan 85 (1868).

⁶⁹Siviter, p. 357. For Dr. Christian's quotation see, *Richmond — The Past & The Present,* (Spartanburg, N.C.: Reprint, 1973), pp. 342-343.

⁷⁰$334,607.56 as of 1 October 1866. See governor's message to the General Assembly, 3 December 1866.

⁷¹*DeRothschilds v. The Auditor,* 22 Grattan 41 (1872).

⁷²The first postwar constitution of Virginia clearly recognized the Alexandria Constitution in its preamble, as did the state's highest court in the cases cited in note 45. Acts of Assembly amendatory of the Code of Virginia 1860 passed at Wheeling and Alexandria are included in the code of 1873, and acts of the *de facto* Legislature in Richmond are omitted as "not valid."

⁷³Margaret V. Smith, *The Governors of Virginia* (Washington, D.C.: W. H. Loudermilk & Col., 1893), p. 382.

PART V
AFTERMATH OF THE WAR
THE AMERICAN UNION

You may not have noticed, but the perpendicular pronoun — that great big capital "I" — does not appear heretofore in the saga; that's because I wanted to refrain (at least insofar as human nature permits) from expressing personal opinions. But now, having told the saga as it actually took place (or should I say "like" it took place to conform to modern (mis)usage?), I think some musings may not be amiss, always keeping in mind that a miss is as good as a mile — if not a smile! (End of pun.)

Whatever may have been the cause or causes of the Civil War, I venture the opinion that each side — North and South — honestly believed that its own cause was fully supported by constitutional law. The question of secession, however, had been little discussed. I know of no book then extant which denied the right of a state to leave the Union, but I have had no occasion to make a diligent search to find one. On the other hand, several writers had presented the opinion that the Union was a confederacy of sovereign states from which any state could withdraw at its own option. De Tocqueville was one such writer, whose book *American Institutions* was published in Philadelphia in 1851 and was widely read in this country. Perhaps the best book in support of the right to secede was *The American Union,* written by a British subject, James Spence, and published in London in 1862, and ran into three editions in just that one year. All that is dwarfed, however, by a book on constitutional law entitled *Rowel on the Constitution,* first published sometime well before the Civil War. In those days Uncle Sam was not in the business of telling schools and colleges what ought to be taught due to the quaint idea then prevailing that it was none of his business. But he did make on exception to this rule in the case of his own cadets at West point (and probably at Annapolis) and this is what was taught such cadets as Robert E. Lee, Jefferson Davis and Thomas Jackson from that book:

"If a faction should attempt to subvert the government

27

of a state for the purpose of destroying its republican form, the paternal power of the Union could be called for to subdue it. Yet it is not to be understood that its interposition would be justifiable if the people of the state should determine to retire from the Union. It depends on the state itself whether it will continue to be a member of the Union."[1]

Having taught that concept to his corps of cadets (and most likely to his brigade of midshipmen as well) over a period of years, Uncle Sam, it seems, ought not be permitted to deny something which he himself had taught those who had relied on his tutelage. But even the principle of "estoppel" becomes moot in this case because there was no forum having adequate jurisdiction to apply or to enfore any such ruling. Thus, if Virginia, having exercised her asserted right to secede, in her own opinion at least, had become a sovereign state, she certainly would not have consented to have the case tried by the United States Supreme Court — or by any other court if any other such court were in existence at the time. Therefore, I respectfully submit, the situation had become akin to that which existed in 1775. Virginia (and her Colonial allies) would have to resort to arms; if she won, she would indeed have become sovereign. But if she lost, she would have been a rebel in the true sense of the word, regardless of anyone's opinion as to the righteousness of her cause.

What had been taught at West Point was the true concept in the opinion of the great majority of citizens in the Southern states; but President Lincoln and a majority of the citizens of the whole country held the contrary opinion. As Pudd'nhead Wilson said, "A difference of opinion is what makes horse racing," although it is doubtful that Mr. Wilson had cavalry and field artillery horses in mind.

That difference of opinion was fought over on the battlefield — that final field of honor from which there is no appeal — and the decision was rendered at Appomattox. But before discussing that decision, let's consider the matter from another angle.

Let's pretend that sometime during August or September of 1863 both England and France recognized the Confederate States of America as an independent, sovereign state (in the ancient usage of that word), and ambassadors or ministers were exchanged between those countries. Let's further pretend that the Copperheads, draft dodgers and others of that ilk in the North then forced President Lincoln to sue for an armistice, which resulted in using words then printed on Confederate currency, until "the ratification of a treaty of peace between the Confederate States of America and the United States of America." Have I gone off my rocker? Maybe so, but I do believe it serves the purpose of bringing out more clearly what the actual results of the Civil War were, especially as they applied to Old Dominion. As Mr. Guy Friddell relates in his delightful little book *What Is It About Virginia,*[2] many Virginian children played war games in which the Confederates always won; Grant surrendered to Lee, but Lee let him keep his sword; yet the games always stopped at that point because none could imagine the

South not being part of the United States.

I, too, cannot imagine a South alien from the nation, and that the South actually won, it is highly improbable that the separation would have existed for any considerable length of time. But let's continue the pretense.

Upon agreeing to an armistice, both sides would have met in a peace conference. Whether each of the sovereign confederated states would have sent her own commissioner or the federal government of the Confederate States of America would have represented all or some of her mother states is immaterial. For the very fact of their representation at the conference would, of itself, have constituted recognition by all parties of the *de jure* status of all parties to the conference. And when the conference got around to the question of what to do about West Virginia — that damn-yankee bunch of "evil disposed and traitorous citizens" of Virgiina — there is no doubt as to what the outcome would have been. Virginia would have asserted — successfully — that she withdrew from the Union on 17 April 1861, at which time western Virginia was undeniably a component part of Virginia and at which time the Consitution of the United States ceased to apply to Virginia — especially to that portion of her geography which, more recently, has come to be recognized as "almost Heaven." Therefore, the so-called "consent" to the transfer of the western counties of Virginia given by a "rump" government in Wheeling was just like the "flowers that bloom in the spring, tra la," having nothing to do with the case!

In a nutshell Virginia could have had just about anything she might have demanded. And so it is with the aftermath of war; the victor invariably prevails, and the loser must accept the results with as much good grace as he can muster.

Now let's go back to the world of reality. *The decision handed down at Appomattox was that this country would continue to be one nation, indivisible (and in those days it was unnecessary to add "under God"); and the Constitution of the United States of America would continue to be the supreme law of the land!*

No peace conference was held nor was one necessary. Although the Constitution of the United States then was — and still is — as silent on the subject of secession as a correspondence school campus at midnight, the decision forged on the battlefields stands written in blood on the pages of history. That, of course, was the primary issue decided by the Civil War. But many historians are prone to overlook another decision rendered at Appomattox, one flowing naturally from that primary decision above stated. Put simply in terms of the common law of Virginia (inherited from the common law of England), the hypothetical "ordinary, reasonably prudent man in any given set of circumstances is presumed to intend the natural and probable consequences of his intentional acts in such circumstances." So it was when the majority of delegates to the Richmond "Secession Convention" in 1861 voted to sever their ties with the Union; they intentionally assumed all risks which might naturally and probably result from their act. Such risks included war with the United States and the loss of Virginia territory west of the Alleghenies, which had been edging toward separation from Old Dominion at an ever-accelerating rate during the past two decades, as is admitted by even the most conservative of Virginia historians of this day. Putting it another way, when Virginia purported to secede, she went to war with the United States and forsook its Constitution; she considered herself to be a separate and sovereign state confederated with a union of other separate states under the combined name of "Confederate of States of America." Nevertheless, she claimed the protection of the United States Constitution in the matter of the status of the Restored Government of Virginia and accepted the consent given by this government to the transfer of her western counties. She asserted something which the doctrine of estoppel forbade. She tried to "eat her cake and have it too." On the other hand, the Unionists considered that the Restored Government represented *all* Virginians who remained loyal to the Union, regardless of their place of residence — be it Richmond or Wheeling. Who else should vote on the matter of separation, or any other matter of concern to Virginia, than those who were eligible to vote by reason of Union loyalty? Nearly all eastern Virginians were at war with the Union and could have had no standing in court in any Union jurisdiction. This is the point which mutes the protest of those historians who cry out that "the real Virginia" had no voice in the Restored Government or in the matter of consent to the transfer of her western counties.

The first postwar General Assembly of Virginia (which could not have come into existence except for the Restored Government of Virginia) was elected in 1865 from the parts of the state that constitute the whole area of Virginia as of today. In its session of 1865-66 its Concurrent Resolution No. 1 proclaimed "We accept the result of the late contest, and do not desire to renew what so conclusively has been determined." So did Mr. George W. Munford, compiler and editor of the Code of Virginia 1873 accept all such results of the Civil War, although it is evident in some instances that he was swallowing a bitter pill. Those contemporary Virginians bowed their heads to no one but they accepted the inevitable with the same dignity and realism of General Lee, who advised all who asked "to go home and go to work" and he did not need to add "without reservation."

As a personal friend of mine — a great-grandson of a Confederate general, a native of Richmond and member of the Virginia State Bar — wrote to me after reading an earlier draft of the manuscript for this book:

> In 1861 the final criterion as to the constitutionality of the Restored Government was: Who would win The War? The federal government recognized Pierpont in Wheeling, and thereafter had to follow through so long as the Wheeling (and Alexandria) government refused to go away. This is what I think Governor Pierpont deserves every commendation for: He preserved this link with the conciliatory posture of Washington towards Wheeling in 1861 and put it to work for the benefit of all Virginians in 1865, despite the hostility in

Republican Washington towards any reasonable southern policy. Because he was there, because he would not go away, and because discrediting him meant discrediting the Act of 1862 creating West Virginia, he possessed leverage that no one else could have possessed. Because he used it for the sake of the conquered state, we do indeed owe him much that has been deliberately forgotten.

Thank you again for the introduction to a former governor of Virginia.

Nevertheless, we have writers who still can't get their facts straight or in accord with the law. In the appendix I shall attempt to show the mass of mythology and misinformation which has accumulated over the years and frustrates efforts to attain accuracy.

---

[1]Robert Edward Lee Strider, *The Life and Work of George W. Peterkin* (Philadelphia: George W. Jacobs & Co., 1929), pp. 40, 41. Also cited in John Goode, *Recollections of a Lifetime* (New York: Neale Publishing Co., 1906), p. 57.

[2](Richmond: Deitz Press, 1969), p. 32.

APPENDIX

Chapter I — Appendix
The Molding of Mythology from Molehills into Mountains

Some twenty years after Appomattox General Grant wrote in his memoirs (I, 69): "We have writers — who profess devotion to the nation — engaged in trying to prove that the Union forces wre not victorious." And now, I respectfully submit, we still have writers who are *successfully* engaged in perpetuating mountains of mythology molded from molehills multitudinous moons ago simply because at their point of departure they failed to see the weather-beaten little arrow pointing to the law library as a source of accurate and vital information concerning the subject matter of this book — the distorted chapters of Virginia and West Virginia history. The Hon. George W. Munford, in his preface to the *Code of Virginia, 1873,* inserted a "synopsis" of Virginia history outlining the changes which occurred between the years 1860 and 1873 that in my opinion ought to be the true Volume I "hornbook" on this subject. In the first volume of *Reports of the West Virginia Supreme Court of Appeals,* published in 1866, the equally Honorable John Marshall Hagans inserted a sketch on the formation of a new state from Virginia territory during the period 1861-1863, that in my opinion ought to be the true Volume II "hornbook" on this subject. Those accounts constitute the very essence of the unpublicized chapters dealth with in this book. Works on the subject include the *Acts of Assembly* of the Restored Government of Virginia, the ordinances of the Wheeling conventions and the Alexandria Convention, the *Acts of Assembly* of the so-called Legislature of Virginia sitting in Richmond from 17 April 1861 until Appomattox, the ordinances of the Virginia Secession Convention, which first assembled in Richmond in February 1861 and *Grattan's Reports of Casses in the Virginia Supreme Court of Appeals* from 1863 until 1873. It is of interest right now to observe that nowhere in these authoritative books is Governor Pierpont referred to as being a "provisional" officer, nor is the Retored Government referred to as a "rump government." On the other hand, Mr. Munford candidly states that the government in Rich-

33

mond was "overthrown" by the Restored Government organized in Wheeling!

So the question here to be answered is: how did the molehills become molded into mountains of mythology?

General Grant wrote with admirable restraint, I believe, when he did not allege that those writers who engaged in trying to prove that the Union forces were not victorious were doing so because of an inborn desire to bend history towards a concept of a "brilliant period" for their beloved "Bonnie Blue Flag." I confess that, human nature being what it is, they could well be excused for their motive, if not their writings.

Perhaps the most objective school history book ever published was *A History of Texas Revised,* written and published by Mrs. Anna J. H. Pennybacker of Austin back in 1908. I believe the following extracts from the preface of her book are worth quoting:

> No pains have been spared to obtain the opinion of the best authorities on every disputed point; accuracy has never been sacrificed for the sake of a "brilliant period."
>
> No occasion should be lost to cultivate true patriotism; this means not the blighted egotism which asserts our State to be without blemish, but the wise love that sees all faults, and seeing, resolves to correct the same.

That Mrs. Pennybacker practiced what she preached is illustrated by this passage on page 225 of her book:

> The Congress of the Republic of Texas in 1836 declared the Rio Grande to be its western boundary; but Mexico asserted (and many of the best historians think she was correct) that the Nueces River formed the dividing line between the two countries.

This book then goes on to tell in the same matter-of-fact manner how Texas purported to secede from the Union against the opposition of her governor Sam Houston, who was removed from office upon his refusal to pledge his allegiance to the Confederacy. The incident is related without the use of adjectives. Unfortunately the example set by Mrs. Pennybacker has not been widely followed.

The other extreme came to my attention within a year or so after World War II in the form of a press wire-service report datelined Victoria, British Columbia. The provincial school authorities announced that they were replacing their textbooks on Russian history because, so they said, these books taught that Russia had a bad habit of violating her treaties. Therefore, in view of the fact that heroic Russia had been their ally in the late war and Canada and the British Commonwealth were on friendly terms with Russia, it was unseemly to teach in the British Columbia schools anything derogatory of the U.S.S.R.! (And I must hasten to add that, since then, I have seen Russian history books in these United States that fail to teach that Russian governments have a habit of telling lies whenever it suits them to do so.)

34

Aside from the very few authors who regard their history doctorates a license to doctor history, I believe it not unfair to anyone to assume that those whose sympathy lies with the Confederacy will feel (as Mr. Munford obviously did) that the Restored Government of Virginia did not, by a very large margin, represent the people of Virginia in giving consent to the formation of West Virginia. That those whose sympathy lies with the Union will fell (as Mr. Hagans obviously did) that the Restored Government representated *all* Virginians — everywhere within the state — *who supported the Union.* Therefore, they were the ones who counted because the Confederate Virginians were levying war against the Union and had renounced their allegiance thereto. On that basis, then, I shall now attempt to sort out some of those molehills which molded into mountains of mythology; admittedly, however, I cannot delve into every molehill because there are just too many!

It is important to note that the life span of the Restored Government of Virginia falls into three distinct eras: (1) The era during which Wheeling was the capital of Virginia and the new state of West Virginia emerged, (i.e., 20 June 1861 — 20 June 1863); (2) The era of the Alexandria capital, August 1863 — May 1865; and (3) The era thereafter, beginning with the fall of Richmond and ending with the removal of Governor Pierpont from office, 4 April 1868. Writers of West Virginia history focus only on the Wheeling era, believing that the other two relate entirely to Virginia and thus overlooking the significance of the continuation of the Restored Government *after* the emergency of the state of West Virginia; for this is evidence of the *bona fides* of that government being truly of Virginia and intending to continue in existence to help bring Old Dominion back into favor in Washington when the Civil War ended. This omission lends credence to assertions made by many historians that the Restored Government was a "legal fiction" or "technicality" whereby a Virginia legislature could be made to appear as having given consent to the transfer of territory of Virginia to form a new state. So it was that the words *rump* and *pretender* came into use.

Virginia historians, on the other hand, focus mainly on the Richmond era; they ignore Wheeling and refer to Alexandria merely to infer that the "pretender" Pierpont governed only one or two counties and that he was picked by President Johnson to go to Richmond as "provisional" governor.[1] And they reserve their verbal artillery fire (quite properly) for the carpetbag period which followed. In following this course the Virginia writers lose sight of the great exertions and valiant endeavors of a western Virginian who, as governor, was doing his best to bring the advantages of a Union state government, which had been in existence throughout the Civil War, to the postwar Commonwealth, which was then deluged with destitution. They also omit from their writings a two-year period of history of the western part of the Commonwealth, for even the city of Wheeling was part of Virginia until 20 June 1863. Furthermore, they ignore events and episodes which are not to their liking though true.

Thus, human nature being what it is, former Virginia Governor Henry A. Wise is reputed to have quipped with West Virginia was "the bastard child of a political rape."[2] This early one-liner, as the current crop of talkshow quips, must have caught on as fast as the proverbial hot cakes and begat sequels such as "shadowy government," first attributed to the Alexandria Virginia government by Maj. Gen. Benjamin ("The Beast") Butler in a letter to a friend:[3] "Pierpont's government, it is true, was and is about as shadowy a representation of State's rights as one could wish."

Surely, Virginians will agree whatever Gen. Butler said would be evidence of the exact oppostie of the truth. Another reference to the Alexandria Capitol as having been within "the shadow of the national capitol" initially implied that because it was so close to Washington it remained in existence only because of support of federal troops (indeed, at times, this was true). Thus, "shadowy" became a general accepted adjective to be bandied about by writers when referring to the Alexandria government and this expression is still in current use: Book published in 1938 uses the term "shadowy government,"[4] and this same term is picked up in another book which went into its sixth printing in 1966.[5]

Supposed "authorities" are not always to be relied on and sometimes they induce errors in books by other writes. Thus, "President" Jefferson Davis in his book *The Rise and Fall of the Confederate Government* (II, 722 and 723), refers to "provisional governors" being appointed by President Johnson for the former Confederate states. In fact, however, he did not *appoint* Mr. Pierpont to any office at all but recognized him as being THE governor of Virginia; but this loose language might well have been the basis for many a writer to have believed that Pierpont was "appointed" as a "provisional governor" as were the others. ("Provisional" has been covered in sufficient detail in the saga itself.) A more serious and spiteful misstatement by Mr. Jefferson Davis, however, appears on page 306 of that Volume II. Herein he refers to the members of the Wheeling convention of June 1861 as having been "disorderly persons"; so I therefore invite attention to the opinion of a respected Virginia historian, Dr. R. A. Brock, on that subject. He states that this convention was "attended by the leading men of Northwestern Virginia" (Page 236 of *Virginia and Virginians,* Hardesty, 1888). It seems appropriate to suggest now that "President" Davis might have been somewhat less than objective in his writings.

But even the truly great historians have, at times, been in error. One example will suffice. Dr. Charles H. Ambler, Mr. Pierpont's biographer, asserts on page 221 of the book that the Alexandria General Assembly of 1864-65 defeated a bill providing for the repeal of those sections of the *Code of Virginia, 1860* which forbade the education of Negroes. He was in error. Chap. 47 of the acts of that sessions, passed 6 March 1865, did indeed repeal such provisions of the Code. And on page 282 of his monumental work of biography Dr. Ambler further avers that the session of 1865-66 repealed the Act of 13 May 1862, which gave Virginia's consent to the formation of West Virginia from her territory. The truth is that only Sec. 2 of the act was repealed, a section which related solely to

Berkeley and Jefferson Counties, which were not then included in West Virginia. It also referred to Frederick County, which was never transferred at all. this error was to the detriment of at least one present-day writer, who, it is fair to say, should have been justified in relying on Dr. Ambler's statement as sufficient authority. But still another error by Ambler, on page 222, was my own undoing: that the Alexandria constitution of Virginia provided *for the first time* a poll tax for the purpose of providing for free schools. Instead, that provision was a carry-over from the 1851 Virginia Constitution. I accepted Dr. Ambler's statement and quoted it in my Pierpont article in *West Virginia Heritage Encyclopedia,* edited and published by Jim Comstock (Richwood, W. Va., 1976). Fortunately, the error is not one of substance. This taught me never to rely on *any other person whomsoever* but to look up myself every reference to law. Dr. Ambler is (or was, as he has since graduated from this life) one of the greatest West Virginia historians in my opinion. And let it be noted that he was not a lawyer, and apparently he did not research in a law library — something that is true of nearly all other historians on the subject of this work.

I could continue this theme umpteen more pages, but I suspect that such dosage would not be digestible and might even lose its savory flavor, so just a few more illustrative errors will be mentioned to nail down my point.

The "Lincoln States," so-called. On 8 December 1863 President Lincoln proclaimed a possible method whereby the people of a state then in rebellion could establish a government and be "recognized as the true government of the State." Generally speaking, the method was simply this: Any ten percent of the former qualified voters who would take oath to "henceforth" support the Constitution of the United State could form such a government. The President went on to provide that his proclamation "has no reference to States wherein loyal state governments have all the while been maintained."[6]

The foregoing is set forth with accuracy by one of the foremost twentieth-century writers on the subject of the Confederacy and Reconstruction — Mr. Robert Selph Henry, in pages eight and nine of his book *The Story of Reconstruction* (New York: Bobbs-Merrill, 1938). But he then goes on to state that President Lincoln:

"had used another method in Tennessee and still another in Virginia, where he recognized and supported the 'restored state of Virginia,' a rudimentary government set up around the fringes of the old state by Francis H. Pierpont, after he had successfully carried through the movement for the separation of West Virginia."

Here we have the implication — amounting to a bald statement — that President Lincoln first recognized Pierpont sometime after 20 June 1863 (the date of West Virginia's admission to the Union). The second bald statement was that the Restored Government was merely a "rudimentary one," although during the period June 1861 to June 1863 it had nearly one-third of the territory of

37

the old state developed, three well-organized and functioning branches of government and was supplying many men and regiments to the Union armies. In fact, *de facto* governor of Virginia William Smith knew and acknowledged this is his message to the so-called "Legislature of Virginia" on 7 December 1864 when he told that body "There are some forty to fifty counties of Virginia within the enemy's lines, most of them under a regular government of the enemy." The "governor," of course, was referring to what had been set up and organized by the Pierpont regime.[7] So much for the "fringes" of the old state and the "rudimentary" nature thereof! And Mr. Henry's statement that the present "had used still another method" with respect to Virginia carries the strong implication, if not a bald statement, that the President was instrumental in the formation of the Restored Government. He was not. The formation was due entirely to those who attended the Wheeling Convention in June of 1861, albeit Mr. Lincon's ardent support thereafter was essential to the continued existence of that resorted government. Yet the notion persists in current history books that Mr. Lincoln set the wheels in motion with West Virginia.

That assumption, however, is not unnatural becaue historians are prone to lump together the states of Arkansas, Louisiana, Tennessee and Virginia under the catchall "Lincoln States." Mr. Henry himself does this in page nine of his book on Reconstruction; he refers to the "fledgling organizations" of those four states and on page 39 he states:

> The four "Lincoln states" were first disposed of. The Lincoln governments in Louisiana, Arkansas and Tennessee were continued without formal action. At the cabinet meeting of May 9 formal recognition of the Alexandria government had already been recognized for acts of the gravest importance — to register the "consent" of old Virginia to the separation of West Virginia in 1862; to "consent" again to the transfer of Jefferson and Berkeley Counties to the new state in 1863. Governor Francis H. Pierpont, who had led the movement to set up West Virginia, was elected "Governor of Virginia," or, as it was usually put, of "restored Virginia." The territory of his government consisted of a few toeholds about the fringes of the state, under United States Army protection; its legislative body numbered six senators and seven delegates, representing among them seven counties; its constitutional convention, when one came to be held, consisted of fifteen members, some without credentials; its powers were just what army officers, sometimes hostile and contemptuous, would allow it — except when it came to take its part in amending the Constitution of the United States, which it did by ratifying the Thirteenth Amendment on February 18, 1865.

There we have a rehash of much that is said on pages eight and nine of his book, although Mr. Henry fails to mention that the 9

May cabinet meeting merely confirmed President Lincoln's previously given recognition of the Restored Government. He implies that Mr. Pierpont was elected governor of Virginia by plan of the President. He neglects to mention that the "Alexandria government," as he calls it, had been in existence since June 1861, that the city charter had been amended by the Wheeling General Assembly, that taxes were regularly levied and collected, that civil courts were functioning as usual and a lot more ets and ceteras as well. But you know all this from having read the saga. Furthermore, the constitutional convention, "when one came to be held" in Mr. Henry's words, was called pursuant to Chap. 2 of the Acts of Assembly of 1863-64, passed 21 December 1863 because *inter alia,* "The President of the United States, by proclamation issued 1 January 1863, did free all the slaves in the Commonwealth of Virginia except [those in the area controled by the Restorted Government]." The then existing constitution of the state charged state officers to enforce slave laws, which were repugnant to the presidental Emancipation Proclamation. In short it was by necessity that there be written and adopted an amended a basic law which would not conflict in any manner with the Constitution and laws of the United States. The Act of Assembly of 1863-64 provided for credentials to be issued to duly chosen convention delegates, and the journal of the convention states that the committee on credentials certified seventeen persons holding proper credentials to be seated as delegates (contrary to Mr. Henry's statement that there were only fifteen and some were without credentials). The federal government did not interfere with the proceedings of the convention; on the contrary, the federal courtroom was provided as a hall for the convention and a convention committee sought advice from the President and Secretary of the Treasury Chase, both of whom were highly praised in a resolution of the convention. An ordinance was adopted whereby money from the sale of the lands due Virginia from the United States was appropriated to reimburse loyal slave owners for loss of their property, and the constitution adopted by the convention abolished slavery completely.

Here is another error by Mr. Henry: the convention did not ratify the 13th (anti-slavery) Amendment to the federal constitution. The only amendment ratified by state conventions was the 21st, which repealed the 18th amendment which had been generally known as the "prohibition amendment." Instead, it was passed by the General Assembly, in its act of 9 February 1865, and none of Mr. Henry's four states ratified the amendment on 18 February of that year, as alleged by him!

But the main point of the Alexandria Constitution was overlooked entirely by Mr. Henry. It was designed to bring (Confederate) Virginia back into the Union upon the end of the hostilities; we may speculate that it would have filled that purpose had not President Lincoln been assassinated and control of the federal government passed to the radical Republicans in 1865.

Mr. Henry's statement that the Alexandria Legislature consisted of six senators and only seven delegates is incorrect. In the saga I cite six senators and thirteen delegates because their names and constituencies are listed on page 361 in Volume I of Miller and Maxwell's *History of West Virginia and its People,* (Chicago: Lewis Historical Publishing Co., 1913).

I believe it a matter of interest to note that "President" Jefferson David, (II, 450) in his work *the Rise and Fall of the Confederate Government,* lumps Louisiana, Arkansas, Tennessee and Virginia together in one chapter, although he does not designate them as "Lincoln" states. These are the states which had reorganized governments of one kind or another prior to the collapse of the Confederacy at Appomattox — their common denominator being (1) a form of government recognized in the supremacy of the Constitution of the United States; (2) incumbent officers loyal to the Union; (3) a considerable geographical area within which writs could run and be enforced; (4) prior recognition by President Lincoln of *de jure* status; and (5) sufficient Union military force within the area to assure uninterrupted continuation of government. It would seem that this was a natural and logical grouping by Mr. Davis; the designation "Lincoln states" must have been given by a lesser-known, or later, historian. Mr. Henry was right, therefore, in stating that President Johnson's action at the 9 May 1865 cabinet meeting, of continuing the governments of Louisiana, Arkansas and Tennessee in effect "without formal action" was correct, because no further action was required.

We have now reached a point which has been and still is generally overlooked, even though its significance would seem to be obvious. Virginia shared all elements of that common denominator except area and military force. In addition, Virginia lacked a permanent state capital. The capital was scheduled to be transferred from Alexandria back to Richmond, which was located in a vast area which had been held securely by Confederate forces until just a few weeks before. In addition, the President saw the immediate need to reinstate within this territory all the usual federal institutions and offices such as post offices, custom houses, courts, marshals' offices and, indeed, all functions of the federal gamut. He also perceived that Governor Pierpont might need some help in reinstating various state functions and offices within that area. Therefore, while the matter of recognition anew of the status of the Resorted Government of Virginia might have been a topic of conversation, the only "formal action" then needed was to publish an executive order directed to members of his cabinet and other officers subject to his orders. The order would promptly reinstate their jurisdiction, allow them to resume their usual duties and functions within the whole area of Virginia and, while they were about it, direct them to give Governor Pierpont a helping hand in getting the state's business set up in proper running order. The President gave no orders whatsoever to the governor; he did not appoint Mr. Pierpont to any office nor send him to any place; he simply recognized the continuation of the *de jure* status of Pierpont's office and the existence of the state government over which he presided. Then, having done this, he proceeded from time to time over the next few months to issue separate proclamations (notice the difference between an executive order and a proclamation) in which he did "appoint" various persons to the office of "provisional governor" while in the same paper, directing various federal officers to reinstitute the functions of the federal government within those state.

An acorn thus appears to have been planted which has grown into a forest, for numerous history books now extant say pretty much the same things about so-called "Lincoln states" and under that same designation.

In a review of Mr. Henry's book by Dr. Henry S. Commanger — himself one of the foremost American historians — in the *New York Times Book Review* of 13 March 1938 we are told that: "here is the not unfamiliar story of Lincoln's reconstruction policy, the rise of radical opposition, the establishment of provisional governments under Johnson." And a stretch of *ets* and *ceteras* running for several inches of print followed by Dr. Commager's comment:

All this has been told time and time again; it is the merit of Mr. Henry's book that he has summarized, most skillfully, the findings of modern scholarship as set forth in scores of monongraphs and thus furnished us with the most convenient book of Reconstruction since Burgess's outmoded volumes.

Dr. Commager goes into more detail for about half a page, and concludes:

For thoroughness, accuracy, comprehensiveness, moderation and balance, it commends itself to every student of reconstruction, and for the argument implicit in its detail, to every student of the present crisis.

There you have it in a nu . . . (I was about to say "nutshell," but my stock thereof is exhausted, so I'll have to substitute "thimble" instead; I have one that belonged to my grandmother) in a thimble — Mr. Henry spent hours in many libraries reading what prior writers had turned out, without checking into the accuracy of what they said.

Furthermore, the Bobbs-Merrill 1938 edition reviewed by Dr. Commager evidently became so established as an "authority" that a later publication of it came on the market, published by Grossett & Dunlap by arrangements with Bobbs-Merrill, but no date of publication is given. Inasmuch as Mr. Commager is included in the fourth edition of *The Oxford Companion to American Literature,* as a professor of history at several prestigious universities and colleges and author and editor of history books, those who turn to Mr. Henry's "Story of the Reconstruction" may naturally feel assured that it is, in fact, "accurate and comprehensive" and its commendation to "every student of reconstruction" is resassuring indeed.

One currently used textbook (I have before me a sixth edition thereof) is *Reconstruction: The Battle for Democracy,* by James S. Allen (New York: International Publishers, 1966). It lumps those same four states together under the caption "The Lincoln Plan" and is a boiled down version of "President" Davis and Mr. Henry.

"The Lincoln States" is, I respectfully submit, an excellent illustration of the molding of a molehill into a mountain of mythology; even the most respected and knowledgeable historians and journalists rely on its preachment as though it came to them by special message from the mouth of Pegasus himself.

More Molehills And Mountains

(1) The so-called "West Virginia's Declaration of Independence," as was spawned by *The Thirty-Fifth State: A Documentary History of West Virginia,* edited by Elizabeth Cometti and the late Festus P. Summers, West Virginia University Library, Morgantown, 1966. They are editor-professors of History at West Virginia University.

This documentary history contains many if not most of the important historical documents relating to West Virginia from colonial days to the date of 1966, EXCEPT that it omits the most important paper of them all, *biz* and *to wit* (as we lawyers are sometimes wont to say) — The Virginia Bill of Rights — but that parchment is set out verbatim in a later chapter of this appendix.

These editors (see page 319 of their book) gratuitously entitle a chapter of their book *West Virginia Declaration of Independence,* based on a resolution of the Wheeling Convention of 17 June, 1861, entitled, "A Declaration of the People of Virginia," which states clearly that it refers to authority contained in the Virginia Bill of Rights.

Nevertheless, these editors would have us believe that their declaration paraphrased the Philadelphia declaration of the Fourth of July, 1776; completely ignoring the fact that Thomas Jefferson — a Virginian — paraphrased the Virginia Bill of Rights which was in *June* of 1776! They put the cart before the horse. This recalls to mind an old horse-cavalry saying that so and so is too stupid to pour water from a boot even if the directions were printed upside down on the heel.

This gross error — published in 1966 — has for twenty years caused misconception in the minds of many students, public-spirited citizens, writers, journalists, newscasters, and other people generally. A building in Wheeling is misnamed; references to that building in the state's *Blue Book* and on state road maps, *inter alia,* now must be revised. And unless another, corrected, edition is published to set the record straight the present edition will surely and rapidly continue to forge forsaken facts into fabulous fables.

(2) *The Civil War in West Virginia: A Pictorial History* by Stan Cohen (Charleston, W. Va., Pictorial Histories Publishing Co., 1976).

This book, for the most part, appears to be accurate in its statement of facts; the contents live up to the expectations raised by the title; and the pictures are both good and interesting. It is unfortunate, therefore, that the author had to rely on the mountains of mythology as the basis for his short synopsis of the Restored Government of Virginia.

Mr. Cohen states that Mr. Pierpont was the "first governor of the Restored Government." He could well have omitted "first," as Pierpont was its only governor. He further states that the Restored Government's congressmen were seated in Congress and recognized by President Lincoln. But it was the houses of Congress that recognized them, including the senators from the Restored Government as well; it was Governor Pierpont who was recognized by the president. But where Mr. Cohen really was misled by the mountains of mythology (from which most authors derive their [mis]information) is his next assertion: "[T]his separation from another state without that state's permission is unparalled in American history and has been questioned for constitutional legality." As you must know from having read the saga iself, and will learn from reading an upcoming chapter ("The Courts looked the Other Way," which follows in this appendix), the constitutionality of the Restored Government was upheld by the highest courts of the United States and the Commonwealth of Virginia as well more than a century ago; West Virginia did not "secede" from Virginia; rather, it was Virginia that purported to secede from the Union, whereupon the loyal people of Virginia "restored" the state to the Union under authority of the Virginia Bill of Rights. And Mr. Cohen's paragraph concerning the debt of West Virginia to Virginia lacks accuracy in many respects; (See the following chapter in this appendix to that subject).

As to the captions under pictures of the Old Custom House, see the following chapter of "Virginia's Old Capitol in Wheeling." And to point out just one more error, Governor Pierpont was removed from office in 1868 instead of 1867. Mr. Cohen is correct in stating that "It was not until January 1, 1863, that the slaves were set free by President Lincoln." But he failed to add that the president's proclamation set slaves free only in the geographical areas of those states which were in rebellion. West Virginia was not in rebellion at any time!

You may say "most of these criticisms verge on triviality." Be that as it may, this book is mentioned here because all of the foregoing errors are contained in just a very few pages! It emphasizes the amount of misinformation which is known to writers generally, and my book is designed to publicize the unpublicized chapters of Virginia and West Virginia history so that the record will be correct and will be known, to writers on this subject everywhere!

(3) *World Book Encyclopedia,* 1958 edition (and how many prior editions?) informs its readers that from 1865 until 1868 Mr. Pierpont was simultaneously governor of Virginia and West Virginia! That error was corrected in a later edition but followed by other errors. My own 1974 edition of *World Book* (which I consider to be as good as encyclopedias go these days) lists two Confederate "governors" of Virginia under a paragraph heading "Governors under the United States Constitution." It also states that after West Virginia became a state Arthur I. Boreman was "appointed" West Virginia's first governor. Mr. Boreman was *elected* at the regular election held in May preceeding his inaugura-

tion of 20 June, 1863. (This is an update — not seen by Messrs. Weeks or Maurice.)

(4) *"Many delegates held irregular credentials; some had none at all."*

That or similar language may be found in many books relating to citizens conventions held in Wheeling and Alexandria; depending upon the points of view and sympathies of the various authors, such language can be, and usually is, amplified so as to connote mischievous conniving to pack a convention to assure the outcome of its proceedings to be favorable to the connivers. On the other hand, various counties and areas of what is now West Virginia were under control of Confederate military forces when such conventions were held, and some delegates went to the conventions without credentials because they were afraid for their bodily safety — while others who did participate in caucuses or mass meetings had no guidelines to follow with respect to drafting such credentials. The 1860 Code of Virginia contained no such provisions, and until the General Assembly of the Restored Government came into existence and first met in July 1861 no such legislation was needed. That being the case, the four delegates from Alexandria and Fairfax counties to the June 1861 Wheeling Convention must have been brave men indeed. Messrs. Close and Hawxhurst were members of the Virginia General Assembly, which *ipso facto* constituted their credentials, but for the other two to have found a jutice of the peace or other Union officials who could have administered an oath would, no doubt, have been difficult in that environment of Confederate sympathizers.

Now it was not my pleasure to have attended any of those conventions, so I cannot speak with the authority of an eye-witness on the subject. But from what I have read (and by now you must suspect that I have become acquainted with many writers on the subject), I have a hunch amounting almost to a conviction that in those days of smaller cities and towns and consequently fewer male citizens of voting age in the state, most of the men of stature and influence knew each other fairly well. Each convention had its own committee on credentials, and I would consider it highly unlikely that more than a very few persons could have been gate crashers, so to speak. And, let's face it, gentle reader (as was the saying back in those days about which I write) I have another hunch which also amounts to near conviction that throughout the South there must have been conventions and meetings and even sessions of state and "federal" legislatures wherein some delegates held equally "irregular" credentials or none at all, but writers of the Confederate persuasion don't touch upon this subject.

The paragraphs of this section are of themselves unimportant insofar as the course of history is concerned. Nevertheless, they so shed light on the molding of molehills into mountains of mythology; each atom of dirt the mole uproots becomes a component of those mountains. Meaning: readers must be wary about the accuracy of connotations and innuendoes involved.

(5) *Chapter Five of "Wheeling: An Illustrated History" by Doug Fetherling, published by civic organizations and private businesses in the fall of 1983.*

Chapter five of this book contains several important errors. Perhaps the most glaring mistake, because it displays the attitude of West Virginia writers generally, is that the Restored Government in Wheeling was actually the government of western Virginia until West Virginia emerged as a separate state. Those writers, including Mr. Fetherling, seem to have displayed that view. The glaring example is the statement that what the Restored Government most needed after its birth was money "and a constitution" — thereby overlooking the fact that they already had a constitution: The VIRGINIA Constitution. The constitution was complete with its oath of allegiance to the United States and its statement that under this a Union government instead of a Confederate one governed the whole state from the Ohio River to the Atlantic. Nevertheless, the author refers to the Restored Government as a government-in-exile.

All that is refuted in Caesar Giffin's case (see "The Courts Looked the Other Way" in this appendix), and in that case it was made clear, step-by-step, that the Pierpont government was *de jure* throughout the whole Commonwealth.

The only other error I shall touch upon is the author's statement that Mr. Pierpont first spelling his name "Pierpoint" and later changed to "Pierpont," but Mr. Fetherling is wrong. Had he consulted *Francis H. Pierpont* by Dr. Ambler (see notes in saga) he would have found that the initial spelling was "Peirpoint" and was changed to "Pierpont." Now Fetherling doesn't mention Dr. Ambler's work in his bibliography, displaying a gross lack of knowledge of West Virginia and Wheeling history. (This is an update — not seen by Messers. Weeks or Maurice).

(6) *West Virginia: A Bicentennial History, by John Alexander Williams, (Morgantown: West Virginia University Press, 1976).*

The dust jacket of this book states that Dr. Williams grew up in White Sulphur Springs and is a descendant of a long line of West Virginians. Nevertheless, the very last paragraph of his book would have believe that bumper stickers such as ones stating "Almost Heaven" hide a sense of inferiority, a sense that there is something of which to be ashamed. Visitors readily see through this pretense. It is to be wondered, then, why Dr. Williams was selected to write the state's bicentennial anniversary (i.e., bicentennial of the United States, 4 July 1976). I can honestly do nothing else than point out Dr. Williams' own point of view without further comment by me.

In the chapter entitled "Droop Mountain" concerning the Civil War period in West Virginia, Dr. Williams states that the procedure by which western Virginia was molded into a separate state could be made to seem "expedient, unprincipled, cheap." But had he done his homework so as to include a law library, he would have found in Caesar Griffin's Case (see chapter of this appendix, "The Courts Looked the Other Way") that a Chief Justice of the United

States, Mr. Salmon P. Chase, while sitting as a circuit justice in Virginia after the Civil War, had pronounced the procedure to have been rooted solidly in constitutional principles and was the most expedient, natural and easiest way to have been taken. Dr. Williams also claims that the first postwar Virginia legislature (Richmond 1865-66) contained numerous former Confederates as members and repealed all the enabling legislation by which the new state had been formed "and that that needle had been in the collective hide of West Virginians ever since!" What a display of powerful imagination! There was so such legislation; the act of assembly to which Dr. Williams refers repealed only the consent given by Virginia for Berkeley and Jefferson Counties. (See *Virginia v. West Virginia* in another chapter of this appendix.)

One last comment on this book: Doctor Williams blamed the courts for "looking the other way." as though the courts could, by their own initiative, have stopped the whole process and were to blame for not doing so. Numerous other writers make the same error, Dr. Williams is to blame for relying on prior "historical" writings which reek with mountains of mythology formed by mere molehills twelve and more decades since the Civil War.

(7) *West Virginia's Bicentennial and Golden Jubilee at Wheeling June 15th-21st 1913, Official Souvenir Book, published by the official committee.*

There is one error; on page 34 it is stated: "West Virginia is also unique in her history. She is the only state carved out of the territory of another." This error has been repeated more or less frequently since then, the latest such statement having been mde by the Rev. Clifford Lewis, S.J., in a sketch of Governor Pierpont.

But what impresses me most concerning this semicentennial observance in Wheeling in 1913 is that there is no mention whatsoever of a "West Virginia Declaration of Independence" or of any such building as "West Virginia Independence Hall." The building now known as such was then the headquarters of a life insurance company.

I was not quite nine years old at the time; I remember a parade in which the Grand Army of the Republic veterans participated — I should say approximately six automobile loads and perhaps twenty-five marches following. Certainly if there had been a declaration document or independence hall, they would have been prominently featured. On the other hand, the old Linsly Institue building was open to the public because it was West Virginia's first capitol.

My mother is mentioned in the booklet several times as being chairman (not "chairperson") of one committee or another (she thrived on this). On the other hand my father, born in Wheeling in 1868, knew where Wetzel's cave was and took me there. Everyone in Wheeling knew the place from which Samuel McCulloch jumped his horse down to Wheeling Creek. I consider these details to be very strong proof indeed that there never was a West Virginia Declaration of Independence of Independence Hall, at least not until a year or so after 1963 when a thought in the minds of two

46

university professors had a brain child which turned out to be their book *The Thirty Fifty State!*

But that 1913 souvenir program contained a historial fact that has been overlooked ever since: West Virginia and Wheeling do indeed have "unique" features in history. West Virginia contains a building in Wheeling which from 20 June 1861 to 20 June 1863 was the capitol of Virginia!! It is the only city in these United States to have been the capitol of two different states and is now not capitol of any state! St. Augustine in Florida makes much of her being the oldest city; the capitol in Texas was once the capitol of a foreign country; and Santa Fe is the only city which has been a capital longer than any other community in this country. Their respective chambers of commerce make money by attracting tourists by such noncostly assets.

This should be a lesson to civic and state agencies in West Virginia and Wheeling!

(8) *A Hornbook of Virginia History, third edition, edited by Emily J. Salmon, Virginia State Library, Richmond, 1983.*

On page 38 it is stated that a convention met in Wheeling on 11 June 1861 and declared all state offices vacant and named a slate of new officers headed by Francis H. Pierpont. Then President Lincoln promptly recognized Pierpont as the governor of Virginia and from the summer of 1861 until the summer of 1863, Pierpont was chief executive of those counties controlled by the Union army. There is an error here — Pierpont was *de jure* governor of Virgina from the Ohio River to the Atlantic Ocean; he was also *de facto* governor of the land held by Union military forces, and his capital was Wheeling. The next statement on that page is that he moved his seat of government to Alexandria in 1862 so as not to be known as a "governor-in-exile." This is incorrect because Alexandria did not become capital until August 1863.

On page 39 it is stated that Congress "admitted" West Virginia to the Union on 20 June 1863, and Pierpont's General Assembly in Alexandria "endorsed" the new state. But what actually happened was that the Wheeling General Assembly gave its consent (not "endorsement") to the formation of the new state from Virginia Territory in May of 1862; and Congress consented by an act signed by President Lincoln on 31 December 1862. Thereafter, on 20 April 1863 the President signed a proclamation stating that West Virginia would become a state from and after sixty days, i.e., 20 June 1863. Following West Virginia's admission, the Governor made a trip to the eastern counties, and in August proclaimed Alexandria to be the new capital of Virginia. There never was any "government in exile" — that must have been a quote from the imagination of the author of a picture book mentioned a page or so ago.

Page 41 tells us that President Andrew Johnson "recognized" Pierpont as "provisional" governor on 9 May 1865. In fact Pierpont had already been established as the *de jure* governor, not as a "provisional" governor. (This is a common error; many governors of other states wee appointed "provisional" governor by pro-

47

clamation of that date, but the president signed an executive order directed to his own officers to resume their duties in Virginia and to help the governor of Virginia, Mr. Pierpont, in any way they could. (See a copy of that order elsewhere in this appendix).

According to page 42, elections were held by the military district commander in 1867 giving Virginia a Republican form of government headed by H. Wells; but this is contradicted on page 80. The contradiction is correct, for Wells was appointed by Gen. Schofield in the same orders that removed Pierpont. He was not elected nor was he a success, but was commonly referred to as a carpetbagger. The first elected governor after Pierpont's removal was Gilbert C. Walker in 1869 under the Underwood Constitution.

It is interesting to note that on page 79 under the heading "Governors Under the Restored Governor" the tenure of Mr. Pierpont is stated to be from 20 June 1861 until 28 August of that year. But he had moved from Wheeling on 20 June of 1863. Then it lists his supposed tenure under the heading of Alexandria and Richmond, a tenure which began on his arrival in Richmond, and not on the date of this executive order of 9 May 1865. I wonder why these tenures are listed as simply *de jure*, while parts of the *de facto* terms of Letcher and William Smith were not *de jure* but *de facto only*. This Hornbook ought, it is respectfully submitted, list in sequence those who had held office but with *de facto* in any such case. The pretense that there were two sets of *de jure* governments is strictly party line; but there is no shame involed here.

General Lee, for example, was a great man, a brilliant general, a true Christian gentleman and respected by friend and foe alike. He was a rebel against the Union; but the cause he espoused was honorable. Here the party line brings the art of trying to justify a cause that needs no such justification.

(9) *Continental Edition, The Writings of Abraham Lincoln, G. P. Putnam's Sons, New York, Vol. 8.*
This series in eight volumes has a foreword in Volume I by Theodore Roosevelt, himself a historian of no little fame, the book was edited by historian Arthur Brooks Lapszey. On page 283 of Volume VIII we are told that Mr. Pierpont was the "first provisional governor of West Virginia." But we know better than that, don't we?

Summary
Is it any wonder, then that after all these decades since Appomattox we still have writers — honest and above reproach — "engaged in trying to prove many things which happened and a lot more other things which did not happen? Where is the school student to go for information if his encyclopedia is fraught with error? And who can blame the newscaster for error when Teddy Roosevelt himself knew not the truth?

The Honorable George Wythe Munford puts it very well in speaking about the causes and effects of the Civil War:

The general historian will recount these causes, and moralize on them; and may give utterance to animated comments, the results of deliberate reflections, without being swayed by passion or prejudice. We [in 1873] can only give a hasty outline, to serve for reference scarcely venturing to express approbation or censure. In a work like this mere rhetorical ornament either in praise or reprobation, would not be justifiable.

Mr. Munford, Sir, I stand and salute you. You have done your commonwealth and your true country a very great service. While I am not a general historian, I do hope that your Spirit, on High, will look down on me with favor, and consider that I have emulated yourself to the best of my ability!

(This item is an update of April of 1986; neither Mr. Weeks nor Mr. Maurice have seen this.)

---

[1]See for example: "The United States government organized a government of Virginia at Alexandria February 13, 1865." See W. Asbury Christian's *Richmond — Her Past and Present* (1912; Spartanburg, N.C.: Reprint, 1973), p. 270.

[2]Ann Pierpont Siviter, *Recollections of War & Peace* (New York: G. P. Putnam's Sons, 1938), p.x. Dr. Paul Brandon Barringer, who was largely instrumental in bringing about the establishment of the University of Virginia Hospital, has told this story at the turn of the century when the "hospital" consisted only of an as-yet incomplete out-patient dispensary, an ox cart containing a bed of straw upon which a girl of fourteen lay in agony on her second day of labor, drew up in front of the door. After hurriedly scrubbing and disinfecting a wooden table and such surgical instruments as happened to be on hand, Doctor Barringer, assisted by the several medical students who chanced to be present, successfully delivered the baby; whereupon one of the students pondered aloud 'what shall we call it?' and was promptly answered 'West Virginia!' "

[3]*Ibid.,* p. 126.

[4]Robert Selph Henry, *The Story of Reconstruction,* (New York: Bobbs-Merrill, 1938), p. 11.

[5]James S. Allen, *Reconstruction, The Battle for Democracy 1965-1876* (New York: International Publishers, 1966), p. 38.

[6]Lincoln's Proclamation of Amnesty, p. 28, Vol. 7. *The Writings of Abraham Lincoln, Constitutional Edition* (New York: G. P. Putnam's Sons, 1906).

[7]John W. Bell, *Memoris of Gov. William Smith* (New York: The Moss Engraving Co., 1891), p. 181. But see page 165 of that book, wherein Mr. Smith tells the audience at his "inauguration" on 6 January 1864 something which needs to be repeated in the 1980s: "The currency of the country, consisting as it does almost exclusively of (Confederate) notes, and which the states and people (thereof) are identified, calls for the most careful consideration.

The facility with which it is created, and the enormous amount which are daily issued, naturally lead to waste and extravagance, and inevitably a vice and depravity.''

Chapter II — Appendix
How Prevalent is Mythology in Other Historical Writings?

The foregoing exposure of the mountains of mythology enveloping Governor Pierpont and the Restored Government of Virginia, and their effect on the writings of learned historians of undoubted integrity, raises a question — at least in my own mind — as to the accuracy of the writings of other equally learned and trustworthy historians in practically all other fields of history. This question first became apparent to me as I read the acknowledgement page of another book by historian Robert Selph Henry, whose *Story of Reconstruction* has been dissected in the preceding chapter.

Mr. Henry was also the author of *The Story of the Confederacy,* published by Bobbs-Merrill, from which I now quote a passage contained in the "acknowledgements" page of the 1957 revised edition:

> One of the principle purposes of this edition of *The Story of the Confederacy* is to correct in print some forty factual errors in previous editions, many of which were first noted by observant readers who were obliging enough to call them to my attention.

Upon reading that very frank acknowledgement and correction of error on his part, I figuratively arose from the comfort of my chair to stand at attention and render a smart salute to Mr. Henry, who, insofar as I know, is unique in this respect. He does indeed meet the standards of Mrs. Pennybacker's book and stands as a shining example for all other writers in this field. Diogenese may now blow out his lamp and go home for a well-earned rest!

But there is still another facet to consider in this matter of perpetuating error unintentionally. The 1936 edition carried a foreword by one of the most respected of all Civil Ward historians, Douglas Southall Freeman, who, being a brother Phi Gam, is in my opinion *ipso facto* foremost in his field. In that foreword Mr. Freeman states "the delighted satifaction with which he breathless-

51

ly read the first edition of Mr. Henry's book'' — supposedly with all the included errors he may or may not have noticed, and we shall never know. That same foreword is contained in the 1957 revised edition although Mr. Freeman had graduated from this life several years before then.

What, if any, significance is this to the subject matter of this book and to history books generally? While Diogenes may be happy with Mr. Henry's acknowledgement and correction of errors, are the historian progeny of Herodotus unhappy that Mr. Freeman should extol a book containing forty errors? What is the duty of a book reviewer in this matter? Must he go back and check a footnote himself in each instance of footnote authority for any statement in the book being reviewed? Sir Winston Churchill wrote a *History of the English Speaking Peoples*. Obviously he could not have had a personal knowledge of every event he recorded and had to draw freely from other sources of competent authority; on the other hand in his monumental volumes of World War II he himself was in many cases the actual source of authority for much of what he wrote. What is the reviewer's duty in each of those instances?

A much later book entitled *Blood Over Texas (The Truth About Mexico's War With the United States)* by Sanford H. Montaigne (Arlington House, 1976) says this in pages 11 and 12 of the introduction:

> Aside from our dealings with American Indian tribes, the earliest case of American ''Imperialism'' cited is usually the Mexican War of 1846. A controversial struggle in its own time, the revisionists have found ample material to paint the portrait of imperialistic, cruel Americans seeking *lebenstraun* at the expense of peace-loving Mexico.
>
> This book is an attempt to right the record of the Mexican War, to show where the burden of responsibility fell, and why.

It occurs to me that Gen. Grant's complaint about writers engaged in trying to prove that the Union forces were not victorious might well have been a precursor for similar complaints in future wars. Such complaints may also be applicable to events in other fields of history not related to war. And historians who review and praise works of other historians ought to check out footnote references and other statements of law and fact *before* according praise — especially in cases wherein, of necessity, many books, monographs and records of accumulated information had to be used by the author whose book is the subject of review.

I do not profess to be an historian (if I were, I would probably have said ''*a* historian,'' although that phrase does not ripple off the tongue nearly so rythmetically); I merely throw out a torch for such historians as may be interested to light and carry it forward. I believe it is an undertaking which might well be worth while and might set many another record straight. I am merely a retired West Virginia lawyer and soldier, who is proud of his state's Old Dominion heritage and has for more than twenty years been a buff on the subject of Governor Pierpont and the Restored Government of Virginia. Therefore, I have explored this field from A to Zed (as our British cousins are wont to say) and, in doing so, have climbed the heights of the mountains of mythology to the very summit. There I became the guest of Pegasus in his imperial stables and learned the truth from the mouth of my host and so can set the record straight.

Chapter III — Appendix
The University Press of Virginia and its Book The Governors of Virginia 1860-1978, Chapters on Messrs. Letcher, William Smith (Second Term Only) and Francis Harrison Pierpont

The Party Line: Conflict of Interests?

My book is about the Restored Government of Virginia. True, it also concerns West Virginia, but its main thrust is Virginia. Therefore, my prime choice for publisher was the University Press of Virginia located in Charlottesville.

A few days before or after Washington's birthday in 1982, my good friend Elie Weeks, (the historian of Virginia who wrote a foreword to this work), and I took my manuscript to the senior editor of that establishment and offered it for publication. Before anything else, however, we told the editor the whole story in the manuscript — how it contradicted all of the party line in Old Dominion; how it exposed the sometimes deliberate lies to favor the party line and how it also refuted statements of law in the then current edition of the state published *Hornbook of Virginia History* and school book history. I even mentioned that while I was a resident of Charlottesville, I left historical notes and court decisions with a friend who is connected with the University of Virginia so as to be able to verify that I had debunked the party line ahead of anyone else. To these statements the editor made no comment but simply took the manuscript and said it would be given due consideration.

About three weeks later the manuscript was returned with a rejection letter saying that I would be happy to know that the University Press is in the process of publishing for fall release a book about the governors which would tell all the nice things about Mr. Pierpont.

The book came on the market about Thanksgiving 1982, as I now recall; and anyone who had had a hand in writing the Letcher,

Smith and Pierpont chapters should now be blushing with shame!

Here's the method that publishing house used to produce its book on the governors: there was a separate author for each governor. How much coordination there was between them I don't know but from reading the book I would guess that there was little cooperation. Each chapter has a picture of its governor, and beneath that the dates of tenure were set out. For example, the chapter for Letcher reads 1860-1864. But he actually served *de jure* from 1860 to 17 April 1861 and he became *de facto* only until the term for which he had been elected expired. The term for Governor William Smith is stated to have been from 1864-1865. But during his tenure he was *de facto* only and he turned over his office to Pierpont when the latter arrived in Richmond around the first of June 1865. Then for Pierpont the term is stated to have been 1865-1868 (i.e., from the fall of Richmond until removed from office on 4 April 1868). All the governors thereafter were, of course, *de jure*. The chapter editors made no changes to distinguish between *de jure* and *de facto* status, but notwithstanding this the Pierpont editor acknowledged in the script that he was *de jure* from 20 June 1861 until 4 April 1868.

You may remember that in previous pages I complained that Virginia writers on the Civil War failed to credit the performance of Pierpont while he was in Wheeling for two years. Well, gentle reader, the Pierpont chapter editor, Richard C. Lowe, who is listed as teaching in Texas, corrected the omission of two years of Virginia history in Wheeling right off the bat! He states that Pierpont was a great governor while in Wheeling, but unsavvy and naive to believe the sincerity of former Confederates in Richmond and a pain to the federal troops while in Alexandria!

The Pierpont chapter editor bowed to the law instead of the party line in the following points:

(1) The Restored Government of Virginia was *de jure* from its inception in Wheeling in June 1861 and thereafter during its sojourn in Alexandria and in Richmond until removal of Pierpont from office in April 1868;

(2) The Richmond government was only *de facto* from the Ordinance of Secession until Appomattox;

(3) The Restored Government was *de jure* throughout all Virginia even during times when Confederate forces prevented it from exercising its lawful authority in any given area of the state; and

(4) The Restored Government was "solidly rooted" in constitutional law in accord with procedure laid down by the Supreme Court of the United States in *Luther v. Borden* (See appendix chapter thereof "The Courts Looked the Other Way); and such procedure constituted the "most reasonable and common sense" path to the formation of a new state.

Thus, some eighteen years after the state magazine *Virginia Cavalcade* refused to let its audience read such uncontravertible facts, another Virginia publisher under an apparent color of authority now publishes them for the first time by any Virginia state agency. But alas! The Pierpont chapter of *The Governors* is otherwise so fraught with error that it is practically useless as a source of history of the Pierpont administration in Richmond.

But despite these sweeping contradictions of the party line, Dr.Lowe forgets himself and returns to the prior practice of declaring that Governor Pierpont was both elected to and removed from office in an extra legal fashion, thus ignoring the authority of the military district commands and the doctrine of *Luther v. Borden.*

Somewhere in the text is another false tenent of the party line that the 1865-66 session of the General Assembly, being composed largely of ex-Confederates, repealed the act of the Restored Government which gave its consent for formation of a new state from territory of Old Dominion, and he serves up the stale allegations that many members of the Wheeling Convention had irregular credentials; but, as you have seen, this allegation doesn't fly. Another allegation which can't take off into orbit is the good doctor's allegation that the legislature, to show its independence from the governor, would not support the governor's proposed free-school bill. If this were a spiteful action, it also reflected an attitude of long standing towards any system for state-wide free schools. In the 1950s at least one county closed its free school system entirely. Now it is highly doubtful that this twentieth century school closing was due to any lingering spite against Governor Pierpont. I suspect there was another reason entirely. I wonder what it must have been — can you guess it?

A technical error by Dr. Lowe is his statement that the government at Wheeling was recognized by the President and Congress in July 1861 after the congressional seating of members from the Restored Government (the President having recognized Pierpont as governor several weeks before then). The error in law is that each such recognition was effective *ab initio*, i.e., dating back to 20 June 1861 when Pierpont took the inaugural oath to support the Constitution of the United States and the Constitution and laws of Virginia not in conflict therewith, all of which became the law of the Restored Government.

Less than a full page is devoted to the Alexandria era of the Restored Government. Included within it is mention of the small area it controlled, disputes with the military authorities and some negative factors, some few of which did not exist.

But as has been pointed out in previous pages, it has been the habit of Virginia writers to gloss over or to ignore totally the Alexandria era of the Restored Government and the Alexandria Constitution, both of which were vital to the continuation of Virginia's connection to Jamestown and Williamsburg.

I believe it worthy to note here the fact that the Alexandria Constitution has been recognized judicially by the postwar Virginia Supreme Court of appeals in 1872 in the case of *De Rothschilds v. The Auditor* which is set out elsewhere in the appendix.

The Pierpont chapter gives a fair account of what took place in Wheeling and the achievements of Governor Pierpont during that period. I concur with the writer's opinion that

> "the tasks to be accomplished and the problems to be overcome seemed endless. A more volatile chief executive might have broken under the pressures. A less committed Unionsist might have concluded the situation was hopeless. But Pierpont, the calm, tireless, systematic workhorse, was a man who could deal with such conditions. The Unionists of the northwest were fortunate to have him as their leader during those desperate days."

I congratulte the over-all editor who allotted him the time and sufficient space for giving Dr. Lowe such account, for this sort of coverage in a Virginia history book is unique indeed!

The Pierpont author opines that the governor, upon establishing is office in Richmond,

> made his first and greatest political mistake. He naively assumed that The War had settled all the important questions and that his only task as governor would be to reestablish local and state government and meet federal requirements . . . and he sincerely believed that former Confederates had learned their lesson at Appomattox and that they would heed the counsels of the north and repudiate their old leaders . . . and do all these things of their own free will.

And the concluding paragraph of the chapter goes on to state the truism that the governor "was plunged into a boiling cauldron of war-inspired fears and hatreds. His record of the Unionist governor of Virginia and 'Father of West Virginia' had already embittered former Confederates." There ends the truism, for the final sentences again express the opinion:

> He had neither the political expeience nor the political instincts to pull suspicious and hostile groups together during the maelstrom of Reconstruction. Francis H. Pierpont was an admirable and successful wartime Unionist but a naive and inept Reconstruction leader.

Now I respectfully submit that, if these opinions be true, the same might well be said of the members of the Virginia "peace delegations," who, after Lincoln's inauguration, went to Washington with the intent to exert every honorable method and without sacrifice of any principle to obtain agreement to stave off impending war. It's an example of the "irresistible force meeting the immovable object!"

The Richmond "Reconstruction" paragraphs are, within space limitations, replete with examples of the General Assembly enacting various measures despite Pierpont's warnings not to do so — to the ultimate detriment of the Commonwealth there are examples of frustration inflicted upon the Governor; and examples of political defeats for him after hard-fought battles; but I respectfully submit that instead of demonstrating naivete or ineptness, these items prove his unalterable determination to fight for the good of the Commonwealth — and especially for the people of Virginia who were being oppressed or imposed upon by persons seeking political power, and by the carpetbaggers and others who were out to make a fast buck (or whatever the dollar was called in those days). When he determined in Wheeling, just before Gettysburg, to continue in office so as to be in a position to help bleeding Virginia after The War, he well knew that his future as a politician would be at stake, but he declined high office in West Virginia and assumed the risk knowingly. There were 19th Century writers (Dr. Brock, Eckenroad, Margaret V. Smith to name a few) as well as 20th Century writers still alive whose books cite many instances of successful activities and important accomplishments by Mr. Pierpont, (many of which are set out in the Saga); and to gratuitiously express my own opinion, I suggest that the Richmond portion of the Pierpont chapter is out-of-balance; but that is a matter for you to decide, after finishing my book and then reading the Pierpont chapter in *The Governors of Virginia 1860-1978.* And then, if you conclude that Governor Pierpont was in fact naive, consider what the late, great, Will Rogers once said: "They call me a 'rube' and a 'hick,' but I'd a lot rather be the man who bought the Brooklyn bridge than the man who sold it." (This is an update from the preface date. Neither Mr. Weeks nor Mr. Maurice has seen this item.)

Chapter IV — Appendix
Sectionalism in West Virginia

Warning to non-Virginians and non-West Virginians: You might find this chapter to be of little interest.

(1) *Delf Norona's Summary,* taken from a pamphlet published in 1963 (West Virginia's centennial year) by the Marshall County Centennial Committee as a public service. It was written by the late Delf Norona, of Moundsville.

Sectionalism which developed between the peoples of eastern and western Virginia was in no small part due to geography. As stated by one writer [not named by Mr. Norona]: "When nature erected a mountain barrier between eastern and western Virginia there was laid the foundation of an intra-state dispute which ended only when the two antagonistic sections were under the authority of different state governments."

A considerable portion of the inhabitants of western Virginia were of Scotch-Irish and German origin who had migrated to the west from Pennsylvania and Maryland, as well as from New England states; whereas eastern Virginians were chiefly of English ancestry and relatively few crossed the Appalachians in search of new homes.

By reason of their different national origins, special customs, and conflicting attitudes towards the established order of things, embracing such matters as religion, slavery, and taxation, the people of the two sections never really became homogeneous.

There was complaint by the westerners that they were denied proper representation in the Commonweath's government, their fair share of internal improvements and public institutions. Proposals were frequently made that a separate government be formed in the west. Even before the American Revolution the suggestion was made in England that Virginia be divided into East and West Virginia.

During the Revolution westerns petitioned the Continental Congress for the formation of a new state to be called Westsylvania.

Many instances can be cited when, during the decades before

the Civil War, the western part of the Commonwealth was referred to as West Virginia, and proposals were made for dividing Virginia into two separate states.

Thus, the people of the northwest generally were in such a state of mind that when Virginia finally cast its lot with the Confederacy, conditions were ripe for a Secession within a Secession.

Biographical note: The West Virginia Heritage Encyclopedia, published by Jim Comstock of Richwood, in 1976, main volume 16, beginning on page 3533, has this to say about Delf Norona:

> Delf Norona, one of West Virginia's leading historians, as well as a philatelic expert and an archeologist, was born in Hong Kong (and thus became a British subject) of a Portuguese father and a French mother in 1895. When he was a young man he moved with his family to the Philippines, and later moved to Canada and then to the United States, where he served in the Army during World War I. He was a court reporter in West Virginia for more than fifty years; he died in Moundsville in 1974 . . . Over the years he accumulated a massive collection of West Virginia memorabilia . . . He was Secretary of the American Philatelic Society for many years; he was a founder of the West Virginia Archeological Society; and he served as President of the West Virginia Historical Society.

(2) *William P. Willey paragraph.* There ends the Norona narration, which, I believe, sums up what other writers have taken a score or pages to say. But it is appropriate to add one more paragraph on geography, by William P. Willey, son of Virginia Senator Waitman T. Willey, who had been a member of the Richmond Session Convention of 1861. The following is a quotation from page 71 of his book *The Formation of the State of West Virginia* (News Printing Co., Wheeling, 1901):

"Nature had divided Virginia. When the boundaries of the States of the Union were being fixed — as far back as 1781 — there was a controversy in the Federal Congress as to the western boundary of Virginia. It was then claimed that the Allegheny mountains should be the real boundary, as it was her natural boundary. Pennsylvania, Delaware, Maryland, and perhaps other states, were inclined to confine Virginia to the Allegheny boundary. It was a question that would not down until it was done. Daniel Webster had, thirty years before The War, with prophetic forecast, advised the South that if it withdrew from the Union that the separation would leave Virginia dissevered, for the natural line of division would leave western Virginia allied with the States of the North rather than with the South. What Mr. Webster foresaw as a natural and inevitable result of a divided nation, was one of the very first results of an attempt to divide."

(3) *Comments by Richard Orr Curry and Virginius Dabney.* Another writer[1] came along in 1964, however, and stated that the "arbitrary" inclusion in West Virginia of twenty-four counties which had voted in favor of secession in the May 1861 referendum,

while it does not detract from the idea of long-standing sectional differences, "except in the geographical sense," but it does point out the "need" for a comprehensive treatment of Reconstruction politics, and he presents an interesting thesis on that subject in much the same manner as Theodore White did in his series on the "making of president," i.e., Mr. Curry cites elections returns in various counties which voted in favor of secession and draws conclusions therefrom. Note, however, that Mr. Curry cites *"ballots* cast" interchangeably with *"votes* cast," which raises the suspicion that he was unaware that the constitution and laws of Virginia in 1861 provided only for *voice* voting; there was then no such thing as the secret ballot. Voters would appear before the precinct election officials, give their names and orally vote "For" or "Against" secession, and their names would be entered in the poll books in columns headed "For" and "Against" according the their respective votes. (The 1863 Constitution of West Virginia abolished voice voting and adopted the secret ballot.)

It is immaterial, however, whether or not Mr. Curry knew about the method of casting votes, for upon reading Mr. Hagan's sketch of the *Formation of West Virginia* in a following chapter of this appendix you will find that a large majority of office holders (including election officers and precinct election officials appointed by them) generally favored the confederacy; and you will also learn that "in the interior of what is now the state of West Virginia the status was not so favorable to the Union. In many of the counties the secessionists had small majorities and claimed to act through authority of the state. Intimidation, therefore, became the order of the day and when this failed, persecution sought to do what arguments and threats failed to accomplish. Being so situated that troops from the east [Confederate] soon found their way into them, and Union people were forced to remain quiet or betake themselves to the mountains to escape the operations of a fierce military despotism which seemed to crush out everything in its path."

And so it was insofar as the referendum on secession is concerned, the late May, 1861. Many of the counties herein discussed were abutting upon the south-western counties of Virginia, and — according to the eminent Virginia historian, Virginius Dabney — by 1864 those counties had become a hot bed of Confederate army deserters.[2] In southwest Virginia, which early in The War appeared to be more secessionist in sentiment than the rest fo the state, a secret organization calling itself Heroes of America had been stimulating desertions since 1863, with devastating results." And furthermore, according to Virginia's *de facto* (Confederate) Governor William Smith in a speech delivered in January of 1864[3], a large number of municipal and county officers of western Virginia, who remained loyal to the Old Dominion and fled to eastern Virginia at the outbreak of hostilities, refused to join the Confederate armed services on the ground that they were political officers of the state government and were exempted from military service!

Comment by Hearne. Whatever may have been the sentiment in any of the counties as of the 1861 referendum on secession, it must be noted that no record exists of any action taken anywhere in

West Virgina after The War to join with the General Assembly of Virginia, as expresed in its Joint Resolution No. 7, adopted 6 February, 1866 (see appendix), to adopt "suitable measures of co-operation in the restoration of the ancient commonwealth of Virginia, with all her people, and up to her former boundaries." Confederate Virgina had renounced the Constitution of the United States and had waged war against it, thereby forfeiting its protection; and the counties which had become West Virginia saw no just reason for returning to the pre-War condition from which they had strived for some three decades to become free; and I see no reason whatsoever to assert or insinuate that the formation of the new state was simply an act of expediency tainted with treason towards the mother Commonwealth, and that the "makers" of the new state acted dishonorably.

Speculation. Inasmuch as some historians engage in speculation-by-statistics, and seem to take pleasure in so doing, I ask forgiveness for indulging in such speculation myself; but I do label it as speculation, which some others neglect to do.

Dr. Oscar D. Lambert, in Volume I of his *West Virginia: Its People and Its Progress* 1958 (pages 80-82) Historical Record Association Press, Hopkinsville, Ky. and Charleston, W. Va., has pointed out that Virginia ratified the Federal Constitution in its 1788 convention by a vote of 89 to 79 — a slim majority of only 10 votes. There were sixteen delegates from that part of Virginia which is now West Virginia, and fifteen of them voted FOR ratification while only one voted against. I have checked this with *Elliott's Debates* and Dr. Lambert is right on target. Thus, it appears that, but for the western Virginia delegation, the Old Dominion would have remained outside the Union, at least for some time. Dr. Lambert then goes on to say:

> It has been related that General Washington, who declined to attend the convention, was kept in daily contact with the progress of events, and then it was seen that the business was growing to a close and that there was grave doubt concerning ratification, he became quite disturbed. It was then that a message was carried from him to the delegates from western Virginia, calling them to rally again for their country's cause as they had so nobly done during the Revolution.

Seventy-three years later, at the Richmond "secession convention," the Ordinance of Secession was adopted by a vote of 88 to 55 — a majority of 33. Of the forty-six delegates from the area which became West Virginia, 29 voted against, 7 were absent, 1 was excused, and 9 voted for ratification.[4] Thus it is seen that the northwestern Virginia delegation was the largest block against the ordinance and in favor of maintaining the the Union — large enough to nearly have upset the secessionists' apple cart! So here's the speculation: The counties which became West Virginia were always more devoted to the Union than were the eastern counties; *ergo*, the eastern counties were more susceptible to seduction by the sirens of secession!! (Remember, this is only speculation; I do not profess to have had it from the mouth of Pegasus or any other horse!)

[1]Richard Orr Curry in *A House Divided,* University of Pittsburgh Press, 1964, see pages 138, 143, 166.

[2]*Virginia, The New Dominion,* Doubleday, 1977, pages 348,9.

[3]*Memoris of William Smith.* Moss Engraving Co., N. Y. 1891, pages 181-188.

[4]*History of West Virginia,* by Virgil A. Lewis, corresponding member of the Virginia Historical Society, published by Hubbard Brothers, Philadelphia, 1889, pages 331 through 337.

Chapter V — Appendix
The Courts Looked the Other Way

That phrase or similar phraseology is used by — as General Grant might have said — "writers engaged in trying to prove that the consent given by the General Assembly in Wheeling to the transfer of Virginia counties to the new state of West Virginia, was invalid, or at least in the nature of a fraud."

Let's examine that phrase.

In the first place, not less than three courts did *not* "look the other way," but faced the issue squarely when called upon to do so. The Supreme Court of the United States, than which there is none higher, took judicial notice of "the Pierpont Government" by name as having been the *de jure* government of Virginia from the time of its inception in 1861 until April of 1868 (*Virginia v. West Virginia,* 78 U.S. (11 Wall.) 39; 20 L. Ed. 67; 1870); and the Supreme Court of Appeals of Virginia on two occasions held that the Richmond (Confederate) state government from the Ordinance of Secession until its demise in Danville in April of 1865 had been merely *de facto* in character and that the Restored Government had been *de jure* throughout the entire area of the Commonwealth, even during the time in which it could not enforce its jurisdiction because Confederate forces occupied most of the Old Dominion; see *Commonwealth v. Chalkley* (20 Grat. 404, 1871), and *De Rothschilds v. The Auditor,* (22 Grat. 41, 1872). There we see the highest court of the Commonwealth of Virginia adding its own "amen" to the holding of the U.S. highest court. (This court had been established under a later Constitution of the Commonwealth and its jurisdiction was beyond dispute.)

A third court also faced the issue squarely — the United States Circuit Court (of appeals) for the District of Virginia — and Mr. Chief Justice Chase sat as Circuit Justice! In *Griffin's Case,* Reported in *11 Fed. Cas. at page 7,* May term, 1869, Mr. Chief Justice Chase held, in pertinent part:

. . . When the functionaries of the state government existing in Virginia at the commencement of the late Civil War took part, together with a majority of the citizens of the state, in rebellion against the government of the United States, they ceased to constitute a state government for the state of Virginia, which could be recognized as such by the national government. Their example of hostility to the Union, however, was not followed throughout the state. In many counties, the local authorities and majority of the people ahered to the national government; and representatives from these counties soon after assembled in convention at Wheeling, and organized a government for the state. This government was recognized as the lawful government of Virginia by the executive and legislative departments of the national government; and this recognition was conclusive upon the judicial department. The government of the state thus recognized was in contemplation of law the government of the whole state of Virginia, though excluded, as the government of the United States was itself excluded, from the greater portion of the territory of the state. It was the legislature of the reorganized state which gave the consent of Virginia to the formation of the state of West Virginia. To the formation of that state, the consent of its own legislature, and of the legislature of the state of Virginia, and of Congress, was indispensable. If either had been wanting, no state, within the limits of the old, could have been constitutionally formed; and it is clear that if the government insituted at Wheeling was not the government of the whole state of Virginia, no new state has ever been constitutionally formed within her ancient boundaries. It can not admit of question, then, that the government which consented to the formation of the state of West Virginia, remained in all national relations the government of Virginia, although that event reduced to very narrow limits the territory acknowledging its jurisdiction, and not controlled by insurgent force. Indeed, it is well known historically that the state and the government of Virginia, thus organized, was recognized by the national government. Senators and representatives from the state occupied seats in Congress, and when the insurgent force which held possession of the principal part of the territory was overcome, and the government recognized by the United States was transferred from Alexandria to Richmond, it became in fact what it was before in law, the government of the whole state. As such it was entitled, under the constitution, to the same recognition and respect, in national relations, as the government of any other state.

Nevertheless, "the courts looked the other way" does prove something after all: The writers using that phrase did not do their homework; they were unfamiliar with points of constitutional law laid down by the United States Supreme Court, some ten years prior to The War, in the landmark case of *Luther v. Borden,* (7

Wall. 1; 12 L. Ed. 581). I have shown in the saga that Governor Pierpont and his colleagues were familiar with that case, and that they prevailed upon the June 1861 Wheeling convention to follow the procedure outlined by the Court to obtain recognition by President Lincoln and the Congress.

A few quotes from the opinion of Chief Justice Taney in *Luther v. Borden* will suffice to show why the judiciary does not take jurisdiction on the spot in cases of dispute between contending parties as to which, in any given case, may be the constititonal authority in any state:

> Where citizens of the same State are in arms against each other and the constituted authorities unable to execute the laws, the interposition of the United States must be prompt or it is of little value. The ordinary course of proceedings in courts of justice would be utterly unfit for the crisis . . . At all events the [power to decide] is conferred upon [the President] by the Constitution and the laws of the United States, and therefore must be respected in its judicial tribunals.

> And if a State court should enter upon the inquiry proposed in this case, and should come to the conclusion that the government under which it acted had been put aside and displaced by an opposing government, it would cease to be a court, and incapable of pronouncing a judicial decision upon the question it undertook to try.

> . . . The Constitution of the United States, as far as it has provided for an emergency of this kind, and authorized the general government to interfere in the domestic concerns of a State, has treated the subject as political in its nature, and placed the power in the hands of that department . . . The Constitution provides that the United States shall guarantee to every State in the Union a republican form of government, and shall protect each of them against invasion; and on the application of the legislature or of the executive (when the legislature cannot be convened) against domestic violence.

In the case of the Restored Government of Virginia, Governor Pierpont called upon the President for aid in repelling an invasion by an enemy purportedly being a foreign country, (the legislature not being immediately available); the President recognized Pierpont as "governor of Virginia," and the Congress in due course seated the representatives and senators from the Restored Government, thus conforming to Mr. Chief Justice Taney's stipulation in *Luther v. Borden.*

> "And when senators and representatives of a State are admitted into the councils of the Union, the authority of the government into the councils of the Union, the authority of the government under which they are appointed, as well as its republican character, is recognized by the proper constitutional authority. And the decision is binding on every other department of the government, and could not be questioned in any judicial tribunal."

Now here is an unusual and unexpected source of support for the doctrine expounded by Mr. Chief Justice Taney in *Luther V. Borden:* Mr. William Smith, the merely *de facto* "governor" of Virginia from 1 January 1864 until Appomattox, who, in his address to the so-called "general assembly" of Virginia on 7 December 1864, urged enactment of a measure "to bring into the field all able-bodied men who are not *necessary* to the State government: "and he went on to cite the state and local officers who left their posts in the western areas to come within Confederate territory, "most of whom have acquired new homes and have formed new social and business relations, and may not return to their counties until this war shall terminate;" and he estimated their number to be about "two thousand," (which might well be something of an exaggeration, but I was not there and he was, so I do not question his statement). The "governor" then went on to complain about the case of *Burroughs v. Peyton* (16 Gratton 470, 1864) which exempted these "refugee" state and local officers from military service because it would be "absurd to suppose that the Government of the Confederate States can rightfully destroy the Government of the States which created it . . . Congress [i.e., the Confederate Congress] can have no right therefore to deprive a State of any officer *necessary* to the action of its government, and the State itself is the sole judge as to the officers who are *necessary* for that purpose." Mr. Smith agreed that *"necessary"* officers should be exempt; but he went on to state that this decision should be regarded as political rather than judicial in nature, and he cited *Luther v. Borden* in support of his position:

> While, however, it may be conceded that the judicial department, in the last resort, is the final expositor of the construction as to all questions of a judicial nature, it is equally clear that it cannot assume jurisdiction of political questions. This doctrine was quite elaborately treated in the case of *Luther v. Borden, et al* (7 How. R.) In the celebrated Dorr case, out of which the one quoted sprung, it was declared that the court shall not take jurisdiction of questions of political power. For instance, that it was the right of the political power to decide which the rightful Constitution of the State of Rhode Island . . . and that it was not a judicial question. So, it was conceded, that the President alone has the right to *decide* when such insurrection or rebellion existed in a State as required him to call out the militia, that it was not a judicial question . . .[1]

Now then: What do *you* think about the argument that "the courts looked the other way"?

---

[1] *Memoris of Gov. William Smith,* The Moss Engraving Co., N. Y. 1891, pages 181-188.

Chapter VI — Appendix
Fables, Facts & a Miracle Too

First, the Miracle: President Lincoln formally recognized the Restored Government of Virginia on 9 May 1865, which took effect some three weeks after his assassination. Glory, Glory, Hallelujah!!

Virginia: A Chronology & Documentary Handbook, Oceana Publications, Inc., Dobbs Ferry, N. Y. 1979, page 22.

A Fact: Virginia Troops Participated in The War on the Union Side as Well as on the Confederate Side until West Virginia became a state on 20 June 1863, at which time all Virginia units in the Federal service became West Virginia units, by operation of an act of the General Assembly of the Restored Government of Virginia, passed in Wheeling on 31 January, 1863.

Acts of Assembly, Wheeling, 1862-63, Chap. 52, p. 40.

A Fable: An Official Publication of the State of West Virginia refers to Mrs. Francis H. Pierpont as the "wife of the first governor of West Virginia," which, if true, reveals that she led a double life, for Arthur I. Boreman was the first governor of West Virginia. (I take responsibility for labeling this a fable; Mrs. Pierpont was an honorable woman who would not have been quilty of bigamy.)

"Wonderful West Virginia" magazine, April, 1982, page 5.

A Fact: Richmond General Assemblies under the Alexandria Constitution during Pierpont's administration granted certain rights to black persons for the first time (1) Legitimized marriages between black persons and provided for the permanent registration thereof; and (2) provided that "hereafter colored pesons shall be competent to testify in this state as through they were white."

(1) Acts of Assembly, Richmond, 1865-66 Chap. 18, passed 27 Feb. 1866; (2) Acts of Assembly, Richmond, 1866-67, Chap. 62, passed 20 April 1867.

A Fable: Numerous publications in West Virginia Claim Stonewall Jackson as a West Virginian. Recognizing that possibly 99% of today's population of the Mountain State claim Stonewall as their own, it is with genuine regret that I must take responsibility for labeling this a fable. While Stonewall was born and reared in western Virginia, he graduated from this life before the new state came into existence, and he had no opportunity to become a Mountaineer, even assuming that he would have wanted to do so had he survived The War; for his heart had been dedicated to the Old Dominion exclusively. Jackson's widow is reputed to have said: "He was born a Virginian and died a Virginian!"

A Fable: The Old Custom House in Wheeling has been called the first capitol of West Virginia by not less than two official state publications. This is a fable, for the real first capitol was the old Linsley (1863 spelling) Institute building, located in Wheeling at the northwest corner of what is now the intersection of Eoff and Eighteenth Streets. The building has been stuccoed and is now known as the first capitol building. It bears a plaque near the entranceway announcing that it was the first capitol of West Virginia.

(1) Wonderful West Virginia, April, 1982, page 14; and again, July, 1982, page 8; and (2) West Virginia Bicentennial Highway Map, 1976.

A Fact: The Old Custom House in Wheeling was the capitol of the Commonwealth of Virginia from 20 June 1861 until noon 20 June 1863. This building stands at the northeast corner of what is now the intersection of Market and Sixteenth Streets. It has been restored to its inner and outer appearance as of June, 1861.

History of the Panhandle of West Virginia Compiled by Messrs. Newton, Nichols, and Sprankle; published by J. A. Caldwell, Wheeling, 1879; page 205; reprinted by Unigraphic, Inc., Evansville, Ind. 1975.

A Fact: Wheeling is the Only Municipality to Have Been the capital of two different states of these United States, although not now a capital of any state. I take responsibility for asserting this information as a fact. Santa Fe was a provincial capital of both Spain and Mexico; it was capital of the Territory of New Mexico; and became capital of the State of New Mexico; but was never capital of any other *state* of the American Union.

A Fable: West Virginia is the only state ever carved from an existing state. This is a fable of the first magnitude, the best example Being the fact that Kentucky had been carved from Virginia some seven decades before West Virginia became a state.

(1) Official Program for Semicentennial Celebration of West Virginia statehood, Wheeling, 1913 (2) Wonderful West Virginia again, April 1982, page 14.

A Fable: Pierpont was the only person to have been Governor of two states of the United States. But how about Sam Houston, who was (1 Governor Tennessee; (2) President of the Republic of Texas; and (3) Governor of the state of Texas? On the other hand — and this is important — Mr. Pierpont was never governor of any state other than Virginia; he was never a governor of West Virginia!

Alas, West Virginia Hillbilly, published in Richwood, has repeated this fable twice during the 1980s. If this page gives the appearance of having drops of liquid spilled on it, you're right — due to my own tear drops, for Hillbilly is my favorite weekly newspaper!

A Fact: The Virginia General Assembly during the Period of the Alexandria capital, Sessions 1863-64 and 1864-65 might well have been the smallest legislative body any of these United States has ever had; and I am hopeful that someone, somewhere, will do the research necessary to determine whether any state (or colony) has had a smaller legislative body, and publish the answer. This general assembly consisted of six senators and thirteen delegates.

History of West Virginia and its People, by Thomas C. Miller & Hu Maxwell, Lewis Historical Publishing Co., New York, 1913, page 361, wherein the senators and delegates, and their constituencies, are named.

A (Curious) Fact: The last session of the Alexandria General Assembly, sitting in Richmond in June, 1865, granted a legislative divorce to a couple I shall not name due to the fact that the validity thereof has not been judicially determined (to the best of my knowledge), and I don't want to prejudice the standing of any living issue of the "divorced" couple. The Alexandria Constitution of 1864 prohibited such action by the General Assembly, as had the constitution of 1851 before it.

Acts of assembly, Extra Session, June, 1865, Chap. 3, p. 4, 21 June, 1865, in force from passage.

A Fact: The General Assembly of Virginia, sitting in Wheeling on 13 February, 1862, gave a big boost indeed to the establishment of Arlington National Cemetery! On that date it authorized the transfer to the federal government of "not more than twenty acres in Alexandria or Fairfax counties for the purpose of providing a cemetery for persons losing their lives in the service of the United States."

Acts of Assembly, Wheeling, 1861-62, Chap. 74, p. 79; repeated verbatim in Code of Virginia, 1873, and 1881. Thereafter by reference in all codes up to and including the present Code of Virginia.

A Fable: by West Virginia governmental departments and agencies: The *West Virginia Blue Book* habitually carries the fable that one Joseph Johnson, resident of Bridgeport, was the only governor of Virginia from western Virginia, thus ignoring the fact that Francis H. Pierpont, of Marion County was also a governor of Virginia; this is just a sample from the *Blue Book. Wonderful West Virginia,* published by the Department of Natural Resources, likewise has published fables cited above, in this chapter. And the Department of Culture and History, not to be outdone by other state agencies, published fables from time to time when writing about the old custom houses. An example of one such fable is told in the March/April, 1984 edition of its free magazine. In referring to the Restored Government during its area of greatest recognition by federal agencies, including the White House and the Congress, states that "from 1861 to 1863 the 'interim' government carried out what duties it could with nominal resources and tenuous official recognition."

The truth is that taxes, license fees, fines, and other regular income from the counties it controlled on the west side of the mountains, plus income from Alexandria and the areas it controlled in the east were ample for all of its governmental functions. Thus, just prior to West Virginia statehood, The Restored Government was able — without any financial pinch — to appropriate $150,000 on hand from prior receipts from the area that was to become West Virginia — and that sum was fabulous in those days! See acts of (Wheeling) General Assembly, Extra Session, December 1862, chapter 72.

Even the Department of Highways road maps refer to the old Custom House in Wheeling as "West Virginia Independence Hall."

Additional Comment By Hearne

The items presented in this chapter are merely samples garnered from a ton or so of books, periodicals, newspaper clippings and the like which contain fables and facts — with a sprinkling of the miracles as well — which together constitue the distorted chapters of Virginia and West Virginia history; and upon assessing what I had sorted out for inclusion I was sorely tempted to change the title of this book to "the Unpublicized Chapters of Virginia and West Virginia History: Two Cans of Worms!"

So much for the fables. I turn now to the facts, and respectfully submit that this book is chock-full of factual items which are of interest to the general public as wella s to Virginia and West Virginia residents; and some of which can be made to bring in revenue to the localities and states concerned. This sort of thing is being done successfully elsewhere. Example: St. Augustine, Florida, founded circa 1565, claims to be and probably is, the oldest municipality continuously in existence anywhere in these United States. Ergo! The city and state advertise this fact, and tourists go out of their way to visit that city, and they spend money en route to and from there, as well as while in the city itself. Another example: Sante Fe, New Mexico, founded circa 1610, is the only municipality which has been continuously since that date the seat of government — the capital — of what is now a state in these United States. ergo! This fact is so advertised, with the same result for Santa Fe and New Mexico as for St. Augustine and Florida. Why? Because each city has something exclusively its own, and makes good use of that unique attribute. Well, gentle reader (to revert to the 19th Century literary usage), here's news for you: Wheeling (and through Wheeling, the State of West Virginia) likewise had an attribute exclusively its own, as heretofore stated: Wheeling is the only city which has been the capital of two different states of these United States; and it may also be noted that Alexandria, Virginia, likewise has an attribute shared by only Jamestown, Williamsburg, Wheeling and Richmond of having been a capital of Virginia. And if that were not enough, how about the fact that Wheeling played a leading role in the establishment of Arlington National Cemetery? Now then, city counselors, state legislators, chambers of commerce, historical societies and so forth *ad infinitum,* how about making good use of these facts? (And, incidentially, governmental historians and archivests, as well as librarians and other persons concerned with providing information to the public, how about setting the record straight, so that there will no longer exist any cans of worms?)

Timely provisions were made for the transfer of judicial functions from Virginia to the West Virginia courts, but as this is a matter of little interest to all but judges and members of the bar of the two Virginias, I do not mention these subjects any further. However, there is considerable information on these subjects in my first article concerning the Restored Government, in *West Virginia Law Review* (College of Law, Morgantown, W. Va., December 1963.)

Chapter VII — Appendix
Virginia's Old Capitol in Wheeling
— Another Independence Hall?

From the hour of Mr. Pierpont's inauguration as Governor of Virginia on 20 June, 1861, until noon on 20 June, 1863, when Mr. Arthur I. Boreman was inaugurated as the first Governor of West Virginia, Wheeling was the capital of Virginia, and the federal building there was Virginia's capitol.

This federal building — located on the northeast corner of what is now the intersection of Market and Sixteenth Streets — was known as the "Custom House," inasmuch as it housed the offices of the surveyor of customs for the port of Wheeling; but it also sheltered the post office, the United States District Courtroom, and offices of various federal government officials. Mr. Thomas Hornbrook was the surveyor of customs, and it seems that he was the general manager of the building as well. He appears to have been deeply smpathetic to the Restored Government, and determined to do all that he lawfully could to further its cause and to keep Virginia within the Union. According to a local history book generally recognized as accurate[1] — written by eyewitnesses in 1897:

> The reorganized state of Virginia found an upper wing [of the Custom House] of the United States beneath which it could bid defiance to the storm of adverse circumstances that surrounded it and the offices thereof. With the consent of Mr. Thomas Hornbrook, the Restored Government occupied, first as a hall for the state convention, the United States court room; and second, as halls for the legislature, the United States court room and his own business office; and third, the state officers, governor, secretary of the Commonwealth, adjutant general, treasurer, and auditor of accounts were ranged consecutively from south to north on the east side of the second floor of the building, and they remained there until the new state of West Virginia [came into being].

It thus appears that the old custom house was indeed the seat

73

of government of Virginia for that two-year period; the General Assembly (legislature) held sessions there; and the offices of the governor, secretary of the Commonwealth, and the other principal officials of the state government were located therein. Therefore, it is entirely proper to refer to that edifice as having been the "capitol" of the Commonwealth of Virginia.

There were four sessions of the general assembly held in Wheeling. The first convened on 1 July, 1861, pursuant to the provisions of an ordinance of the citizens' convention of 11 June, and it adjourned before the end of the month. The second session convened 2 December, 1861, and continued until around mid-February, 1862; this was the biennial regular session. The third was an extra session, called primarily to give consent to the transfer of Virginia territory to the proposed state of West Virginia; it convened 6 May 1862 and ajourned prior to the end of that month. The fourth and last session held in Wheeling convened 4 December, 1862 and lasted until the middle of February 1863; it was an extra session.

it seems to have been, and continues to be, the habit of historians — when writing about the making of treaties, enactment of legislation, holding conventions, and other actions of significance — to refer to the cities in which such events occurred, and it is indeed seldom that any specific building or structure within the city is mentioned. thus, we hear of "the Treat of Ghent," "the Congress of Vienna," "the Chicago convention of such-and-such a year," *et cetera* almost without exception, without being told the name of the palace, building or hall in which any such event occurred. Virginia and West Virginia historians, alas, run true to form; but fortunately for the sake of the record there were a few contemporary writers who did name the legislative halls of the General Assembly in the city of Wheeling. With respect to the first session — July, 1861 — both John Marshall Hagans and Granville Davisson Hall have written that the Custom House was the meeting place, thus reinforcing the statements made in the 1879 history of the Panhandle; and further verification is to be found in the appropriation act which was passed during the following session, which contained this item: "To Thomas Hornbrook, Esq., for expenses in preparing halls for the Senate and House of Delegates, gas, fuel, etc., $490.33." That first session, by the way, was a very important one, in that it supplemented the actions of the June convention to compelte the reorganization of the state government by *inter alia,* electing certain state officers as provided in the Constitution of Virginia; electing two Virginia senators as provided in the Constituton of the United States; making county jails lawful for the confinement of felons (as the penitentiary in Richmond was no longer available in western Virginia); organizing militia units; and making appropriations for various purposes of the reorganized government of the Commonwealth.

The second session — being the regular session of 1861-62, appears to have been held in the old building of Linsley Institute, located on the northwest corner of what is now the intersection of Eoff and Fifteenth Streets. This is according to S. Myers,[2] and is confirmed by an item in the appropriation act of that session which provided "To the trustees of Linsley [as it was then spelled] Institue for the use of their building during the session of the General Assembly commencing December 2, 1861, five dollars per day." An act of Assembly which continues to have national significance was passed during this session, to authorize the transfer of realty in Alexandria or Fairfax counties to the United States government for a national cemetery, which was the beginning of Arlington National Cemetery!

I have found but one item which I consider accurate with respect to the place or places in which the third and fourth sessions were held; but even this accurate item is inconclusive. It is Chapter 65, Acts of Assembly 1862-63 (pages 62 *et seq.*), passed 4 February, 1863, which appropriated: "to the principal of Linsley Institute for the use of the building during the extra session commencing December 4, 1862, $2.50 per day." This item, of course, refers only to the fourth Wheeling session; and I have found nothing that can be pinpointed toward the very important third session (May, 1862) which granted Virginia's consent to the transfer of counties to the proposed new state! I have consulted with a former high officer of Linsly, who has access to the old minute books of the trustees, who could find no reference therein to the use of the building by the Restored Government of Virginia, although he did find an entry after 1863 whereby Linsly leased the building to the new state of West Virginia for its first capitol. I shall not belabor the point, however, for this book is concerned mainly with *what* took place in Wheeling rather than *where* in Wheeling the events occurred. The present trustees of the Old Custom House, however, have been and continue to be diligent in ferreting out even the minutest details, such as the type of brick used in the sidewalk abutting this building, and I have no doubt that they will come up with the answers to these questions.

Returning to the fourth (1862-63) session and an appropriation to Linsly of only $2.50 per day for use of their building suggests that perhaps only one house of the Assembly met there during that session, and that the other house may have met in the Custom House. That is only a guest, but inasmuch as Linsly was paid five dollars per day during the 1861-62 session and only half of that for the 1862-63 session, it seems to make sense. There was no appropriation to Mr. Hornbrook, however, for either the third or fourth sessions, although he probably could have been paid out of general appropriations for "expenses of the General Assembly" as enacted each year . . . Strangely enough, I could find no contemporary newspaper accounts of *where* any session was held during the entire two-year period of Wheeling's having been the capital of Virginia, although there were daily reports of *what* the assembly did.

Another Independence Hall?

The centennial celebration of West Virginia statehood occurred during the year 1963, and several years before or after — the precise time is immaterial herein — the late Delf Norona, (a respected West Virginia historian), discovered that the old custom house had played an important role in the formation of the state, for it was in the court room of that edifice that a document entitled "A Declaration of the People of Virginia" had been adopted by the Wheeling Convention on 17 June, 1861; and that on the yeas and nays being called there were fifty-six "for" and none "against," whereupon Delegate Carlile observed, within hearing of reporters, that fifty-six persons had signed the Philadelphia Declaration of 1776. Mr. Norona believed Carlile's remark to have been the basis of an item in the *Baltimore Sun* of 18 June headed "The Wheeling Declaration of Independence," which was repeated in the *Richmond Enquirer,* while the *Wheeling Intelligencer* the same day referred to the "signing of the Declaration of Independence." Mr. Norona went on to relate that although such title was never mentioned in the official journal of the convention, the document had been during "the past century" refereed to frequently as "West Virginia's Declaration of Independence;" and it was largely due to Mr. Norona's persuasion that the custom house property was bought by the state for a museum.

But is the old custom house actually an independence hall? Is there such a document as a true West Virginia Declaration of Independence?

The editors-compilers of *The Thirty-Fifth State* (West Virginia University Library, Morgantown, 1966) would have us believe so; they chose "West Virginia's Declaration of Independence, June 17, 1863" as the heading for a chapter which sets out the document adopted by the Wheeling convention on the date under the title "A Declaration of the People of Virginia," which was also known to the convention as a "declaration of rights" (i.e., rights of loyal Virginia citizens to be free of the actions of the secession convention in Richmond and acts by Confederate Governor Letcher in furtherance of the purposes of the secessionists); and they go on to express their opinion that the document, "as an inspired paraphrase of the famous Declaration adopted at Philadelphia, July 4, 1776," its pronouncement was "in a very real sense West Virginia's Declaration of Independence." Other writers and jouranlists then followed suit by referring to the old Custom House as "West Virginia's Independence Hall;" and when the state chartered "The West Virginia Independence Hall Foundation" to operate to the building the name became official. Nevertheless, the foregoing is but another example of a molehill being molded into a mountain of mythology!

Let's look at the facts.

In the first place, the document itself tells us the "Bill of Rights of Virginia" is the authority on which it is based. See Virginia Bill of Rights in this appendix.

In the second place, neither newspaper headlines nor eyecatching words used by writers generally are *per se* guarantees that they are used accurately. Thus, as has been amply demonstrated in preceding chapters, the use of "provisional," "rump convention," "pretender," "shadowy," and many more *ets* and *ceteras,* as used with respect to the subject matter of this book, has been, and continues to be, incorrect much more often than not. By the same token, giving any maxim or doctrine the stamp of "official" does not guarantee the truth of whatever it is that bears such stamp; as, for example, it no doubt was "official" in the era of Christopher Columbus that the earth was flat.

In the third place, a reading of the document (set out in full in the chapters of this appendix containing the sketches by Messrs. Munford and Hagans) will reveal that instead of declaring western Virginia's independence from Virginia it declares the continuance of Virginia's existence as a whole state — within the federal union, however, and under new management loyal to the United States; and it further declares that the acts of the secession convention and of Governor Letcher in the furtherance of those acts to be null and void.

In the fourth place, the delegates themselves in no way regarded this document as a declaration of western Virginia's independence, and they took pains to do nothing at all towards a division of the state prior to the organization of a loyal government for Virginia and its recognition by both the president and the Congress as the true government of Virginia. They did not want to be accused of "jumping the gun," and in fact the call (or charter) for this June 11th Wheeling convention, which had been adopted by a prior large mass meeting in Wheeling on 14 May, contained limitations on its authority with respect to the matter of formation of an new state:

> . . . it being a conceded political axiom that government is founded on the consent of the governed and instituted for their good, and that the course of the ruling power of the State was utterly subversive and destructive of the interests of North-western Virginia, that the people of the same could rightfully and successfully appeal to the proper authorities of Virginia, to permit them to peacefully and lawfully separate from the residue of the State, and form a government that would give effect to the wishes and views and interests.

But on 17 June (the date of adoption of the so-called "declaration of independence") there were no "proper authorities" to whom such an appeal could have been made under the Constitution of the United States; the Restored Government did not come into existence until 20 June; and it was not recognized by the Congress of the United States until sometime after the United States senators and representatives had been chosen and seated, although the President had accorded his recognition prior to the first session of the General Assembly early in July. The charter did, however, set out some specific action for the convention:

> . . . that was the imperative duty of the citizens to maintain the constitution of the State and the laws made in pursuance of the same, and all officers acting thereunder; that, in

the language of Washington, expressed in his letter to the President of Congress, on the 17th September, 1780: 'In all our deliberations on this subject, we keep steadily in view that which appears to us the greatest interest to every true American, the consolidation of our Union, in which is involved our property, felicity, safety and perhaps our national existence."

The call went on to provide that, in the event of the ordinance of secession being ratified by the voters [as it was so ratified at the regular election of 23 May], all counties disposed to cooperate [note that this phrase includes an invitation to counties east of the Alleghenies — and two delegates from Fairfax and two from Alexandria counties did attend] were to send delegates to a place chosen by a committee [Wheeling] to meet on 11 June "to advise such measures as the safety and welfare of the people they represented should demand." Mr. Pierpont, a delegate from Marion County, took this view of the call:

> . . . The government of the state is in rebellion against the United States — against the laws and loyal people of Virginia. We, representing those people here, are bound to take immediate action to protect their lives and property . . . I am sure that the President and Congress must and will recognize us as the rightful government of the State . . . Everything is in our favor and everything must aid and sustain us in our effect . . .

And in the debate which preceded adoption of the so-called "declaration of independence," the statement of Delegate Hubbard of Ohio County went directly to the point, and may have been the clincher which won over the delegates who wanted an amendment inserted to the effect that the convention would at a later date take steps to dismemeber Virginia:

> We are not here to create a state but to save one; not here to create a government but to help save a government.

The forgoing quotations are from *The Rending of Virginia* pages 317 and 322, by Granville Davisson Hall (Press of Myer & Miller, 85 Fifth Avenue, Chicago, 1902). Mr. Hall was a contemporary writer, and may have covered the convention for the *Wheeling Intelligencer.*

And in the fifth place, this Virginia convention did, during its adjourned session on 20 August, 1861, adopt an ordinance whereby a new state could be formed from Virginia territory, subject, however to affirmation by the voters of the counties concerned and election by them of delegates who were to meet in Wheeling on 26 November "to organize themselves into a convention" for the purpose of drafting a constitution for the proposed state and to provide for its submission to voters and, to the general assembly for its consent; whereupon the assembly would approve and forward the matter to Congress for its needed consent. Here we have an entirely new convention, composed only of western Virginia delegates, the June convention of Virginia having adjourned *sine die*. No declaration, ordinance, resolution or other document having even a remote resemblance to a declaration of independence was adopted, nor was such a declaration needed or appropriate.

Wheeling convention delegates may not have thought of it, but there was good Virginia precedent for the formation of a new state from her own territory. Some seventy years before then the residents of what was then south-western Virginia held several conventions to provide for a new state and its government, to which the General Assembly in Richmond gave its consent by act of 18 December, 1789. They then petitioned Congress for its concurrence, which was granted by act approved 4 February, 1791, which provided that Kentucky be admitted to the Union on 1 June 1792 (as the 15th state, Vermont having preceded her to statehood.) Now then: Have you ever heard of a Kentucky declaration of independence, or a Kentucky independence hall? Neither have I.

In retrospect, it becomes apparent that the Wheeling conventions followed the right course; the delegates were able to distinguish between "spasmotic disruption" and "authorized resistence," in the words of Waitman T. Willey.[3] And Granville Davisson Hall tells of a meeting, "many years later," with ex-delegate Daniel Lamb, who stated "If it were all to do over again, looking back to it now after all these years, I cannot see where a single one of our steps could have been more wisely taken."

I was born in Wheeling in 1904 and grew up there. My father was born there in 1868 and there graduated from this life in 1949. His maternal grandfather was Joseph B. Ford, who during the period under discussion was general agent for the Baltimore & Ohio Railroad in Wheeling, and one who had become a personal friend to Governor Pierpont. Both my father and I attended Linsly Institute; I can remember that over the door of a large assembly room was the caption "House of Delegates" and over another door was the caption "Senate;" but both these titles had belonged to the West Virginia legislature when that building had been West Virginia's first capitol. At no time did my father mention any such thing as a West Virginia declaration of independence, nor did I ever hear of any such instrument from anyone else. Neither did I know that there had been a Custom House in Wheeling, much less an "independence hall"! I have more recently inquired of friends of my own age here in Wheeling, including Attorney Chester R. Hubbard, grandson of the 1861 Wheeling conventions delegate Chester Dorman Hubbard, above quoted, and none of these friends had heard any such story. My first recollection of the building which I more recently learned had been a Custom House was the old Conservative Life Insurance building which, following repeal of prohibition in the early 1930s, became the first state liquor store in Wheeling. What it had become earlier and until it was taken over for a museum I don't know, for I was employed elsewhere. All of which is by way of saying that it was not until the 1960s — a century after the birth of West Virginia — that the people of that state suddenly exclaimed, "Oh goodie, goodie; West Virginia declared her independence from that horrid old Virginia 100 years ago, and here's the building which is our state's equivalent of Independence Hall in Philadelphia!!!"

Well, as a boy I used to celebrate the Fourth of July as President Reagan did; and I would fight imaginary British Redcoats with a cap pistol. It wasn't until World War I that I found out that England and the English speaking countries of the now British Commonwealth were our best friends in the world, and I see no reason now to suddenly renew resentment for past actions of our Mother Country's King and Parliment which have had no ill effects on this side of the Atlantic for something more than one and a half centuries. I wish, instead, that we had more such loyal friends and allies as those countries which constitute the British Commonwealth of Nations!

Similarly, I see no reason now to dredge up old differences with our Mother State which no longer exist, nor to pretend that there is another "independence hall" in Wheeling. Historical writers — mythologists who could not distinguish a "spasmodic disruption" from an "authorized resistance" — chose to give a different title to an historical document than the writers thereof gave it, thus molding another molehill to that already Alpine mountain of mythology. As a matter of fact, I am proud of our state's heritage from the Old Dominion, and I offer the guess that a tremendous majority of present-day West Virginians feel as I do.

In conclusion, I venture to suggest that a more truthful and more appropriate name for the old Custom House would be "Virginia's Old Capitol in Wheeling," which indeed it was, but which casts no shadow on the honor or dignity of our Mother Commonwealth.

The Building Itself

The picture of this building which is elsewhere in this book portrays the edifice as it was during the time period 1860-1863. The property was sold to commercial enterprise by Uncle Sam in 1912, and from that time until an undetermined period a fourth floor was added and the face of the building on Market Street was considerably stretched some six feet or more. The building was purchased by the State in the 1960s and a board of trustees was appointed to restore the edifice to its original condition and to assume the management thereafter. Those trustees deserve great thanks for their devotion to duty, for they followed the original plans of the architect faithfully, even to the type of brick for the abutting sidewalks. Visitors to Wheeling should make it a point to go through this old Custom House which served the Commonwealth of Virginia, and the embryo state of West Virginia, so well during the era which is the subject of this book.

---

[1]*History of the Panhandle of West Virginia,* compiled and written by Messrs. J. H. Newton, G. G. Nicholas, and A. G. Sprankle; published by J. A. Caldwell, Wheeling, 1879 — and later

reprinted by Unigraphic, Inc., 4400 Jackson Avenue, Evansville, Indiana, 1975.

[2]See *Myers' History of West Virginia,* Vol. 1, page 428, apparently published in New Martinsburg, W. Va., in 1915.

[3]As recorded by Granville Davisson Hall.

Chapter VIII — Appendix
The West Virginia Debt Case

Hearne note: This chapter has no direct — and only a remote — bearing upon the Restored Government of Virginia and the Pierpont administration. It is included here because it was a subject of bitter dispute between the Virginias for more than fifty years after The War; and it is, perhaps, one explanation for errors and omissions, whether intentional or not, in historical writings by historians on both sides of the Alleghenies.

Members of the Wheeling convention which reconvened in August of 1861 were aware that a division of the Commonwealth into two separate states involved the matter of a division of the public debt of the Old Dominion as well; and in an ordinance adopted 20 August they provided that the new state should assume a just proportion of such a debt incurred prior to 1 January, 1861, to be ascertained by charging to it all state expenditures within the limits thereof, and a just proportion of the ordinary expenses of the state government, since any part of such debt was contracted; and deducting therefrom the monies paid into and included within the new state during the same period. Pursuant to this provision, the constitutional convention of 1862 provided, in Section 8 of Article VIII of the proposed constitution for West Virginia, that "an equitable proportion of the public debt of the Commonwealth of Virginia, prior to the first day of January, 1861, shall be assumed by this state; and the legislature shall ascertain the same as soon as may be practicable, and provide for the liquidation thereof, by a sinking fund sufficient to pay the accuring interest, and redeem the principal within thirty-four years."

The Virginia General Assembly in 1866 provided for the appointment of commissioners to meet with West Virginia commissioners to determine the debt situation, and the following year West Virginia's legislature followed suit; but in the meanwhile Virginia had instituted proceedings in the Supreme Court to recover Berkeley and Jefferson Counties, and no action on the debt could be taken until the status of those counties had been determined. The court held for West Virginia, and that state appointed another commission in 1861, one member having been Jonathan M. Bennett of Weston. That appointment was sigificant, for Mr. Bennett had been auditor of accounts of the Commonwealth of Virginia for eight years, including the Confederate period dating from the Ordinance of Secession until Appomattox; and he was, quite likely, the most knowledgeable person on the subject of that debt that either state could have chosen. This commission went to Richmond in November, but by that time Virginia General Assembly had enacted that the debt matter should be decied by arbitration, and no one in authority would meet with the West Virginia delegation, and the members went home. Nevertheless, they felt obligated to ascertain the West Virginia portion of the debt and report it to the legislature, in accord with their commissions; and after consideration of such facts and figures known to them, they reported that slightly less than $1,000,000 of money represented by the debt had been expended within the territory which had become West Virginia, and that they did not have sufficient data to determine the amount of the offset against that amount. Several years later, during which time Mr. Bennett had been busy gathering the missing facts and figures, he reported to the legislature that the offset exceeded the debt, and that the Old Dominion in fact was the debtor in the case.

It appears that one reason — if not *the* reason — Virginia authorities would not meet with the West Virginia commissioners in Richmond in 1871 was that the Old Dominion had decided upon a new course of action: To issue bonds for the reduction of the entire debt. The debt itself was determined to be divisible by three, and West Virginia was to bear one-third of the total amount, on the theory that the Mountaineers constituted, in both area and population, about one-third of the area and population of the Old Dominion prior to 1861. On that basis, the old state issued bonds against herself, and issued "West Virginia certificates" totaling one-third of the entire amount, these certificates not bearing the full faith and credit guarantee and, instead were to be redeemed from time to time as West Virginia made payments thereon. West Virginia seems to have taken a dim view of this procedure, and it appeared that Virginia might be left holding the entire bag, so to speak; and in 1906 Virginia brought a suit in equity against West Virginia in the Supreme Court of the United States, praying for recovery in the full amount of one-third of the total debt as of 1 January, 1861, plus accrued interest. West Virginia demurred; technicalities were argued, and the Court appointed a master who was directed to hold hearings, take testimony, etc., and report his findings and recommendations back to the full Court. Nine years and several thick volumes of testimony later (in 1915) the master made his report; and the upshot was that the Court determined that the basis for division of the debt between the two states was to be the amount of taxable property (exclusive of slaves) in each of the states, (as though only the whole state of Virginia as of 1861 were involved) less such equities as West Virginia might have in the proceeds of securities held in Virginia, and other technical details which need not be elaborated, including the determination of interest on the debt. A specific amount — $12,393,929.50 — was held to be due from West Virginia to Virginia as of 1 July, 1915. Neither party was entirely happy and costs were divided equally between them, so that neither side could fairly be said to have "won" the case. One thing was quite clear, however: West Virginia was obligated to Virginia to the tune of something more than $12,000,000 by decree of the highest court in the land, from which there was no appeal. One would be justified in supposing that West Virginia would dutifully pay-up, and that over the years the two states came to live happily together ever after. Right?

Wrong!

My face is red as I write this, for as a West Virginian I must dutifully admit that my state came very close to welching on the payment of that debt; and that in 1917 Virginia found it necessary to go back to the Court to seek mandamus or its equivalent to enforce payment of the 1915 decree; and so it came about that West Virginia has the very dubious honor of having had its legislative session of 1917 interrupted by process-servers going from aisle to aisle in the chambers of the house of delegates and senate serving show-cause orders on the members to appear in court on the 6th day of March, 1917, or else! Well, those legislators were fully represented in Court on that day in March, just two days after the second inauguration of President Woodrow Wilson and the only inauguration of Governor John J. Cornwell of West Virginia, and the Court (1918) held in no uncertain terms that it had the means to enforce payment, but graciously gave the defendant one last chance to come to terms without further order of the Court. Thereafter, and due in considerable part to the good-faith efforts of Governor Cornwell, the legislature of West Virginia in 1919 finally made adequate provisions for the retirement of the debt. Following is an extract from West Virginia Acts, Extraordinary Sessions, 1919, Chapter 10 (page 19 et seq.), passed 31 March, 1919, approved by governor 1 April, 1919, in effect from passage:

Whereas the Supreme Court of the United States, by its decree in the cause of Commonwealth of Virginia against the State of West Virginia on the 14th of June, 1915 adjudged, ordered and decreed that . . . Virginia recover from West Virginia the sum of $12,393,929.50, with interest thereon from July 1, 1915, until paid, at the rate of 5% per annum, and that each party pay one-half of the costs . . . which, as of January 1, 1919, amounts to (total principal and interest plus ½ of the costs), $12,562,867.16; and

Whereas the State of West Virginia desires to comply with the decree of the Court and satisfy it as soon as possible; and

Whereas this legislature has been informed by the report of the West Virginia debt commission, as well as by the representatives of the Commonwealth of Virginia, that the bonds of West Virginia dated January 1, 1919, bearing interest at 3½ per centum per annum, payable semi-annually on the first days of July and January of each year (hereinafter described), and to the face amount of $13,500,000, together with a cash payment of $1,062,867.16, with interest thereon at the rate of 5% per annum from January 1, 1919 until the date of payment thereof, (West Virginia to pay one-half of the court costs), will be accepted at par in full satisfaction of the said judgment.

Now, therefore,

Be it enacted by the Legislature of West Virginia:

(This section of the act directs the state auditor to draw his warrant on the state treasurer for the amount of the cash payment as above specified, payable to the Commonwealth of Virginia; and following sections provide for the issuance of bonds as above specified so that the entire amount of the debt would be fully paid on the 1st day of January, 1939.)

And so it was that West Virginia's adjudged share of the public debt of the Old Dominion as of 1 January, 1860, was paid in full — but not until 1939!

Virginians and West Virginians may argue in good faith as to the merits of the Court's 1915 decree, and plausible grounds for the contentions of citizens of both states existed at the time and must be recognized even today. But for West Virginia to attempt avoidance of the decree, with the resulting action of plaintiff Virginia having to seek mandamus to compel payment, is something for which West Virginia must be ashamed; and the restraint which Virginia writers have shown in relating the debt proceedings is something for which West Virginians ought to be thankful and for which they should display great humility.

The Supreme Court citations for the several decisions in Virginia v. West Virginia are (1) 206 U.S. 290, in 1906; (2) 220 U.S., in 1911; (2) 238 U.S. 202, in 1915; and (3) 246 U.S. 565, submitted 6 March 1917, decided 22 April, 1918. Other references, for those who seek to delve further: *The Life of Jonathan M. Bennett,* by Harvey Mitchell Rice, University of North Carolina Press, 1943; *West Virginia Encyclopedia,* edited by Phil Conley, page 939, West Va. Pub. Co., Charleston, 1929; *West Virginia Heritage Encyclopedia,* edited and published by Jim Comstock, Richwood, W. Va., main Vol. 22, page 4811 et seq.; and *Virginia The New Dominion,* by Virginius Dabney, Doubleday, New York, 1971, pp. 376-77, 386-87.

Chapter IX — Appendix
West Virginia Political Chronology
1860-1863

Note: A chronological synopsis of events leading to the formation of West Virginia, from the time of the election of Abraham Lincoln as President of the United States to the admission of West Virginia as the thirty-fifth State of the Union. It was written by the late Delf Norona, who was a member of the West Virginia Centennial Commission and was published as a courtesy to the public by the Marshall County Centennial Committee in 1963. (A short biographical sketch of Mr. Norona is set out in the "Sectionalism" chapter of this Appendix.)

This should be regarded as "must reading" by journalists, news broadcasters, pamphleteers, Sunday editors, presidents of historical societies, and all windjammers who speak at banquets, pageants and what-have-you on an occasion commemorating anything about this history of West Virginia, who almost to a man (whose name escapes me at the moment) make some booboo as, for example, "On 20 June 1863 President Lincoln signed the bill making West Virginia a state of the Union," or "the day Mr. Pierpont became the first provisional governor of West Virginia," or the "the *day that the old Custom House* became the capitol of the new state;" I've heard all these bloopers by people who ought to have boned up on the subject before holding forth to the public.

Warning to non-Virginians and non-West Virginians: I recommend that you skip this chapter, unless you like to recite the multiplication tables or memorize such useful information as "on 30 February 1755 one Bostolsov Iskivitch invented the first machine-driven fly swatter," etc., etc., world without end, amen.

1860
Nov. 6. Abraham Lincoln elected president of the United States.

Of some 167,000 votes recorded cast in Virginia, Lincoln

received less than 2,000, of which 1,400 were from the Northern Panhandle.

Nov. 7. Members of the Virginia Assembly petitioned Governor John Letcher of Virginia to convene an extra session to consider the crisis which Lincoln's election had produced. Letcher selects January 7, 1861, for such session.

Letcher owed his election as Governor to the tremendous majorities received in the Northwest. He was at that time strongly attached to the Union.

Nov. 12. Mass meeting of citizens in Kingwood. Resolutions adopted opposing secession, that any action of Virginia looking toward secession will meet with opposition of the people of Preston County.

It was the practice at that time to hold mass meetings to consider matters of public interest. Speeches would be made, resolutions adopted, and the proceedings were frequently published.

A study of resolutions adopted at such meetings in 1861 illustrates the feelings of the people at the grassroots level as to the formation of a new state out of Virginia.

Prior to the extra session of the Assembly commenced on January 7th at Richmond, at mass meetings held in Morgantown, Grafton, Parkersburg, Wheeling, and elsewhere, resolutions were adopted deploring the election of Lincoln but calling on maintenance of the Union declaring that the election of Republican candidates did not justify secession, opposing the dissolution of the Union for existing causes, calling on the people to maintain the Union, and condemning the action taken by South Carolina in seceding.

Dec. 1. Discourse at Wheeling, "Secession is Revolution; the dangers of the South . . ." by George W. Thompson, Judge of the Wheeling Circuit Court.

This speech was published in pamphlet form.

A strong opponent of secession, when Virginia finally did secede Judge Thompson felt his first allegiance was to the state. He refused to take a loyalty oath to the Union, and was removed from office and was arrested.

Dec. 20. South Carolina secedes from the Union.

By February 1, 1861, six additional Southern states had adopted ordinances of secession.

Dec. Toward the end of December suggestions made in the press that a new state be erected. "There is no affinity between Eastern and Western Virginia." Proposal that panhandle counties be annexed to Pennsylvania.

1861

Jan. 7. General Assembly of Virginia convenes at Richmond in extra session to "take into consideration the condition of public affairs.

Jan. 14. Assembly passes act for election of members to a Convention to meet February 13th, election of delegates to be held February 14th and a poll taken whether any action of the convention dissolving connection with the Union "shall be submitted to the people for ratification or rejecton."

The delegates-elect from the northwest were almost all in favor of reference.

Jan. 21. Resolution adopted by the Assembly that if efforts to reconcile differences between the two sections of the country shall prove abortive, then Virginia should unite with slaveholding states of the South.

Feb. 4. Election to select delegates to convention and to take a separate poll on submission to the people of the question of ratification or rejection of the action of the convention.

The face of the returns indicated an overwhelming victory of the Unionists, with "scarcely left a vestige of secession in Western Virginia."

Of 152 delegates elected about 120 were opposed to secession at that time.

By a vote of about 100,000 to 45,000 the people voted that the findings of the convention should be submitted to the people for ratification or rejection.

Feb. 13. Convention convenes.

Forty-seven of the 152 delegates were from present West Virginia.

This is popularly known as the Secession Convention.

At first favorable to maintaining the Union, with changing conditions many delegates veered from Unionism towards Secessionism.

Apr. 12. Bombardment of Fort Sumter commenced.

Apr. 15. President Lincoln issues proclamation calling for 75,000 militia "to suppress said combinations" against the United States.

Apr. 17. Convention adopts ordinance of secession (88 to 55), with provision that a poll be taken of the voters on May 23rd on the question of ratifying or rejecting the ordinance.

32 delegates from present West Virginia voted against secession.

A provision was made that the election of members of Congress of the United States, due to be held on May 23rd, be suspended.

Most members of the convention from northwestern Virginia immediately returned to their homes.

Frequent mass meetings were held during and after the time the secession convention was in session, and a new state movement was well under way in the northwest by the time the secession ordinance was adopted.

Most of these meetings held in present West Virginia were Union in character, but there were a number of States Rights meetings, mostly in southern and eastern counties.

Apr. 22. Mass meeting of citizens at Clarksburg.

Resolution adopted calling for a convention at Wheeling on May 13th composed of delegates from counties in northwestern Virginia, each county to send not less than five persons, to determine the action "the people of northwestern

Virginia should take in the present fearful emergency."

May 13-15. First Wheeling Convention.

This was held at Washington Hall and was composed of 430 "delegates," many of whom were elected irregularly.

Immediate division of Virginia and the creation of the state of New Virginia was at first generally favored; others insisted and finally prevailed that action be deferred until after the May 23rd vote; that if the ordinance of secession was ratified, then a second convention be held in Wheeling on June 11th, at which each county would be entitled to double the number of delegates to which it would be entitled in the next House of Delegates; that senators and delegates to be elected on May 23rd be also seated at the Convention.

Committee of nine selected to carry into effect the objects of the convention.

May 23. People of Virginia vote overwhelmingly for ratification of the Secession Ordinance, but a considerable majority of persons in the northwest vote against ratification.

Union forces under General McClellan, with the acquiescence of Union leaders in western Virginia, entered the state immediately afterwards; the famous skirmish at Philippi took place on June 3rd.

June 11-25. Second Wheeling Convention.

This was attended by about 100 delegates, representing 34 counties. It convened at Washington Hall, but on June 13th the Convention adjourned to the Federal building.

June 13. Declaration of the People of Virginia presented.

The Declaration was adopted, with amendments, on June 17th.

It asserted that the Secession Convention had been illegally called, consequently its acts and the acts of the Executive tending to separate Virginia from the United States were without authority and void.

It declared that the offices of all who adhered to the Convention and the Executive were vacated.

The Declaration further demanded a reorganization of the state government.

June 14. Ordinance for the reorganization of the state government presented as adopted, with amendments, on June 19th.

June 20. Declaration signed. Francis H. Pierpont elected governor of the reorganizaed government of Virginia; and other officers were also elected.

This Declaration is popularly [but incorrectly][1] known as "West Virginia's Declaration of Independence."

June 25. Convention ajdourns to meet again August 6th.

July 1-26. Extra session of the reorganized General Assembly.

The Assembly met at the Federal building in Wheeling which thereby became the capitol of the Union government of Virginia.

Waitman T. Willey and John S. Carlile were elected United States senators on July 9th.

Action on the formation of a new state was deferred, it being considered that such action should be initiated in a constituent assembly rather than in a legislature.

Aug. 6-21. Adjourned session of the Second Wheeling Convention.

An ordinance was adopted August 20th providing that the state of Kanawha be formed out of the state of Virginia and that on October 24th a vote of the people be taken on the matter of ratifying the ordinance and electing delegates to a Constitutional Convention to prepare a constitution of the new state, the convention to convene at Wheeling on November 26th.

Oct. 24. Ordinance for the formation of a new state ratified by a vote of 18,408 for, to 781 against. Delegates selected for the Constitutional Convention.

Nov. 26-Feb. 18 (1862). First Constitutional Convention.

The convention met at the Federal building in Wheeling.

A constitution was adopted on February 18th providing that the new state be named West Virginia, to consist of 44 counties but that seven additional counties under certain conditions might be added.

A "slavery section" was included: "No slave shall be brought or free person of color be permitted to come, into this State for permanent residence."

An interim committe was appointed to superintend and certify the result of a referedum to be held April 3rd on the question of adopting the Constitution and later to reconvene the convention if necessary.

1862

Apr. 3. Vote on the question of adoption of the Constitution of West Virginia.

18,862 voted for adoption; 514 for rejection.

May 6-15. Extra session of the reorganized General Assembly.

Act passed May 13th, giving consent to the formation of the state of West Virginia, to consist of 48 counties, with a provision for the inclusion of Berkeley, Jefferson, and Frederick counties under certain conditions.

May 29-June 3. Senator Waitman T. Willey presents memorial to U.S. Senate on May 29th asking for admission of the state of West Virginia into the Union, and Congressman William G. Brown presents the same memorial to the House of Representatives on June 3rd.

Jul. 14. Senate passes act for the admission of West Virginia into the Union.

This act (Senate bill 365) contained provisos:

(a) Changing the slavery section of the proposed West Virginia Constitition to provide for the gradual emancipation of slaves.

(b) That the Constititional Convention of West Virginia should agree to the change in the slavery clause and that after an affirmative vote of the people ratifying such change the

President should issue a proclamation that the act would take effect "from and after sixty days from the date of said proclamation."

Jul. 16. House postpones consideration of the statehood bill until the next session of Congress to be held in December.

This session of Congress adjourned July 17th to resume December 1st.

Between the sessions of Congress numerous petitions were sent from West Virginia asking the House to concur with the Senate bill.

Dec. 10. House passes Senate bill 365 for the admission of West Virginia into the Union.

Dec. 22. Bill presented to President Lincoln.

Dec. 23. President Lincoln requests opinion of members of the Cabinet: "1st. Is the said Act constitutional? 2nd. Is the said Act expedient?"

Three members replied affirmatively; three negatively.

Dec. 31. President Lincoln signs statehood bill.

1863

Jan. 14. Commissioners of the Constitutional Convention issue call reconvening the convention on February 12th and providing for election of delegates on February 5th to fill vacancies.

Feb. 12-20. Recalled session of the Constitutional Convention.

Feb. 18. Constitutional Convention unanimously adopts the new slavery clause to comply with the act of Congress.

The Convention passed ordinances for the holding of a poll on the question of adopting or rejecting the amended Constitution and the election of officers for the state of West Virginia; that the senators and delegates so elected shall assemble at Wheeling at eleven a.m. on the sixty-first day after the President shall have issued his proclamation and organize as the Legislature of West Virginia.

Mar. 26. Poll taken on question of adoption of the amended Constitution.

Apr. 16. Executive committee of the Constitutional Convention certifies to President Lincoln that at the poll taken on March 26th, 26,632 votes were cast for ratification and 534 votes for rejection of the amended constitution.

Apr. 20. President Lincoln issues proclamation that the act of Congress admitting West Virginia into the Union "shall take effect and be in force, from and after sixty days from the date thereof."

Apr. 22. Executive committee of the Constitutional Convention sets the date of May 28th for the election of officers for the state of West Virginia.

May 28. Election of state and county officials generally throughout the state.

Arthur I. Boreman elected governor.

June 20. West Virginia becomes "one of the United States of America" with Wheeling as its capital.

Inaugural ceremonies were held in front of the Linsley Institute building, which became West Virginia's first capitol.

West Virginia had 48 counties on June 20, 1863. Berekely and Jefferson counties were added later in the year.

July 4. Thirty-fifth star added to Old Glory, representing West Virginia. [This note added by Hearne].

---

[1]Bracket by Hearne.

Chapter X — Appendix
Virginia Bill of Rights

Hearne note: The following text is taken verbatim from pages 32-34 of the Code of Virginia, 1860, which was in effect during the years 1860-1863 (and through the entire period of time covered by the subject matter of this book). The historical note preceding the Bill of Rights is by the editor of the Code, the late Hon. George W. Munford, who was Secretary of the Commonwealth.

When, on the 15th of May 1776, the Convention of Virginia instructed their delegates in Congress to propose to that body to declare the United Colonies free and independent States, it, at the same time, appointed a committee to prepare a declaration of rights and such a plan of government as would be most likely to maintain peace and order in the Colony and secure substantial and equal liberty to the people. On subsequent days the committee was enlarged; Mr. George Mason was added to on the 18th. The declaration of rights was on the 27th reported by Mr. Archibald Cary, the chairman of the committee, and, after being twice read, was ordered to be printed for the perusal of members. It was considered in committee of the whole on the 29th of May and the 3rd, 4th, 5th, and 10th of June. It was then reported to the house with amendments. On the 11th the convention considered the amendments, and having agreed thereto, ordered that the declaration (with the amendments), be fairly transcribed and read a third time and passed *nem. con.* A manuscript copy of the first draft of the declaration, just as it was drawn by Mr. Mason,[1] is in the Library of Virginia. The declaration as it passed was adopted without alternation by the Convention of 1829-30, and re-adopted with amendments by the Convention of 1850-51, and as amended is as follows:[2]

A Declaration of Rights made by the Respresentatives of the good people of VIRGINIA, assembled in full and free Convention, which rights do pertain to them and their posterity as the basis and foundation of government.

1. That all men are by nature equally free and independent, and have certain inherent rights, of which, when they enter into a state of society, they cannot, by any compact, deprive or divest their posterity; namely, the enjoyment of life and liberty, and the means of acquiring and possessing property, and pursuing and obtaining happiness and safety.

2. That all power is vested in, and consequently derived from the people; that Magistrates are their trustees and servants, and at all times amendable to them.

3. That government is, or ought to be, instituted for the common benefit, protection and security of the people, nation, or community: of all the various modes and forms of government, that is best, which is capable of producing the greatest degree of happiness and safety, and is most effectually secured against the danger of mal-administration; and that, when any government shall be found inadequate or contrary to these purposes, a majority of the community hath an indubitable, unalienable, and indefeasible right, to reform, alter, or abolish it, in such manner as shall be judged most conducive to the public weal.

4. That no man, or set of men, are entitled to exclusive or separate emoluments or privileges from the community, but in consideration of public services; which not being discernable, neither ought the offices of Magistrate, Legislature, or Judge, or be hereditary.

5. That the legislative, executive and judicial power should be separate and distinct; and that the members thereof may be restrained from oppression, by feeling and participating the burthens of the people, they should, at fixed periods, be reduced to a private station, return into that body from which they were originally taken, and the vacancies be supplied by frequent, certain, and regular elections, in which all, or any part of the former members, to be again eligible, or ineligible, as the laws shall direct.[3]

6. That all elections ought to be free; and that all men, having sufficient evidence of permanent common interest with, and attachment to, the community, have the right to suffrage, and cannot be taxes or deprived of their property for public uses, without their own consent, or that of their representatives so elected, nor bound by any law to which they have not, in like manner, assented, for the public good.[4]

7. That all power of suspending laws, or the execution of laws, by any authority, without consent of the representatives of the people, is injurious to their rights, and ought not to be exercised.

8. That, in all capital or criminal prosecutions, a man hath a right to demand the cause and nature of his accusation, to be conformed with the accusers and witnesses, to call for evidence in his favor; and to a speedy trial by an impartial jury of twelve men of his vicinage, without whose unanimous consent he cannot be found guilty; nor can he be compelled to give evidence against himself; that no man be deprived of his liberty, except by the law of the land or the judgment of his peers.[5]

9. That excessive bail ought not to be required, nor excessive fines imposed, nor cruel and unusual punishments inflicted.

10. That general warrants, whereby an officer or messenger may be commanded to search suspected places without evidence of a fact committed, or to seize any person or persons not named, or whose offence is not particularly described and supported by evidence, are grievous and oppressive, and ought not to be granted.

11. That, is in controversies respecting property, and in suits between man and man, the ancient trial by jury of twelve men is preferable to any other, and ought not to be granted.[6]

12. That the freedom of the press is one of the great bulwarks of liberty, and can never be restrained but by despotic governments.

13. That a well regulated militia, composed of the body of the people, trained to arms, is the proper, natural and safe defense of a free state; that standing armies in times of peace, should be avoided, as dangerous to liberty; and that in all cases, the military should be under strict subordination to, and governed by, the civil power.

14. That the people, have a right to uniform government; and therefore, that no government separate from, or independent of, the governor of Virginia, ought to be erected or established within the limits thereof.

15. That no free government, or the blessings of liberty, can be preserved to any people, but by a firm adherence to justice, moderation, temperance, frugality, and virtue, and by a frequent recurrence to fundamental principles.

16. That religion, or the duty which we owe to our Creator, and the manner of discharging it, can be directed only by reason and conviction, not by force or violence; and therefore all men are equally entitled to the free exercise of religion, according to the dictates of conscience; and that it is the mutual duty of all to practice Christian forbearance, love, and charity towards each other.

---

[1]Va. Hist. Reg. Jan. 1849, p. 29.

[2]See Acts 1852, p. 320-21. Sections amended are 5, 6, 8, and 11. The Bill of Rights as originally passed, is found in the Revised Code of 1819, p. 31-2, and Code of 1849, p. 32, 33, 34, 1st. edition.

[3]Amended. Acts 1852, p. 321, Sec. 5. The 5th section, without amendment, read: "That the legislative and executive powers of the state should be separate and distinct from the judiciary, and that the members of the two first" &c.

[4]Amended. Acts 1852, p. 321, Sec. 6. The 6th session was: "That election of members to serve as representatives of the people in assembly" &c.

[5]Amended. Acts 1852, p. 321, Sec. 8, 11. In the 8th and 11th sections, the words "of twelve men" inserted after the word "jury."

[6]See note 4 supra.

Chapter XI — Appendix
Act of Assembly in Wheeling, 13 May 1862, giving Virginia's Consent to Transfer of Counties from Virginia to West Virginia

Extra Session Held May Sixth, 1862
In the City of Wheeling

AN ACT

giving the consent of the Legislature of Virginia to the formation and erection of a new State within the jurisdiction of this State.

Passed May 13, 1862

1. Be it enacted by the General Assembly, That the consent of the Legislature of Virginia be, and the same is hereby given to the formation and erection of the State of West Virginia, within the jurisdiction of this State, to include the counties of Hancock, Brooke, Ohio, Marshall, Wetzel, Marion, Monongalia, Preston, Taylor, Tyler, Pleasants, Ritchie, Doddridge, Harrison, Wood, Jackson, Wirt, Roane, Calhoun, Gilmer, Barbour, Tucker, Lewis, Braxton, Upshur, Randolph, Mason, Putnam, Kanawha, Clay, Nicholas, Cabell, Wayne, Boone, Logan, Wyoming, Mercer, McDowell, Webster, Pocahontas, Fayette, Raleigh, Greenbrier, Monroe, Pendleton, Hardy, Hampshire and Morgam, according to the boundaries and under the provisions set forth in the Constitution for the said State of West Virginia and the schedule thereto annexed, proposed by the Convention which assembled at Wheeling, on the twenty-sixth day of November, 1861.

2. Be it further enacted, That the consent of the Legislature of Virginia be, and the same is hereby given, that the counties of Berekely, Jefferson and Frederick, shall be included in and form part of the State of West Virginia whenever the voters of said counties shall ratify and assent to the said Constitution, at an election

held for the purpose, at such time and under such regulations as the Commissioners named in the said schedule may prescribe.

3. Be it further enacted, That this Act be transmitted by the Executive to the Senators and Representatives of this Commonwealth in Congress, together with a certified original of the said Constitution and Schedule — and the said Senators and Representatives are hereby requested to use their endeavors to obtain the consent of Congress to the admission of the State of West Virginia into the Union.

4. This Act shall be in force from and after its passage.

Chapter XII — Appendix
President Johnson's Executive Order, 9 May 1865, Recognizing Pierpont as Governor of Virginia

(Messages and Papers of the Presidents
Volume VI, pages 337, 338)

EXECUTIVE CHAMBER,
Washington City, May 9, 1865.

EXECUTIVE ORDER TO REESTABLISH THE AUTHORITY OF THE UNITED STATES AND EXECUTE THE LAWS WITHIN THE GEORGRAPHICAL LIMITS KNOWN AS THE STATE OF VIRGINIA.

Ordered, first. That all acts and proceedings of the political, military and civil organizations which have been in a state of insurrection and rebellion within the State of Virginia against the authority and laws of the United States, and of which Jefferson Davis, John Letcher, and William Smith were late the respective chiefs, are declared null and void. All persons who shall exercise, claim, pretend, or attempt to exercise any political, military, or civil power, authority, jurisdiction, or right by, through, or under Jefferson Davis, late of the city of Richmond, and his confederates, or under John Letcher or William Smith and their confederates or under any pretended political, military, or civil commission or authority issued by them or either of them since the 17th day of April 1861, shall be deemed and taken as in rebellion against the United States, and shall be dealt with accordingly.

Second. That the Secretary of State proceed to put in force all laws of the United States the administration whereof belongs to the Department of State applicable to the geographical limits aforesaid.

Third. That the Secretary of the Treasury proceed without delay to nominate for appointment assessors of taxes and collectors of customs and internal revenue and such other officers of the

Treasury Department as are authorized by law, and shall put in execution the revenue of laws of the United States within the geographical limits aforesaid. In making appointments the preference shall be given to qualified loyal persons residing within the districts where their respective duties are to be performed; but if suitable persons shall not be found residents of the district, then persons residing in other States or districts shall be appointed.

Fourth. That the Postmaster-General shall proceed to establish post offices and post routes and put into execution the postal laws of the United States within the said State, giving to loyal residents the preference of appointment; but if suitable persons are not found, them to appoint agents, etc., from other states.

Fifth. That the district judge of said district proceed to hold courts within said State in accordance with the provisions of the act of Congress. The Attorney-General will instruct the proper officers to libel and bring to judgment, confiscation, and sale property subject to confiscation, and to enforce the administration of justice within said State in all matters, civil and criminal, within the cognizance and jurisdiction of the Federal courts.

Sixth. That the Secretary of War assign such assistant provost-marshal-general and such provost-marshals in each district of said State as he may deem necessary.

Seventh. The Secretary of the Navy will take possession of all public property belonging to the Navy Department within said geographical limits and put in operation within said geographical limits and put in operation all acts of Congress in relation to naval affairs having application to the said State.

Eighth. The Secretary of the Interior will also put in force the laws relating to the Department of the Interior.

Ninth. That to carry into effect the guaranty by the Federal Constitution of a republican form of State government and afford the advantage and security of domestic laws, as well as to complete the reestablishment of the authority and laws of the United States and the full complete restoration of peace within the limits aforesaid, Francis H. Pierpont, governor of the State of Virginia, will be aided by the Federal Government so far as may be necessary in the lawful measures which he may take for the extension and administration of the State government throughout the geographical limits of said State.

In testimony whereof I have hereunto set my hand and caused the seal of the United States to be affixed.

[SEAL]   ANDREW JOHNSON.
By the President:

W. HUNTER,
Acting Secretary of State.

Chapter XIII — Appendix
President Johnson's Proclamation Appointing a Provisional Governor of North Carolina

(Messages and papers of the Presidents,
Volume VI, Pages 312-314)

Hearne Note: This proclamation was used as a model for the appointment of provisional governors in Mississippi, Georgia, Texas, Alabama, South Carolina and Florida during the period 29 May 13 July 1865.

BY THE PRESIDENT OF THE UNITED STATES OF AMERICA

A PROCLAMATION

Whereas the fourth section of the fourth article of the Constitution of the United States declares that the United States shall guarantee to every State in the Union a republican form of government and shall protect each of them against invasion and domestic violence; and

Whereas the President of the United States is by the Constitution made Commander in Chief of the Army and Navy, as well as chief civil executive officer of the United States, and is bound by solemn oath faithfully execute the office of President of the United States and to take care that the laws be faithfully executed; and

Whereas the rebellion which has been waged by a portion of the people of the United States against the properly constituted authorities of the Government thereof in the most violent and revolting form, but whose organized and armed forces have now been almost entirely overcome, has in its revolutionary progress deprived the people of the State of North Carolina of all civil government; and

Whereas it becomes necessary and proper to carry out and enforce the obligations of the United States to the people of North

Carolina in securing them in the enjoyment of a republican form of government:

Now, therefore, in obedience to the high and solemn duties imposed upon me by the Constitution of the United States and for the purpose of enabling the loyal people of said State to organize a State government whereby jutice may be established, domestic tranquillity insured, and loyal citizens protected in all their rights of life, liberty, and property, I, Andrew Johnson, President of the United States and Commander in Chief of the Army and Navy of the United States, do hereby appoint William H. Holden provisional governor of the State of North Carolina, whose duty it shall be, to the earliest practicable period, to prescribe such rules and regulations as may be necessary and proper for convening a convention composed of delegates to be chosen by that portion of the people of said State who are loyal to the United States, and no others, for the purpose of altering or amending the constitution thereof, and with authority to exercise within the limits of said State all powers necessary and proper to enable such loyal people of the State of North Carolina to restore said State to its constitutional relations to the Federal Government and to present such a republican form of State government as will entitle the State to the guaranty of the United States therefor and its people to protection by the United States against invasion, insurrection and domestic violence: *Provided,* That in any election that may be hereafter held for choosing delegates of any State convention as aforesaid no person shall be qualified as an elector or shall be eligible as a member of such convention unless he shall have previously taken and subscribed the oath of amnesty as set forth in the President's proclamation of May 29, A.D. 1865, and is a voter qualified as prescribed by the constitution and laws of the State of North Carolina in force immediately before the 29th day of May, A.D. 1861, the date of the so-called ordinance of secession; and the said convention, when convened, or the legislature that maybe thereafter assembled will prescribe the qualification of electors and eligibility of persons to hold office under the constitution and laws of the State — a power; the people of the several States composing the Federal Union have rightfully exercised from the origin of the Government to the present time.

And I do hereby direct —

First. That the military commander of the department and all officers and persons in the military and naval service aid and assist the said provisional governor in carrying into effect this proclamation; and they are enjoined to abstain from in any way hindering, impeding, or discouraging the loyal people from the organization of a State government as herein authorized.

Second. That the Secretary of State proceed to put in force all laws of the United States the administration whereof belongs to the State Department applicable to the georgraphical limits aforesaid.

Third. That the Secretary of Treasury proceed to nominate for appointment assessors of taxes and collectors of customs and internal revenue and such other officers of the Treasury Department as are authorized by law and put in execution the revenue laws of the

United States within the geographical limits aforesaid. In making appointments the preference shall be given to qualified loyal persons residing within the districts where their respective duties are to be performed; but if suitable residents of the districts shall not be found, then persons residing in other States or districts shall be appointed.

Fourth. That the Postmaster-General proceed to establish post-offices and post routes and put into execution the postal laws of the United States within the said State, giving to loyal residents the preference of appointment; but if suitable residents are not found, then to appoint agents, etc., from other States.

Fifth. That the district judge for the judicial district in which North Carolina is included proceed to hold courts within said State in accordance with the provisions of the acts of Congress. The Attorney General will instruct the proper officers to libel and bring to judgment, confiscation, and sale property subject to confiscation and enforce the administration of justice within said State in all matters within the cognizance and jurisdiction of the Federal courts.

Sixth. That the Secretary of the Navy take possession of all public property belonging to the Navy Department within said geographical limits and put in operation all acts of Congress in relation to naval affairs having application to the said State.

Seventh. That the Secretary of the Interior put in force the laws relating to the Interior Department applicable to the geographical limits aforesaid.

In testimony whereof I have hereunto set my hand and caused the seal of the United States to be affixed.

[SEAL.]   Done at the city of Washington, this 29th day of May, A.D. 1865, and of the Independence of the United States the eighty-ninth.

ANDREW JOHNSON.

By the President:
    WILLIAM H. SEWARD,
    Secretary of State.

Chapter XIV — Appendix
First (Congressional) Reconstruction Act, 2 March 1867

The First Reconstruction Act
(Congressional)

Passed Over Veto On 2 March 1867
14 Stat. 428

CHAP. CLIII. — *An Act to provide for the more efficient Government of the Rebel States.*

WHEREAS no legal State governments or adequate protection for life or property now exists in the rebel states of Virginia, North Carolian, South Carolina, Georgia, Mississippi, Alabama, Louisiana, Florida, Texas, and Arkansas; and whereas it is necessary that peace and good order should be enforced in said States until loyal and republican State governments can be legally established: Therefore,

Be it enacted by the Senate and House of Representatives of the United States of America in Cognress assembled, That said rebel States shall be divided into military districts and made subject to the military authority of the United States as hereinafter prescribed, and for that purpose Virginia shall constitute the first district: North Carolina and South Carolina the second district; Georgia, Alabama, and Florida the third district; Mississippi and Arkansas the fourth district; and Louisiana and Texas the fifth district.

SEC. 2. *And be it further enacted,* That it shall be the duty of the President to assign the command of each of said districts an officer of the army, not below the rank of brigadier-general, and to detail a sufficient military force to enable such officer to perform his duties and enforce his authority within the district to which he is assigned.

SEC. 3. *And be it further enacted,* That it shall be the duty of each officer assigned as aforesaid, to protect all persons in their rights of person and property, to subpress insurrection, disorder, and violence, and to punish, or cause to be punished, all disturbers of the public peace and criminals; and to the end he may allow local civil tribunals to take jurisdictions of and to try offenders, or, when in his judgment it may be necessary for the trial of offenders, he shall have power to organize military commissions or tribunals for that purpose, and all interference under color of State authority with the exercise of military authority under this act, shall be null and void.

SEC. 4. *And be it further enacted,* That all persons put under military arrest by virtue of this act shall be tried with unnecessary delay, and no cruel or unusual punishment shall be inflicted, and no sentence of any military commission or tribunal hereby authorized, affecting the life or liberty of any such person, shall be executed until it is approved by the officer in command of the district, and the laws and regulations for the government of the army shall not be affected by this act, expect in so far as they conflict with its provisions: *Provided,* That no sentence of death under the provisions of this act shall be carried into effect without the approval of the President.

SEC. 5. *And be if further enacted,* That when the people of any one of said rebel States shall have formed a constitution of government in conformity with the Constitution of the United States in all respects, framed by a convention of delegates elected by the male citizens of said State, twenty-one years old and upward, of whatever race, color, or previous to the day of such election, except such as may be disfranchised for participation in the rebellion or for felony at common law, and when such constitution shall provide that the elective franchise shall be enjoyed by all such persons as have the qualifications herein stated for electors of delegates, and when such constitution shall be ratified by a majority of the persons voting on the question of ratification who are qualified as electors for delegates, and when such constitution shall have been submitted to Congress for examination and approval, and Congress shall have approved the same, and when said State, by a vote of its legislature elected under said constitution, shall have adopted the amendment to the Constitution of the United States, proposed by the Thirty-ninth Congress, and known as article fourteen, and when said article shall have become a part of the Constitution of the United States, said State shall be declared entitled to representation in Congress, and senators and representatives shall be admitted therefrom on their taking the oath prescribed by law, and then and thereafter the preceding sections of this act shall be inoperative in said State: *Provided,* That no person excluded from the privilege of holding office by said proposed amendment to the Constitution of the United States, shall be eligible to election as a member of the convention to frame a constitution for any of said rebel States, nor shall any such person vote for members of such convention.

SEC. 6. *And be it further enacted,* That, until the people of said rebel States shall be by law admitted to representation in the Congress of the United States, any civil governments which may exist therein shall be deemed provisional only, and in all respects subject to the paramount authority of the United States at any time to abolish, modify, control, or supersede the same; and in all elections of any office under such provisional governments all persons shall be entitled to vote, and none others, who are entitled to vote, under the provision of the fifty section of this act; and no person shall be eligible to any office under any such provisional governments who would be disqualified from holding office under the provisions of the third *article* of said constitutional amendment.

SCHUYLER COLFAX,
Speaker of the House of Representatives.
LA FAYETTE S. FOSTER,
President of the Senate, pro tempore.

IN THE HOUSE OF REPRESENTATIVES,
March 2, 1867.

The President of the United States, having returned to the House of Representatives, in which it originated, the bill entitled "An act to provide for the more efficient government of the rebel States," with his objections thereto, the House of Representatives proceeded, in pursuance of the Constitution, to reconsider the same; and
Resolved, That the said bill do pass, two thirds of the House of Representatives agreeing to pass the same.
Attest: 　　　　　　　　　EDWARD McPHERSON
Clerk of H. R. U. S.

IN SENATE OF THE UNITED STATES,
March 2, 1867.

The Senate having proceeded, in pursuance of the Constitution, to reconsider the bill entitled "An act to provide for the more efficient government of the rebel States," returned to the House of Representatives by the President of the United States, with his objections, and sent by the House of Representatives to the Senate, with the message of the President returning the bill:
Resolved, That the bill do pass, two thirds of the Senate agreeing to pass the same.
Attest: 　　　　　　　　　J. W. FORNEY,
Secretary of the Senate.

Chapter XV — Appendix
Resolutions of First Post-War
General Assembly in Richmond,
under Alexandria Constitution

(See Acts of Assembly, 1865-66)

No. 1 — Joint Resolutions approving the Policy of the President of the United States, in reference to the Reconstruction of the Union.

Adopted February 6, 1866.

1. Resolved by the General Assembly of Virginia, That the people of this Commonwealth, and their respresentatives here assembled, cordially approve the policy pursued by Andrew Johnson, president of the United States, in the reorganization of the Union. We accept the result of the late contest, and do not desire to renew what has been so conclusively determined; nor do we mean to permit any one, subject to our control to attempt its renewal, or to violate any of our obligations to the United States government. We mean to co-operate in the wise, firm and just policy adopted by the president, with all the energy and power we can devote to that object.

2. That the above declaration expresses the sentiments and purposes of all our people; and we denounce the efforts of those who represent our views and intentions to be different, as cruel and criminal assaults on our character and our interests. It is one of the misfortunes of our present political condition, that we have among us persons whose interests are temporarily promoted by such false representations; but we rely on the intelligence and integrity of those who wield the powers of the United States government, for our safeguard against such malign influences.

3. That involuntary servitude, except for crime, is abolished and ought not to be re-established; and that the negro race among us should be treated with justice, humanity and good faith; and every means that the wisdom of the legislature can devise,

should be used to make them useful and intelligent members of society.

4. That Virginia will not voluntarily consent to change the adjustment of political power as fixed by the constitution of the United States; and to constrain her to do so in her present prostrate and helpless condition, with no voice in the councils of the nation, would be an unjustifiable breach of faith; and that her earnest thanks are due to the president for the firm stand he has taken against amendments of the constitution, forced through in the present condition of affairs.

5. That a committee of eight be appointed, five on the part of this house and three on the part of the senate, whose duty it shall be to proceed to Washington city, and present the foregong resolutions to the President of the United States.

No. 7 — Joint Resolution of the Restoration of the State, and the Adjustment of the Public Debt.

Adopted February 28, 1866.

1. Resolved by the General Assembly of Virginia, That the people of Virginia deeply lament the dismemberment of the "Old State," and are sincerely desirous to establish and perpetuate the reunion of the states of Virginia and West Virginia; and that they do confidently appeal to their brethren of West Virginia to concur with them in the adoption of suitable measures of co-operation in the restoration of the ancient commonwealth of Virginia, with all her people, and up to her former boundaries.

2. That three commissioners, resident citizens of this state, shall be appointed by the joint vote of the two houses of the general assembly to proceed forthwith to the seat of government of West Virginia, for the purpose of communicating to the governor and general assembly of that state a copy of the foregoing resolution, and the report of the committee accompanying the same, with authority to treat on the subject to the restoration of the state of Virginia to its ancient jurisdiction and boundaries: provided, that the result of such negotiation, if favorable to such restoration on any terms, shall be subject on the approval or disapproval of the legislatures or conventions of the respective states, as may be hereafter mutually agreed upon.

3. The commissioners appointed under the foregong resolution, are also empowered and directed to treat with the authorities of West Virginia, upon the subjects of a proper adjustment of the public debt of the state of Virginia, due or incurred previous to the dismemberment of the state, and of a fair division of the public property; subject, however, to the approval or disapproval of this general assembly.

4. The said commissioners are hereby authorized to treat upon either or both the subjects mentioned in the two preceding resolutions, as circumstances may demand, with instructions to suspend or forbear any action on the subject to adjusting the debt of the state, or a division of the public property, if in their opinion the

probable restoration of the state of Virginia to its ancient boundaries may render an effort at such adjustment unnecessary. The action of said commissioners to be subject to the approval or disapproval of this General Assembly.

Chapter XVI — Appendix
Orders Terminating Governor Pierpont's Administration and Appointing Henry H. Wells Governor of Virginia

Headquarters, First Military District
State of Virginia
Richmond, Va., April 4th, 1868

General Orders
No. 36

The office of Governor of Virginia having become vacant by expiration of the term of service by His Excellency Francis H. Pierpont, and the Governor being ineligible to the same office for the term next succeeding that for which he was elected, His Excellency Henry H. Wells has this day been appointed Governor of Virginia, and will be obeyed and respected accordingly.

By command of Brevet Major General Scholfield.
Official:

S. F. Chalfan
Assisted Adjutant General

Hearne note: And so it was that a governor — not "provisional governor" — was removed and replaced by another "governor." In the words of Senator Oliver of Pennsylvania, spoken at the ceremony of unveiling Pierpont's statue at Statuary Hall in 1910:

. . . He would do neither wrong himself nor tolerate it in those around him. In his later years it was his proud boast that in his three year's administration at Richmond he restored stable government in Virginia without a whisper of scandal or even a suspicion of that corruption which unfortunately stained the annals of so many Southern States during that trying period.

Chapter XVII — Appendix
Reports of Cases in Supreme Court of Appeals of Virginia, Richmond

Commonwealth v. Chalkley
20 Grattan 404; 13 March 1871

N. was elected storekeeper of the penitentiary prior to 1861, for a term commencing on the 1st of January, 1861, and to continue for two years. In the last of the year 1861, and the first of the year 1862 N., as such storekeeper, purchased of C. leather and findings to be manufactured by the convicts in the penitentiary — both N. and C. recognizing the authority of the Richmond government. C., as having been able to obtain payment of his debt from the Richmond authorities, he, in December, 1866, instituted proceedings to recover the amount due him from the present government of Virginia. HELD: He has no claim, either in law or equity, upon the present government for its payment.

This was an appeal by O. H. Chalkley from the refusal of the auditor of public accounts to pay a claim presented by Chalkley against the State for leather and findings, furnished by him to the penitentiary, from November 4th, 1861, to February 25th, 1862, amounting to $6,750.08. There was no doubt that the articles were furnished to the penitentiary by Chalkley. At the time, Robert M. Nimmo was the storekeeper of the penitentiary, under an election of the General Assembly, his term having commenced on the 1st of January, 1861, and continuing for two years; but he did not take the oath prescribed by the Wheeling government. It was his duty to purchase the articles used in manufacture at the institution, upon the order of the board of directors; and though the record does not show that he purchased these goods, or that the directors either ordered the purchases, or approved them afterwards, yet there was no reason to doubt either fact.

Nimmo having got into pecuniary difficulties, the amount due upon the account, though applied for by Chalkley during the war; was not paid, and in the session of 1864-65, he petitioned the

General Assembly for its payment, and a bill was reported to the House of Delegates for the purpose, but, owing to the press of more important matters, was not acted on.

The auditor, in his answer to the petition, relies upon the provision of the constitution, article 4, §27, which declares that the General Assembly "shall not provide for the payment of any debt or obligation created in the name of the State of Virginia, by the usurped and pretended authorities at Richmond:" And he insisted that Nimmo, not having taken the oath prescribed by the Wheeling government, his office of storekeeper or the penitentiary was vacated, and he had therefore, no authority to purchase the articles.

Upon the hearing, the parties dispensed with a jury, and submitted the case to the court; and the court ordered a judgment for the sum of $5,496.65, the value in gold of Confederate money at the time of the sales. The Attorney General thereupon excepted to the opinion of the court; and applied to a judge of this court for a *supersedeas,* which was awarded.

The Attorney General, for the Commonwealth
J. Alfred Jones, for the appellee.

JOYNES, J. To entitle the defendant in error to recover in this case, it was incumbent on him to establish that his claim rests upon a "legal ground;" in other words, that it could be sustained upon principles of law or equalty. Code, ch. 45, §12, ch. 46, §§1-3. The question before us is, therefore, a legal one purely; beyond that view of the case we cannot go. We have nothing to do with any consideration of justice, policy or good faith, which might appeal to the Legislature, if any such consideration exists, except so far as they may bear on the legal question.

The claim in this case is for the price of leather and findings furnished to the penitentiary from November 1861, to February, 1862, for the purpose of carrying on its manufactories. It is not disputed that they were proper and necessary supplies. During that period the State of Virginia was one of the States associated under the name of the Confederate States. The government of Virginia, at Richmond, had the possession and control of the penitentiary, supplied it with materials, sold and appropriated the proceeds of the goods manufactured there. Robert M. Nimmo was then acting as the general agent and storekeeper of the penitentiary, having been elected before the secession of the State, for a term of two years from January 1, 1861; and having continued to hold the office and perform its duties after secession as before. It is the duty of the general agent, "on the requisition of the board of directors, to purchase all materials and other things required for work done in the penitentiary. Code, ch. 213, §55. It does not appear in this case, by an express proof, that there was any requisition of the board for the purchase of the articles which are the subject of this claim, nor that there was any general requisition that would cover such purchases, not that the purchase of them was subsequently ratified by the board. It does not even appear, by an express proof, that they were

111

purchased by the general agent. The answer of the auditor, however, does not deny that they were purchased by Nimmo, acting as general agent, and at the requisition of the board. And I think it may be fairly inferred, from all the evidence, that the purchases were made by Nimmo, as general agent, and that they were made on a requisition of the board given beforehand, or were ratified afterwards; which would have the same effect as a previous requisition.

The question is, whether the purchases, so made, impose a legal claim upon the Commonwealth, which can be sustained by the court.

It must be conceded, that Chalkley, when he sold these goods, looked to the Richmond State government, and to that alone, for payment. He must be presumed to have known of the existence of that government; that it was exercising supreme and exclusive control in this part of the State; that it had exclusive management and control of the penitentiary, furnished its supplies and appropriated its work; and that Nimmo, however and whenever he was appointed general agent, was then acting as such under the authority, direction and control of that government; in short, that he was acting as an officer of that government. It may fairly be inferred, that Chalkley recognized that government was as a lawful government, because it appears that he was, what the witness calls, "a good Southern man." He, no doubt, believed that that government would survive the efforts to overthrow it. Why, then, should he not be willing to sell goods to it upon its credit alone? That he sold the goods on the credit of that government alone, further appears from the fact that he was willing to accept Confederate money in payment in 1865, when it had depreciated to not more than one-twentieth, or perhaps one-fortieth, of its value, at the time he was entitled to receive it, under the contract. That he reposed confidence in the credit of that government, or in its ability to bind the State by its contract, is shown by the fact that he continued to sell to it as before, notwithstanding the non-payment of the present claim, and from the other fact that he sold to the penitentiary cheaper than to other manufactories, because he "considered the State (meaning, of course, as it might be bound by the Richmond government) safer than individual credit."

We must now enquire what that government was, and what was its legal relation to the people of the State — to the State itself.

I shall not go into a discussion of the right of a State to secede from the Union in 1860 and 1861, or of the effects resulting from its exercise, or attempted exercise. It was understood in the States which seceded, to be nothing more than a withdrawal from all connection with the other States, under the constitution; not the creation of a new State; the original State retaining its integrity and identity. In Virginia, the officers of government continued; there were so new elections in consequence of secession. In June, 1861, the "restored government," as it was called, was established at Wheeling, and claimed jurisdiction, as did the Richmond government, over the whole territory of the State. After the establishment of the restored governments became unable to render its jurisdiction practical and effectual as to a large part of the territory of the State. The actual jurisdiction became practically divided between them — the Richmond government exercising exclusive jurisdiction over about two-thirds of the State, and the restored government excercising jurisdiction over the other third.

I need not follow up the history of these conflicting governments, or discuss their respective claims, upon principles of public and constitutional law, to be considered the true and lawful government of the State. It has been held by the Supreme Court, that when there are two governments in a State, each claiming to be the lawful government, the question which of them is really the lawful one, is not a judicial question, but a political one, to be determined by the political authorities of the United States. *Luther v. Borden,* 7 How U. S. R. 1.

Now, whatever opinion we, or any other citizen, may entertain upon the respective claims of these two governments, upon principles of law, of reason or justice, all must agree that the opinion of the authorities of the United States has been unmistakably expressed. The conqueror, as might have been expected, has resolved the question in favor of his ally in the conflict, and against his enemy. This question was fully discussed by Chief Justice Chase in *Caesar Griffin's case,* 8 Am. Law Register, N. S., 358; and he accordingly held that the restored government was the lawful government of Virginia.

The present constitution of the State recognizes the restored government as having been the lawful government, and denounces the authorities which carried on a government at Richmond during the war as "usurped and pretended authorities." This constitution was adopted by the people at the polls. Whether the people adopted it willingly and because they approved it, or only adopted it as the best alternative within their reach, is a matter of no consequence — the constitution is equally obligatory in either case. Sitting here under the authority of that constitution, and exercising only the jurisdiction it confers upon us, directly or indirectly, we are not at liberty to disregard its provisions, or the principles on which it evidently rests. Whatever we might have thought about it, as an original question, it was our province to decide it as such, we are not at liberty now, in the circumstances in which we are placed, to hold judicially, in opposition to the constitution, that to have been the lawful government which the constitution has declared to have been unlawful. The most that would be conceded by the Federal authorities, and the most that can be maintained upon the principles of the present constitution, the Richmond government was a *de facto* government. That is all that the Supreme Court has conceded to the governments of seceded States, which had complete and exclusive control of the whole territory, with no other government asserting a conflicting claim. *Texas v. White,* 7 Wall. U. S. R. 700; *Thorington v. Smith,* 8 Ib. 1.

The constitution of the State provides that "no appropriating shall ever be made for the payments of any debt or obligation created in the name of the State of Virginia, by the usurped and pretened authorities assembled at Richmond during the late war."

This provision makes no reference to the character or consideration of the debt, further than to describe it as a debt "created in the name of the State of Virgina, by the authorities at Richmond." The evident meaning is, that every such debt or obligation is void on *principle,* independent of this provision, and that the Legislature shall never treat any such debt or obligation as valid, by providing for its payment. And the convention seems to have treated such debts and obligations as invalid, because they considered the Richmond government as having no lawful authority to bind the State by any contract. This provision of the constitution, though in terms a restraint upon the Legislature only, is virtually a restraint upon the courts likewise.

It was contended at the bar, that notwithstanding the general and comprehensive terms of this provision it could not have been designed to prohibit the payment of such a debt as that claimed in this case. The support of the penitentiary, it was said, was imposed upon the State by laws passed long before secession and never repealed; and the restraint and punishment of offenders were necessary to the protection of society. And reference was made at the bar, and in the opinion of the Circuit Court, to a report made by the majority of the committee for courts of justice, in the house of delegates of 1865-'6, in reference to the right of the Legislature, under the constitutional provision above quoted; to provide for the payment of claims for bread and other necessary supplies for the inmates of the penitentiary during the war, and for which the claimants alleged that, after the exercise of due diligence, they had been unable to obtain payment from the Richmond authorities. I do not purpose to express any opinion under the soundness of the view presented in that report, or in the counter report of the minority; for the question then before the Legislature was not the same as that now before this court. The Legislature, if not restrained by the constitution, might choose to recognize an obligation founded on considerations of justice, policy, or good faith, when it might not think there was any obligation in point of law. This court, before it can sustain a claim rejected by the creditor, must find a ground of legal obligation. The majority of the committee held that the claims under its consideration, being founded on long-established laws, never repealed by the restored government, and essential to the preservation of civil society; being what they called *debts of the people;* not debts of the government; not arising originally out of the action of the "usurped" authorities, and not burdens thrown upon the people of the State in consequence of secession, over and above what they have borne had there been no secession; but being such only as they must have borne under any circumstances, could not properly be regarded as debts or obligations "created by the usurped authorities." Upon that ground, among others, the majority of the committee expressed the opinion that the payment of these claims was not inhibited. But these views, if we should hold them to be sound, will not help us, unless we can hold that there is some ground of legal obligation upon the state.

Chalkley cannot sustain his claim upon the ground of his contract with the Richmond authorities, *proprto vigore,* for we must hold that they had no right to make a contract that could, as such, impose a legal obligation on the State. It is insisted, however, 1st, that there was no contract with the Richmond authorities, as called, but that the contract was made with Nimmo, an officer appointed by the lawful government, before secession, and never removed by the restored government; and 2d, that Chalkley does not seek to recover on the basis of the express contract, if it should be held that it was made with Richmond authorities, but upon an implied obligation, arising out of the duty of the State to maintain the penitentiary. Let us consider those grounds.

1. While it is true that Nimmo was appointed by the lawful government before secession, and while the counsel is probably right in saying that he was not removed from his office by force of any ordinance or statute of the restored government, I cannot hold that he is to be regarded as acting under the authority of the restored government, or as possessing any authority from that government, while he was daily acting in the service of the Richmond government, and recognizing its authority. The Richmond government was hostile to the restored government. The two positions were, therefore, incompatible. When Nimmo recognized the authority of the Richmond government and continued in its service, he must be regarded as repudiating and turning his back on the restored government. When he thus repudiated and turned his back on upon the restored government, he abdicated his office under the government, if he was ever entitled to hold it under that government, and virtually resigned it. The suggestion that an officer of the Richmond government was, at the same time, an officer of the restored government, would have shocked the common understanding of that day; and any officer who would have aserted such a pretension would, without doubt, have been thrust from his office, with the least possible ceremony.

2. Chalkley must avail himself of the alleged obligation of the restored government to provide for the penitentiary, if at all, either on the principles applicable to the action of assumpsit upon what the laws call an implied contract, or on the equitable doctrine of the substitution. The case was put by the Circuit Court on both grounds. And first as to the principles of assumpsit.

I have already said that Chalkley made an express contract with the Richmond government, upon whose credit alone he relied, at that time, for the payment of his debt. The precise question to be now considered is, whether the law imply another contract on the part of the restored government, or on the State presented by it for the payment of this debt.

If this debt to Chalkley can be considered as a debt "created" by the Richmond government, within the meaning of the constitution, it might be contended, with great force, that the provision of the constitution referred to imposes a restraint upon the courts as well as upon the Legislature, and that it would be an evasion of the constitution thus indirectly to give substantial effect to an invalid and reprobated contract. But I do not propose to consider these questions.

A conclusive reason why the law will not imply an assumpsit to pay Chalkley's debt, by the State, or by the restored government, is, that the sales upon which his claim is based were made at the Richmond government. The principles appliable to this case, putting it in the strongest light for Chalkley, may be illustrated by reference to the case of husband and wife. When a wife is living with her husband, he is bound to provide her with necessaries, and a person who provides them for her may sue him for the price. So, if a husband turns his wife out of his house, and refuses to provide for her, a person who supplies her with necessaries may sue the husband for the price, upon an assumpsit implied from his obligation to provide for her. But if, in either case, the goods are not furnished upon the credit of the husband, but upon the credit of another person, the husband cannot be held liable. This is so when the goods are sold upon the credit of the wife only, and although she is living with her husband, and so he is undoubtedly bound to provide for her. The person who supplies the articles, may, if he chooses, rely upon the credit of the husband the duty which the law casts upon him to provide for his wife, or, if he chooses, he may rely upon the agreement and the crdit of some other person, whom he prefers to trust, even though that person be a married woman. When he has fairly, and with a knowledge of the facts, chosen his debtor, the law will not allow him to change his contract. He cannot "repudiate his choice and choose again." *Metcalf v. Shaw,* 3 Camp. R. 22; *Bently v. Griffin,* 5 Taunt. R. 356, (1 Eng. C. L. R. 131); *Stammers v. Macomb,* 2 Wend. R. 454. So if, at the time of a sale, the seller knows that the person with whom he is dealing is an agent, and that he is acting within the scope of his authority so as to bind his principle, and notwithstanding this knowledge, he chooses to make the agent his debtor, and looks to him along for payment, he cannot, after the failure of the agent, turn round and charge the principal; having made his election when he had the power to choose between the one and the other: *Addison v. Grandapequin,* 4 Taunt. R. 574; *Paterson v. Grandapequin,* 15 East. R. 62; *Paige v. Stone,* 10 Mete. R. 160.

Now, as much as could be claimed in behalf of Chalkley, would be, that the obligation of the State, represented by the restored government, to provide for the support of the penitentiary, should be placed upon as high ground as the obligation of a husband to support his wife; and that a person furnishing supplies for the penittentiary should have the same rights as a person furnishing supplies for a wife. If that were conceded, it would not help Chalkley, because he did not furnish the articles sold by him upon the credit of the State, or of her lawful representative, the restored government; but upon the credit of certain parties in Richmond, who did not lawfully represent the State, and could not pledge her credit.

If Chalkley had found the penitentiary abandoned or neglected, and the necessary wants of the prisoners unprovided for; and had, in that state of things, supplied them with food, clothing and other necessaries, relying upon the restored government alone to reimburse him, he would have had a claim of the strongest character upon the justice and the gratitude of the present government. Perhaps his claims might have been sustained by the court in that case; but as to that I give no opinion. But that is not the case. Chalkley supplied neither food, clothing fuel, or any other article of necessity for the prisoners. He supplied leather and findings to the Richmond government, upon its credit, to be used in carrying on its workshops in the penitentiary. It does not appear from anything in this cause, that the proceeds of the goods manufactured from these materials, or any part of such proceeds, went to the use of the penitentiary in any way, much less to the use of the prisoners, by supplying them with necessaries. They may have been part of the funds which were soon after sunk in the hands of Nimmo.

It was argued, however, that the business of manufacturing in the penitentiary is part of the discipline of the prison, employed to promote the good behavior, the contentment, and the health of the prisoners. Does it follow that Chalkley, who supplied materials for carrying on one of the workshops, ought to be regarded as furnishing necessaries for the prisoners, in like manner as one who furnished bread? I think not. It may be true, and doubtless it is, that it is of great advantage to the prisoners, and to the discipline of the prison, that they should be kept at work; but those advantages are incidental. The primary purpose in carrying on the workshops is to make money. The great object is to make the penitentiary support itself, and, if possible, yield a surplus to go into the general treasury. In some of the States these institutions yield large profits, over and above expenses. The Richmond government was in deadly hostility to the restored government, in the pending war, and had, with its adherents and allies, excluded the restored government from the greater part of the territory over which it claimed jurisdiction, and from the control of the public institutions within those limits. All this, we are bound to presume, was well known to Chalkley. It would seem to be too clear for argument, that, under such circumstances, the State, or the restored government, was under no obligation to pay for supplies furnished by Chalkley to the Richmond government to be worked up into goods for its benefits; to enable that government to carry on a profitable business, and thereby to augment its resources and lessen the burden of taxation. When there is no obligation, no duty, the law will not imply an assumpsit.

As to the claim to rest this case upon the ground of substitution, I need say but little. The claim is, that Chalkley is entitled to be substituted to the rights of the prisoners, to be provided for by the State, as represented by the restored government. Certainly the Richmond authorities had no claim against the State to which he could claim to be substituted; and no such claim has been asserted. Whatever right of substitution to the prisoners a man might have who supplied their necessary wants, the claim could not be extended to articles not, in themselves, necessaries for the prisoners, without proof that they or their proceeds were actually applied to the procurement on such necessaries. As I have said heretofore, there is no proof that the articles furnished by Chalkley, or any part of them, or their proceeds, went to the procurement of necessaries

117

for the prisoners, or even that the proceeds of them went to the use of the penitentiary at all. Besides, as I have already shown, the articles furnished by Chalkley were only materials to be worked up into goods, to be sold for the benefit of the Richmond government. Under the "circumstances then existing," there was no obligation, legal or equitable, upon the restored government to pay for things furnished to the Richmond government to enable it to make money. It would be inequitable, in the last degree, to impose such an obligation. And a court of equity will not lend its aid to enforce payment, but its extraordinary remedies, of claims that are not sustained by justice and good conscience.

Moreover, it was incumbent on Chalkley, before he could claim relief upon the principles of equity, to show that he had used due diligence in his efforts to collect his debt from the Richmond government. And in considering the measure of diligence which he ought to have used, it must be borne in mind that the Richmond government was a revolutionary government, not recognized as lawful, and whose very existence was involved in the war then pending. He seems to have been diligent in importuning the officers of the penitentiary for payment up to the end of 1862. He does not appear to have done anything in 1863 or 1864. The next thing he seems to have done was on the 27th day of January, 1865, when he obtained a certified copy of his account from the books of the penitentiary, and a certificate from the superintendent of his refusal to pay the claim, and of the grounds of his refusal. These were obtained, no doubt, with a view of the application to the Legislature, spoken of by Judge Sheffey. Why was no legal proceeding taken in all this time? Why was no application made to the Legislature at the session of 1862-'3, or at that of 1863-'4? Why was it postponed until 1865, when, as the Legislature no doubt well knew, the Confederate cause had come to extremities well nigh desperate — utterly desperate, as the event soon proved — and when the minds of members were so engrossed by the perils of the situation that no wonder they could give but little attention to claims? My opinion is, that Chalkley has not shown that he used due diligence to collect his claim from the Richmond government.

Upon the whole, I am of opinion that the claim of Chalkley cannot be sustained upon any ground of law or equity. The decree must, therefore, be reversed and the petition dismissed.

ANDERSON, J. I very reluctantly, and with considerable doubt, concur in the judgment, upon the ground of the inhibition of the constitution. But am not prepared to concur in all the positions and the reasoning of the opinion of J. *Joynes*.

The other judges concurred in the opinion of *Joynes*.
JUDGMENT REVERSED.

Virginia Cases Continued

De Rothschilds v. The Auditor
22 Grattan 41; 27 March, 1872

Between May and November 1860, D. deposited tobacco, for inspection and storage, in the public warehouse at Richmond, and paid the inspection fees. The tobacco remained in the warehouse until March 1863, when the warehouse was accidentally consumed by fire, and the tobacco was burned. The present State government is not responsible to D. for the loss.

This was a bill filed in the Circuit Court of the city of Richmond, by De Rothschild Brothers against the Auditor of Public Accounts, to recover the value of two hundred and fifty hogsheads of tobacco, which had been destroyed by fire on the 10th of March 1863, in the public warehouse in the city of Richmond. The Auditor filed his answer, and the parties agreed to the facts; and dispensing with a jury, submitted the case to the court.

From the facts agreed, it appears that the "public warehouse" in the city of Richmond belonged to the State of Virginia, from the time of its erection until after its practical destruction by fire in March 1863. That between the 13th of May 1860, and the 2nd of November in the same year, the plaintiffs deposited in said warehouse, for inspection and storage, three hundred and seventy-eight hogsheads of leaf tobacco; that said tobacco was received by the regularly appointed and and qualified inspectors of said warehouse, and was actually inspected thereat; the inspectors giving, in the usual form, a tobacco note for each hogshead at the time at which it was received; and that the plaintiffs have never sold the tobacco, and still hold the tobacco notes. That said tobacco remained in said warehouse until the night of the 10th of March 1863, when the warehouse was partially destroyed by fire, and two hundred and fifty hogsheads of said tobacco were consumed; and that each of said hogsheads of tobacco so destroyed was then worth $105.88 in gold coin, making an aggregate of $26,470.

It appears, further, that the inspectors who received and inspected the tobacco continued in office during the year 1860; that inspectors were regularly appointed and qualified for the year 1861; but that no inspectors were appointed for 1862 or 1863 by the restored government of Virginia; but that the inspectors of 1861 were reappointed for these years by the government of Richmond, and qualified and acted as inspectors at said warehouse, for the years 1862 and 1863, under the Richmond government. It appears, further, that the fees for inspection were paid to the inspectors at the date of the inspection; that no other charges than for inspection had been paid on said tobacco, and that nothing has been received on account of the same by the restored government of Virginia; that tobacco in a warehouse, by universal custom in Richmond, is held bound for all charges due the State, which are to be paid when the tobacco is removed; and that all unpaid charges due the State on said two hundred and fifty hogsheads of tobacco amount to $462.50, as of 10th of March, 1868.

It appears, further, that the said warehouse consisted of large connected sheds, one story in height, except that over a portion thereof a second and third story had been built, which were not and

119

could not be used for the inspector or storage of tobacco. That these rooms were at the time of the fire occupied by an officer of the Confederate States army, with the sanction of the Richmond government; and the fire originated in the rooms in the second story, by accident or carelessness, and not by design; and at the time of the fire the inspectors of the warehouse remained in the exclusive charge and control of the first story. That from the 17th of April 1861, to the 3rd day of April 1865, the city of Richmond, and the public property of the State therein, was under the control of the Richmond State government; and that the authority of the government of Virginia at Wheeling, and afterwards located at Alexandria, was not recognized or enforced in said city of Richmond. And that the Richmond government was, between the periods aforesaid, aiding, and assisting in the war against the Government of the United States.

The cause came on to be heard on the 17th of November 1870, when the court dismissed the bill with costs. And thereupon the plaintiffs applied to this court for an appeal, which was allowed.

Old & Carrington, for the appellants.
The Attorney-General, for the Commonwealth.

STAPLES, J. This case brings before the court the question of the liability of the State for plaintiffs' tobacco, stored in a public warehouse in the city of Richmond, and destroyed by fire on the 10th March 1863. It is a question of novelty, and considerable difficulty. As there is no adjudged case, no precedent, to guide the court in its decision, we must act according to our best convictions of the principles of law controlling the rights and obligations of the parties.

This court held, in *Chalkley's case,* 20 Gratt. 404, that the present government is not legally responsible for any debt contracted, or liability incurred, by the authorities having control of the State after the ordinance of secession was adopted. This decision has been the subject of some complaint and criticism. It is easy, however, to demonstrate that this is not the Richmond government, nor the successor to that government, and consequently that it is not answerable for the debts contracted by that government. It is well known that on the 19th June 1861, a convention assembled at Wheeling, adopted an ordinance reorganizing the State government, providing for the election of officers, prescribing an oath of fidelity to the Constitution of the United States and of the States, and declaring vacant all offices upon the failure of the incumbents to take the oath so prescribed.

The government thus restored, as it was termed, continued until the adoption of the Alexandria constitution on the 12th February 1864. Under this constitution a legislature assembled on the 19th June 1865, in the city of Richmond. It passed an act for the election of the members of the General Assembly, and for taking the sense of the people in relation to the disqualifications for office imposed by that constitution; and it required that all persons voting in such election should take an oath to uphold and defend the government restored by the convention at Wheeling. Under the authority of this act, the legislature of 1865-1866, and 1866-1867, assembled in the city of Richmond. The various acts passed by that body constitue important and valuable laws for the adjustment of many perplexing questions growing out of the war.

The government thus organized at Alexandria contintued in existence until superseded by the reconstruction laws under which the present constitution was framed, and adopted by the people. How is it possible, in the light of these facts, to maintain that the present government is identical with, or is the successor to the Richmond government? Besides all this, the constitution expressly prohibits the payment of any debt or obligation created in the name of the State of Virginia, "by the usurped and pretended State authorities assembled at Richmond during the late war." It is not our province to discuss the propriety of this provision, or the language in which it is expressed. We are sworn to expound the constitution and laws as they are written, and not as we would have them. The Richmond government may have been the true and lawful government of Virginia, as maintained by some. No doubt it represented the views and wishes of a large majority of the people; but neither its contracts nor its liabilities can impose any legal obligation upon the State which the courts can recognize, under the present constitution and laws.

In *Chalkley's case,* the contract was made with the Richmond authorities, and the credit given to them or their agents exclusively; and this court held that the present government could not be held accountable for the debt thus contracted. In the present case, it is true, the original contract, if such it be, was made in 1860 with the regular State government; but we are to consider the true import and operation of that contract, and how far it was modified or affected by subsequent events. This renders necessary a brief consideration of the statutes in regard to the inspection and storage of tobacco. They are too numerous and complex to justify a citation in this opinion. It is clear, however, that they contemplate in the first instance an inspection and storage for a year; in which case the owner is not responsible for the payment of a rent. He may at the expiration of that period, or sooner, remove his property upon the payment merely of the officers' fees for inspection, and the State charges. These charges and fees amount to sixty cents for each hogshead of tobacco inspected, stored, or delivered, and a special charge of thirty cents upon the hogshead, supposed to be intended for the risk of insurance. They are to be paid, as is conceded, whether the deposit be for inspection merely, or inspection and storage, embracing one day or one year. But this compensation did not embrace a longer time than the year. At the expiration of that period, the State might have repeated its statutes, or discontinued the arrangement, without any just cause of complaint. At the date of the inspection, or storage, it was bound to know the owner might continue the same for the year; but it was not required to know that he would exceed that period. If the year being ended, he elected to continue the storage, he might so do for three years, inclusive of that first year. In that event, however, a new contract arose — a new charge was made of five cents on the hogshead per month, in the nature of a rent for the use of the warehouse upon such extended storage. In this case the storage was commenced between the 10th May and the 2nd November 1860. Upon the expiration of the year, they elected to continue the use and occupation of the warehouse. At that time the government with which the original contract was made had been overthrown, and another established in its place, officers owing allegiance to, and deriving their authority from, the new government, had the management and control of the warehouse in which the tobacco was stored. The Confederate authorities had also established their capital in this city; their officers and employees were in the occupancy of every available building, public and private, and their armies quartered within and without the city limits, in every direction. Under these circumstances the owners of this tobacco thought proper to continue its storage indefinitely in a warehouse not in the possession of the government with which they had contracted, nor under the direction of officers appointed by, and responsible to, that government. They made this election *flagrante bello,* and they persisted in it from month to month, and year to year, although the city was in continued danger of bombardment and conflagration. The plaintiffs must have had some information of the extraordinary events occurring here; they must have been apprised that war existed; that old governments were being overthrown, and new ones struggling into existence. If they were ignorant of these matters, it was their fault or their misfortune. By the exercise of a very moderate share of diligence, they might easily have informed themselves of occurrences which so much concerned them. The French consul resided in this city throughout the war. He should have kept them advised, and no doubt did, of the condition of affairs in this State. It is true, that the blockade would probably have prevented the removal of the tobacco from the country but there was nothing to interfere with its storage in some other and more secure place, under the supervision of the plaintiffs' own agents. It is to be presumed that they preferred to continue the storage of the tobacco as it was, and to take the chances of its preservation. They must be held to have done so with full knowledge of the consequences; and they should be willing to bear the loss resulting from their advanture.

The learned counsel for the plaintiffs, in their petition for an appeal here, say that the State of Virginia insured against its own acts of omission and commission. It insured against any loss by fire in consequence of its abandonment, even if such a case were made out. All this might be true if the State had made a contract of insurance for any specific period beyond the first year of the storage, founded upon a valid consideration paid or stipulated to be paid for such risk. But I have already shown, or attempted to show, there was not such contract. The plaintiff's tobacco at the time of its descrution had been on deposit nearly three years. For all this they had only paid certain inspectors' fees at the date of the inspection. When they elected to continue the storage beyond the year, they well knew the government had been re-established at Wheeling. This fact was made known through its laws and its proclamations, through the recognition of the Federal Government, with which plaintiff's government was in friendly and constant communication.

But the position of the counsel is not sound in other respects. The insurance of the State, if such it be, only extended to losses by fire. It did not comprehend the damage or loss of the tobacco occasioned by floods, tempests, or captured by hostile armies or superior powers. With the single exception of the promise of indemnity in case of fire, the position of the State was that of any other bailee for hire. Such bailee is only liable for the use of ordinary case and common prudence in the preservation of the property intrusted to him; but he is not an insurer in any sense of that term. There is no foundations for the pretension that the State insured against is abandonment in the face of overwhelming numbers. It insured against fire, but not against capture. Even as against insurance companies, to which the most stringent rules are always applied, it is well settled, that if there be an insurance against fire, and an exception by the assured in favor of capture, and the vessel is captured, and before she is delivered from that peril she is afterwards destroyed by fire, the loss is properly attributable to the capture alone. In *Magoun v. New England Marine Ins. Com.*, 1 Story R. 157, 164, Mr. Justice Story said it would be an over refinement and metaphysical subtlety to hold otherwise. In the case of *Dale v. New England, Mutual Marine Ins. Co.*, 6 Allen R. 373, 395, Bigelow, C. J. said, "there is no stipulation in the policy that the insurers were to remain liable after the ship had passed into the hands of her captors.

The cases in which it is held that where the insured is liable for capture, if followed by condemnation or detention for a prescribed period, and a subsequent abandonment, he is also liable for any supervening peril occurring during the intermediate period, are not applicable to cases like the present, where the risk of capture is not assumed by the underwriters. See, also, *Lewis v. Springfield Fire and Marine Ins. Co.*, 10 Gray R. 159.

These views are founded on good sense and upon sound reasoning. I do not perceive why they do not equally apply to this case. If the tobacco had been captured and appropriated by the Confederate government, or captured and destroyed by Federal soldiers, it will scarcely be maintained that the State is responsible for a loss occurring under such circumstances. As a general rule, it is true, where the property is destroyed by fire, the insurer is liable, though it were absolutely certain it would have been afterwards captured but for such destruction. But where the capture is made, and the damage from fire is the consequence of the capture, to impose the loss upon the bailee is to make him an insurer against both capture and fire. In this case the injustice is the more palpable because the owners, after the warehouse was taken by the Confederate government and appropriated by the Confederate authorities, might have taken possession of their property without the least difficulty.

The condition of the country at the time of the destruction of this tobacco, and indeed long before, is within the recollection of all. In the language of Mr. Justice Nelson, *Mauran v. Insurance Company,* 6 Wall. U.S. R. 14, a government in fact was erected greater in territory than many of the old governments of Europe, complete in the organization of all its parts, containing within its lines more than eleven millions of people, and of sufficient resources in men and money to carry on a civil war of unexampled demensions; their vessels captured recognized as prized of war, and dealt with accordingly; their property seized on land referred to the judicial tribunals for adjudication; their ports blockaded, and the blockade maintained by a suitable force, and duly notified to neutral powers, the same as in open and public war.

No one can for a moment entertain the opinion that either the plaintiffs or the State ever contemplated this state of things. The compensation agreed to be paid had no reference to such a risk. The State could hardly have been expected, for a charge of five cents per month on each hogshead of tobacco, to assume all the hazards of war, invasion, and conquest. It did not undertake, it was not asked to insure against any peril except that of fire. But as the fire occurred long after the warehouse had been wrested from the possession of the insurer by overwhelming numbers, the loss must be regarded as attributable to the capture, and not by any reasonable intendment within the terms of the contract. For these reasons I am of the opinion the judgment of the Circuit Court should be affirmed.

The other judges concurred in the opinion of *Staples, J.* DECREE AFFIRMED.

Chapter XVIII — Appendix Virginia v. West Virginia, 78 U.S. 39, Dec. Term, 1870 (Abstract), Relating to Berkeley and Jefferson Counties

ABSTRACT OF U.S. SUPREME COURT CASE VIRGINIA V. WEST VIRGINIA

78 U.S. (11 All.) 39; 20 L.Ed., 67 — Dec. term, 1870

Syllabus by the Court

1. This court has original jurisdiction, under the Constitution, of controversies between States of the Union concerning their boundaries.

2. The jurisdiction is not defeated because in deciding the question of boundary it is necessary to consider and construe contracts and agreements between the States, nor because the judgment or decree of the court may affect the territorial limits of the jurisdiction of the States that are parties to the suit.

3. The ordinance of the organic convention of the Commonwealth of Virginia, under which the State of West Virginia was organized, and the act of May 13th, 1862, of the said Commonwealth, constitute a proposition of the former State that the counties of Jefferson and Berkeley and others might, on certain conditions, become part of the new State; and the provisions of the constitution of the new State concerning those counties are an acceptance of that proposition.

4. The act of Congress admitting the State of West Virginia into the Union at the request of the Commonwealth of Virginia, with the provisions for the transfer of those counties in the constitution of the new State, and in the acts of the Virginia legislature, is an im-

plied consent to the agreement of those States on that subject.

5. The consent required by the Constitution to make valid agreements between the States need not necessarily be by an express assent to every proposition of the agreement. In the present case the assent is an irresistible inference from the legislation of Congress on the subject.

6. The condition of the agreement on which the transfer of these two counties was to be made was, that a majority of the votes cast on that question in the counties should be found in favor of the proposition.

7. The statutes of the Virginia legislature having authorized the governor of that State to certify the result of the voting on that proposition to the State of West Virginia, if, in his opinion, the vote was favorable, and he having certified the fact that it was so, under the seal of the State to the governor of West Virginia, and the latter State having accepted and exercised jurisdiction over those counties for several years, the State of Virginia is bound by her acts in the premises.

8. The State of Virginia cannot under such circumstances be permitted to set aside the whole transaction in a court of equity, on the ground that no fair vote was taken, that her own governor was deceived and misled by the election officers, with no charge of fraud or improper conduct on the part of West Virginia, nor can she withdraw her consent two years after the vote was taken and the transfer of the counties accomplished.

By the court
Statement of purpose of suit; judicial
Notice of de jure status of new state.

An original bill to settle the boundary line between the States of Virginia and West Virginia, the case was existing is well-known public history and from the record being thus:

A convention professing to represent the State of Virginia, which assembled in Richmond in February, 1861, attempted by a so-called "ordinance of secession" to separate that State from the Union, and combined with certain other Southern States to accomplish that separation by arms. The people of the northwestern part of the State, who were separated from the eastern part by a succession of mountain ranges and had never received the heresy of secession, refused to acquiesce in what had been thus done, and organized themselves to defend and maintian the Federal Union. The idea of a separate State government soon developed itself; and an organic convention of the State of Virginia, which in June 1861, organized the State on loyal principles — "the Pierpont government" — and which new organization was acknowledged by the President and Congress of the United States as the true State government of Virginia — passed August 20, 1861, an ordinance by

126

which they ordained that a new State be formed and erected out of the territory included within certain boundaries (set forth) including within those boundaries of the proposed new State the counties of, &c [thirty-nine counties being named.]

Abstract by Hearne begins.

Neither Berkeley nor Jefferson County was included by name in the foregoing list. But the ordinance also provided that other contiguous counties may be included, subject to vote of approval in such counties.

The ordinance provided for a convention to meet to form a constituion for the proposed new state, the delegates were to be elected from the counties contemplated to form such new state.

The ordinance provided that an election would be held on the first Thursday in April of 1862 in the counties proposed to form the new state, but it appeared that "no one voted in either Berkeley or Jefferson, on the matter; "owing, it was said by the defendant's counsel, to the fact that 'from the 1st of June 1861 to the 1st of March 1862, during which time these proceedings for the formation of a new state were held, those counties were the possession, and under the absolute control, of the forces of the Confederate States; and that an attempt to hold meetings in them to promote the formation of the new state have been followed by immediate arrest and imprisonment.' "

All this being done, the legislature proceeded to enact its bill passed 13 May, 1862, giving the consent of Virginia to the formation of the new state. This act is set out elsewhere in the appendix.

Under that act it appears that no elections were held, and on 31 December 1862 Congress passed the act for the admission of the State of West Virginia into the Union. (12 Stat. at page 633). It should be noted, however, that the preamble to this act recounted, *inter alia,* previous action of the convention, the vote of the people, and the assent of the legislature specified the names of the counties to be included but neither Berkeley nor Jefferson County was named.

The court then recites two more "consent acts" of the Virginia General Assembly, the first being that of 31 January, 1863, which includes, inter alia, Berkeley. The election to be held on the fourth Thursday in May of 1863.

The second "consent act" was passed on 4 February 1863, which provided for more counties to vote on the fourth Thursday of April, and this act included Jefferson County. Both of these acts provided that if the governor of Virginia was satisfied that the elections were held and that the vote was in favor of annexation to the new state, he should so certify, and the annexation would take place when the new state entered the Union. These acts further provided that if an election could not be held on the date specified, another date could be set.

Under these two acts elections "of some sort" were held, and the governor of Virginia certified to the Governor of West Virginia

127

and that state extended her jurisdiction over both counties and still maintained it.

By the court.

Next came an act of the State of Virginia, passed December 5th, 1865:

An Act to repeal the second section of an act passed on the 13th day of May, 1862, entitled An act giving the consent of the legislature of Virginia to the formation and erection of a new State within the jurisdiction of this State; also, repealing the act passed on the 31st day of January, 1863, entitled An act giving the consent of the State of Virginia to the county of Berkeley being admitted into, and becoming part of, the State of West Virginia; also, repealing the act passed on the 4th day of February, 1863, entitled An act giving consent to the admission of certain counties into the new State of West Virginia, upon certain conditions, and withdrawing consent to the transfer of jurisdiction over the several counties in each of said acts mentioned.

Whereas, It sufficiently appears that the conditions prescribed in the several acts of the General Assembly of the restored government of Virginia, intended to give consent to the transfer, from this State to the State of West Virginia, of jurisdiction over the counties of *Jefferson* and *Berkeley*, and the several other counties mentioned in the act of February 4th, 1863, hereinafter recited, have not been complied with; and the consent of Congress, as required by the Constitition of the United States, not having been obtained in order to give effect to such transfer, so that the proceedings heretofore had on this subject are simply inchoate, and said consent may properly be withdrawn; and this General Assembly, regarding the contemplated disintegration of the Commonwealth, even if within its constitutional competency, as liable to many objections of the gravest character, not only in respect to the counties of Jefferson and Berkeley, over which the State of West Virginia has prematurely attempted to exercise jurisdiction, but also as to the several other counties above referred to:

1. *Be it therefore acted by the General Assembly of Virginia,* That the second session of the act passed on the 13th day of May, 1862, entitled An act giving the consent of the legislature of Virginia to the formation and erection of a new State within the jurisdiction of this State be, and the same is hereby, repealed.

2. That the act passed on the 31st day of January, 1863, entitled An act giving the consent of the State of Virginia to the county of Berkeley being admitted into and becoming part of the State of West Virginia, be, and the same is, in like manner, hereby repealed.

3. That the act passed February 4th, 1863, entitled An act giving consent to the admission of certain counties into the new State of West Virginia upon certain conditions, be, and the same is, in

like manner, hereby repealed.

4. That all consent in any manner heretofore given, or intended to be given, by the General Assembly of Virginia to the transfer, from its jurisdiction to the jurisdiction of the State of West Virginia, of any of the counties mentioned in either of the above-recited acts, be, and the same is hereby, withdrawn; and all acts, ordinances, and resolutions heretofore passed purporting to give such consent are hereby repealed.

5. This act shall be in force from and after the passage thereof.

On the 10th of March, 1866, Congress passed a *Joint Resolution giving the consent of Congress to the transfer of the Counties of Berkeley and Jefferson to the State of West Virginia.* (14 Stat. 850).

Be it resolved, &c., That Congress hereby recognizes the transfer of the counties of Berkeley and Jefferson from the State of Virginia to West Virginia and consents thereto.

In this state of things, the Commonwealth of Virginia brought her bill in equity against the State of West Virginia in this court on the ground of its original jurisdiction of controversies between States under the Constitution, in which it was alleged that such a controversy had arisen between those States in regard to their boundary, and especially as to the question whether the counties of Berkeley and Jefferson had become part of the State of West Virginia or were part of and within the jurisdiction of the Commonwealth of Virginia; and the prayer of the bill was that it might be established by the decree of this court that those counties were part of the Commonwealth of Virginia, and that the boundary line between the two States should be ascertained, established, and made certain, so as to include the counties mentioned as part of the territory and within the jurisdiction of the State of Virginia.

The stating part of the bill was largely composed of the substance of four acts of the General Assembly of the Commonwealth, already presented at large, in the statement, copies of them being made exhibits and filed with the bill.

The bill, in addition to the substance of these statutes, alleged that no action whatever was had or taken under the second section of the act of 1862, but that afterwards the State of West Virginia was admitted into the Union, under an act of Congress and proclamation of the President, without including either the counties of Berkeley, Jefferson, or Frederick.

It further alleged that an attempt was made to take the vote in the counties of Jefferson and Berkeley at the time mentioned in the acts of January 31st, and February 4th, 1863, but that, owing to the state of the country at that time, no fair vote could be taken; that no polls were opened at any considerable number of the voting places; *that the vote taken was not a fair and full expression;* all of which was well known to the persons who procured the certificate of such election. It also alleged that it having been *falsely and fraudulently suggested, and falsely and untruly made to appear to*

129

the governor of the Commonwealth, that a large majority of the votes was given in favor of annexation, he certified the same to the State of West Virginia, and that thereupon, without the consent of Congress, that State extended her jurisdiction over the said counties of Berkeley and Jefferson, and over the inhabitants thereof, and still maintained the same.

The State of Virginia, of course, in coming before this court with this case, relied upon that clause of the Federal Constitution which ordains that "no State shall, *without the assent of Congress,* enter into any agreement or compact with any other State," and that one also which ordains that "the judicial power shall extend . . to controversies between two or more States."

To the bill thus filed the State of West Virginia appeared and put in a general demurrer. It was not denied that West Virginia had from the beginning continued her assent to receive these two counties.

The case was elaborately argued at December Term, 1866, by *Messrs. B. R. Curtis and A. Hunter, in support of the bill, and by Messrs. B. Stanton and Reverdy Johnson, in support of the demurrer; and again at this term by Mr. Taylor, Attorney-General of Virginia, Messrs. B. R. Curtis, and A. Hunter, on the former side, and Messrs. B. Stanton, C. J. Faulkner, and Reverdy Johnson, contra.*

Hearne Note: Arguments of counsel and several paragraphs of majority opinion have been omitted.

The State of Virginia, in the ordinance which originated the formation of the New State, recognized something peculiar in the condition of these two counties, and some others. It gave them the option of sending delegates to the constitutional convention, and gave that convention the option to receive them. For some reason not developed in the legislative history of the matter these counties took no action on the subject. The convention, willing to accept them, and hoping they might still expres their wish to come in, made provision in the new constitution they might do so, and for their place in the legislative bodies, and in the judicial system, and inserted a general proposition for accession of territory to the new State. The State of Virginia, in expressing her satisfaction with the new State and its constitution, and her consent to its formation, by a special session, refers again to the counties of Berkeley, Jefferson, and Frederick, and enacts that whenever they shall, by a majority vote, assent to the constitution of the new State, they may become part thereof; and the legislature sends this statue to Congress with a request that it will admit the new State into the Union. Now, we have here, on two different occasions, the emphatic legislative proposition of Virginia that these counties might become part of the of West Virginia; and we have the constitution of West Virginia agreeing to accept them and providing for their place in the new-born State. There was one condition, however, imposed by Virginia to her parting with them, and one condition made by West Virginia to her receiving them, and that was the same, namely, the assent of the majority of the votes of the counties to the transfer.

It seems to us that there was an agreement between the old State and the new that these counties should become part of the latter, subject to that condition alone. Up to this time no vote had been taken under any but a hostile government. At all events, the bill alleges that none was taken on the proposition of May, 1862, of the Virginia legislature. If an agreement means the mutual consent of the parties to a given proposition, this was an agreement between these States for the transfer of these counties on the condition named. The condition was one which could be ascertained or carried out at any time; and this was clearly the idea of Virginia when she declared that *whenever* the voters of said counties should ratify and consent to the constitution they should become part of the State; and her subsequent legislation making special provision for taking the vote on this subject, as shown by the acts of January 31st and February 4th, 1863, is in perfect accord with this idea, and shows her good faith in carrying into effect the agreement.

2. But did Congress consent to this agreement?

Unless it can be shown that the consent of Congress, under that clause of the Constitution which forbids agreements between States without it, can only be given in the form of an express and formal statement of every proposition of the agreement, and of its consent thereto, we must hold that the consent of that body was given to this agreement.

The attention of Congress was called to the subject by the very short statute of the State of Virginia requesting the admission of the new State into the Union, consisting of but three sections, one of which was entirely devoted to giving consent that these two counties and the county of Frederick might accompany the others, if they desired to do so. The constitution of the new State was literally cumbered with the various provisions for receiving these counties if they chose to come, and in two or three forms express consent is there given to this addition to the State. The subject of the relation of these to the others, as set forth in the ordinance for calling the convention, in the constitution framed by the convention, and in the act of the Virginia legislature, must have received the attentive consideration of Congress. To hold otherwise is to suppose that the act for the admission of the new State passed without any due or serious consideration. But the substance of this act clearly repels any such inference; for it is seen that the constitution of the new State was, in one particular at least, unacceptable to Congress; and the act only admits the State into the Union when that feature shall be changed by the popular vote. If any other part of the constitution had failed to meet the approbation of Congress, especially so important a part as the proposition for a future change of boundary between the new and the old State, it is reasonable to suppose that its dissent would have been expressed in some shape, especially as the refusal to permit those counties to attach themselves to the new State would not have endangered its formation and admittion without them.

It is, therefore, an inference clear and satisfactory that Congress by that statute, intended to consent to the admission of the

State with the contingent boundaries provided for in its constitution and in the statute of Virginia, which prayed for its admission on those terms, and that in so doing it necessarily consented to the agreement of those States on that subject.

There was then a valid agreement between the two States consented to by Congress, which agreement made the accession of these counties dependent on the result of a popular vote in favor of that proposition.

3. But the Commonwealth of Virginia insists that no such vote was ever given; and we must inquire wheather the facts alleged in the bill are such as to require an issue to be made on that question by the answer of the defendant.

The bill alleges the failure of the counties to take any action under the act of May, 1863, and that on the 31st of January and the 4th of February thereafter the two other acts we have mentioned were passed to enable such vote to be taken. These statutes provide very minutely for the taking of this vote under the authority of the State of Virginia; and, among other things, it is enacted that the governor shall ascertain the result, and if, he shall be of opinion that said vote has been opened and held and the result ascertained and certified pursuant to law, he shall certify that result under the seal of the State to the governor of West Virginia; and if a majority of the votes given at the polls were in favor of the proposition, then the counties became part of the State. He was also authorized to postpone the time of voting if he should be of opinion that a fair vote could not be taken on the day mentioned in these days.

Though this language is taken mainly from the statute which refers to Berkeley County, we consider the legal effect of the other statute to be the same.

These statutes were in no way essential to evidence the consent of Virginia to the original agreement, but were intended by her legislature to provide the means of ascertaining the wishes of the voters of these counties, that being the condition of the agreement on which the transfer the counties depended.

The State thus showed her good faith to that agreement, and undertook in her own way and by her own officers to ascertain the fact in question.

The legislature might have required the vote to have been reported to it, and assumed the duty of ascertaining and making known the result to West Virginia; but it delegated that power to the governor. It invested him with full discretion as to the time when the vote should be taken, and made his opinion and his decision conclusive as to the result. The vote was taken under these statutes, and certified to the governor. He was of opinion that the result was in favor to the transfer. He certified this fact under the seal of the State to the State of West Virginia, and the legislature of that State immediately assumed jurisdiction over the two counties, provided for their admission, and they have been a part of that State ever since.

Do the allegations of the bill authorize us to be behind all this and inquire as to what took place at this voting? To inquire how many votes were actually cast? How many of the men who had once been voters in these counties were then in the rebal army? Or had been there and were thus disfranchised? For all these and many more ambarrassing questions must arise if the defendant is required to take issue on the allegations of the bill on this subject.

These allegations are indefinite and vague in this regard. It is charged that no fair vote was taken; but no act of unfairness is alleged. That the governor was misled and deceived by the fraud of those who made him believe so. This is the substance of what is alleged. No one is charged specifically with the fraud. No particular act of fraud is stated. No charge of any kind of moral or legal wrong is made against the defendant, the State of West Virginia.

But, waiving these defects in the bill, we are of opinion that the action of the governor is conclusive of the vote as between the States of Virginia and West Virginia. He was in legal effect the State of Virginia in this matter. In addition to his position as executive head of the State, the legislature delegated to him all its own power in the premises. It vested him with large control as to the time of taking the vote, and it made his *opinion* of the result of the condition to final action. It rested of its own accord the whole question on his judgment and in his hands. In a matter where that action was to be the foundation on which another sovereign State was to act — a matter which involved the delicate question of permanent boundary between the States and jurisdiction over a large population — a matter in which she took into her own hands the ascertainment of the fact on which these important propositions were by contract made to depend, she must be bound by what she has done. She can have no right, years after all this has been settled, to come into a court of chancery to charge that her own conduct has been a wrong and a fraud; that her own subordinate agents have misled her governor, and that her solemn act transferring these counties shall be set aside, against the will of the State of West Virginia, and without consulting the wishes of the people of these counties.

This view of the subject renders it unnecessary to inquire into the effect of the act of 1865 withdrawing the consent of the State of Virginia, or the act of Congress of 1866 giving consent, after the attempt of that State to withdraw hers.

The demurer to the bill is therefore sustained, and the bill must be dismissed.

Mr. Justice DAVIS, with whom concurred CLIFFORD and FIELD, J.J., dissenting.

Being unable to agree with the majority of the court in its judgment in this case, I will briefly state the grounds of my dissent.

There is no difference of opinion between us in relation to the construction of the provision of the Constitution which affects the question at issue. We all agree that until the consent of Congress is given, there can be no valid compact or agreement between States. And that, although the point of time when Congress may give its consent is not material, yet, when it is given, there must be a reciprocal and concurrent consent of the three parties to the contract. Without this, it is not a completed compact. If, therefore, Virginia withdrew its assent before the consent of Congress was

133

given, there was no compact within the meaning of the Constituion.

To my mind nothing is clearer, than that Congress never did undertake to give its consent to the transfer of Berkeley and Jefferson Counties to the State of West Virginia until March 2, 1866. If so, the consent came too late, because the legislature of Virginia had, on the fifty day of December, 1865, withdrawn its assent to the proposed cession of these two counties. This withdrawl was in ample time, as it was before the proposal of the State had become operative as a concluded compact, and the bill (in my judgment) shows that Virginia had sufficient reasons for recalling its proposition to part with the territory embraced within these counties.

But, it is maintained in the opinion of the court that Congress did give its consent to the transfer of these counties by Virginia to West Virginia, when it admitted West Virginia into the Union. The argument of the opinion is, that Congress, by admitting the new State, gave its assent to that provision of the new constitution which looked to the acquisition of these counties, and that if the people of these counties have *since* voted to become part of the State of West Virginia, this action is within the consent of Congress. I most respectfully submit that the facts of the case (about which there is no dispute), do not justify the argument which it attempted to be drawn from them.

The second section of the first article of the constitution of West Virginia is merely a proposal addressed to the people of two distinct districts, on which they were invited to act. The people of one district (Pendleton, Hardy, Hampshire, and Morgan) accepted the proposal. The people of the other district (Jefferson, Berkeley, and Frederick) rejected it.

In this state of things, the first district became a part of the new State, so far as its constitution could make it so, and the legislature of Virginia included it in its assent, and Congress included it in its admission to the Union. But neither the constitution of West Virginia, nor the assent of the legislature of Virginia, nor the consent of Congress, had any application whatever to the second district. For though the second section of the first article of the new constitution had proposed to include it, the proposal was accompanied with conditions which were not complied with; and when that constitution was presented to Congress for approval, the proposal had already been rejected, and had no significance or effect whatever.

Hearne Note: I concur with the dissenting opinion, but I was not a justice of that court and my vote doesn't count! See Munford's "synopsis," elsewhere in this appendix, under his subheading "Berkeley and Jefferson Counties Annexed"; his reasoning is as sound as a frog's eye, which is waterproof!!!

Chapter XIX — Appendix
Historical Synopsis of the Changes in Virginia Law and Constitution 1860-1872
By George W. Munford

HISTORICAL SYNOPSIS OF THE CHANGES IN THE
LAWS AND CONSTITUTION OF THE STATE OF
VIRGINIA
During the period of 1861-1872

by the Hon. George W. Munford, as set out verbatim from the
Code of Virginia 1873; but the last few pages of Mr. Munford's account, of events after 4 April 1868 are omitted because Mr. Pierpont's term of office as governor ended at that time.

Biographical sketch of the author of Synopsis. George Wythe
Munford was born in Richmond on 8 January, 1803; he was the
son of William Munford, Esq. Upon graduating from the College
of William and Mary he studied law with the intent to be a practicing lawyer. But his father, clerk of the House of Delegates, called
upon him for assistance in carrying on his duties, and on the death
of his father he became Clerk of the House. When the Virginia constitutional convention of 1829 assembled, Mr. Munford's reputation as clerk of the House of Delegates was so high, he was elected
secretary of the convention. During the convention Mr. Munford
became acquainted with many distinguished Virginians of those
days, and he got to know much history of the Commonwealth and
the events of the time; and he became a member of a famous
military organization, The Richmond Blues; and became president
of the Blues Association. Later he became Secretary of the Commonwealth, and in that capacity he assembled and edited the Code
of Virginia, 1860. It was while serving in that capacity that The
War broke out. Later, Mr. Munford became clerk of the House of
Delegates committee for courts of justice. Mr. Munford lived until
10 January, 1882, when he graduated from this life in his native city

of Richmond. The House of Delegates honored his memory with this resolution:

"*Resolved,* That in the death of Colonel George Wythe Munford, the Commonwealth of Virginia has lost a loyal son, who devoted the best days of his life to her service; one whose mind was stored with useful knowledge; who knew how to say what was best to say, and what was best to do; whose whole life was but the expression of the goodness, wisdom and purity of his heart and soul; and who in all the relations of life, was the honorable and honored gentleman." *Biographical sketch provided by courtesy of the Virginia State Library, Richmond.*

Hearne note. The following text is taken verbatim from Mr. Munford's "synopsis" without editing by me or by anyone else. It is to be taken as the feelings of an honorable and distinguished Virginian, whose point of view was that of secessionist, but true to the facts and realizing that the federal — and later on, the state courts — determine the law, regardless of what any one's opinion may be as to the righteousness thereof. Note generally that Governor Pierpont is nowhere referred to as a "provisional" governor. Note also, in the first paragraph, that he concedes the point that the Richmond Confederate government of Virginia was "overthrown" by the Restored Government in Wheeling. And observe closely the first paragraph of the synopsis, which recites a sequence of events. Thus the first event was the organization of the Restored Government (comma), which dismembered the State by; (semicolon to denote one avent); subjected people to military rule (comma) without representation, (comma), as a military district (semicolon); indicating end of another event; and finally, subjected the district to military rule, etc. (Period, end of recital of events.) Thus, he does not mean to infer that the dismemberment of the state by events which took place in Wheeling was of necessity brought about events which followed.

BEGINNING OF THE SYNOPSIS

A condensed statement of the events which caused the overthrow of the government of Virginia, and induced the establishment of a new organization, denominated the "Restored government;" which produced the dismemberment of the Commonwealth and the creation of the state of West Virginia out of its limits; subjected the people to military rule, without representation, as a mere military district; and finally culminated in the reconstruction of the state by Federal laws and its qualified restoration into the Union.

These results had been for many years the subject of speculation and deep concern. They were the inevitable products of seed sown in the past history of the country, which, though slow in germinating, and slow in subsequent growth, continued spreading their roots and throwing out branches until they pervaded and overshadowed the entire Union. The general historian will recount these causes, and moralize upon them; and may give utterance to animated comments, the results of deliberate reflection, without being swayed by passion or prejudice. We can only give a hasty outline, to serve for reference, scarcely venturing to express approbation or censure. In a work like this, mere rhetorical ornament either in praise or reprobation, would be justifiable.

It is well known, that after prolonged agitation on one side and great excitement and complaint on the other, producing acrimony between the northern and southern states, the people of some of the latter had resolved with almost entire unanimity upon assuming a separate existence and forming an independent confederacy. Several of the more ardent states had adopted ordinances of secession dissolving their connection with the United States, and invoked the aid of Virginia, through considerations of identity of interest, suffering and feeling, to make common cause with them in the impending struggle.

The people of Virginia, with accustomed patient endurance, fully developed in this narrative, could not avoid looking on with intense anxiety and excitement, watching the manifestation of hostile preparation around them, but sympathizing deeply with their southern sisters.

This being the condition of the country, Governor John Letcher, the then governor of the state, well aware of the total want of adequate preparation for so great a conflict, immediately convened the General Assembly, to meet in extra session on the 7th of January, 1861. His proclamation and message to that body exhibited much of the temper and spirit of the time. He was certainly opposed to the ultra measures then current and popular, but when the state once assumed her position, he like every true son of Virginia, both by official action and by private influence, displayed a patriotic ardor and devotion rarely surpassed.

There can be no doubt that the legislature thus convened, and the executive by whom they were called, were the constitutional authorities of the state. They had been recognized by the government of the United States and by all the states separately, and as such they exercixed the right to invoke an expression of the will of the people in this emergency.

Accordingly, on the 14th of January, one week after the meeting of the General Assembly, they passed an act to provide for electing members of a convention and to convene the same.

The act required a poll to be opened "to take the sense of the qualified voters as to whether any action of said convention dissolving our connection with the Federal Union, or changing the organic law of the state, shall be submitted to the people for ratification or rejection." The delegates were elected on the 4th of February, 1861, and the question submitted to the people was decided affirmatively by a large majority. The convention assembled in Richmond on the 13th of February following.

The General Assembly, as expressive of the conciliatory spirit which then animated it, adopted joint resolutions inviting the other states to send commissioners to meet commissioners on the part of Virginia, extending the invitation to all such states as were willing to unite with Virginia in an earnest effort to adjust the present unhappy controversies in the spirit in which the constitution was originally formed, and consistently with its principles, so as to afford to the people of the slave-holding states adequate guarantees for the security of their rights. The resolutions were adopted on the 19th of January, 1981, and the commissioners were invited to meet on the 4th of February following.

The commissioners on the part of Virginia were Ex-President John Tyler, William C. Rives, Judge John W. Brockenbrough, George W. Summers and James A. Seddon. The legislature also appointed Ex-President John Tyler a commissioner to the President of the United States, and Judge John Robertson to the state of South Carolina and the other seceding states, with instructions to request the President and the authorities of such states to agree to abstain, pending the proceedings contemplated by the act of Virginia, from all acts calculated to produce a collision of arms between the states and the government of the United States. Acts 1861, p. 337 to 339.

In pursuance of these resolutions, the first commissioners repaired to the city of Washington, and fruitlessly attempted to effect the object contemplated by the General Assembly. In their report to Governor Letcher, which was communicated by him to the convention on the 6 of March 1861, they say:

"The undersigned commissioners, in pursuance of the wishes of the General Assembly, expressed in their resolutions of the 19th of January last, repaired in due season to the city of Washington. There they found, on the 4th February — the day suggested in the overture of Virginia for a conference with the other states — commissioners to meet them from the following states, viz: Rhode Island, New Jersey, Delaware, Maryland, New Hampshire, Vermont, Connecticut, Pennsylvania, North Carolina, Ohio, Indiana, Illinois, and Kentucky. Subsequently, during the continuance of the conference, at different periods, appeared likewise commissioners from Tennessee, Massachusetts, Missouri, New York, Maine, Iowa and Kansas; so that before the close, twenty-one states were represented by commissioners appointed either by the legislature or governor of the respective states.

"The undersigned communicated the resolutions of the General Assembly to the conference, and both before the committee appointed to recommend a plan of adjustment, and the conference itself, urged the propositions known as the

138

Crittenden resolutions, with the modifications suggested by the General Assembly of Virginia, as the basis of an acceptable adjustment.

"They were not adopted by the conference; but in lieu thereof, after much discussion, and the consideration of many proposed amendments, an article with seven sections, intended as an amendment to the constitution (a copy of which article is hereto adjoined), was adopted by sections (not under the rules — being voted on as a whole), and by a vote of the conference (not taken by states), was directed to be submitted on Congress, with the request that it should be recommended to the states for ratification, which was accordingly done by the president of the conference.

"The undersigned regret that the Journal showing the proceedings and votes in the conference has not yet been published or furnished them, and that consequently they are not able to present it with this report. As soon as received it will be communicated to your excellency. In the absence of that record it is deemed appropriate to state that on the final adoption of the first section, two of the states, Indiana and Missouri, did not vote, and New York was divided, and that the vote by states was ayes 9; noes 8 — Virginia, by a majority of her commissioners, voting in the negative. The other sections were adopted by varying majorities, (not precisely recollected,) and on the 5th and 7th sections the vote of Virginia was in the negative. The plan when submitted to Congress failed to receive its recommendation; and as that body, having adjourned, can take no further cognizance of it, the undersigned feel the contingency has arrived on which they are required to report, as they do, the result of their action.

Respectfully,

JOHN TYLER,
G. W. SUMMERS,
W. C. RIVES,
JAMES A. SEDDON.

[See Journal Con., Doc. No. 11.]

Thus the hopes of effecting any satisfactory adjustment were blasted, there being no manifestation of such a compromising spirit as would give a prospect of recolciliation. In the report of Ex-President Tyler it is stated "that the President of the United States complained that the south had not treated him properly; that they had made unnecessary demonstrations by seizing unprotected arsenals and forts, and thus perpetrating acts of useless bravado which had quite as well be let alone." The President stated that he was impressed with the sense of the obligation which rested upon him, could give no pledges but those contained in his public acts, but expressed his intention to send a special message to Congress accompanied with a strong recommendation to avoid the passage of any hostile legislation.

The report states that the morning newspapers contained a statement that guns had been mounted on the land side of Fortress Monroe, and Mr. Tyler states that he had deemed it in no way inappropriate to call the attention of the president to these rumors.

In the report of Judge Robertson, made to Governor Letcher on the 20 January 1861, writing from Charleston, South Carolina, he says: The intelligence of the sailing of the Brooklyn from Hampton Roads, received here on the 25th instance, determined me at once not to press an immediate reply to my note of that date, communicating the mediatorial propositions of the General Assembly of Virginia. It was arranged between Ex-President Tyler and myself, previous to our depature from Richmond, that we would endeavor to obtain from the government at Washington and the authorities of the seceded states mutual assurances of abstinence from acts calculated to produce hostile collision during the period designated by the General Assembly, which assurances being interchanged would be reciprocally binding. Last evening I received a dispatch from Mr. Tyler informing me that the president declines to give a written pledge. I do not understand that he has given or proposes to give a verbal one. Under these circumstances — informed moreover that South Carolina does not consent to send commissioners to Washington as proposed by Virginia — it seems wholly unnecessary, if not unreasonable, to ask from the authorities of that state assurances of the character contemplated, which the government at Washington declines to give. At the same time he informed the authorities of South Carolina, "though regarding my mission as terminated it will afford me sincere pleasure to be the bearer of any response which the authorities of South Carolina may think proper to make through me to the friendly interposition of the state I have the honor to represent."

In the final report of Judge Robertson to the governor on the 25 February 1861 among other matters he says: "The trust confided to me by the General Assembly was cheerfully accepted, and in earnestly endeavoring to the best of my ability to accomplish the object desired by them, my judgment and feelings have gone hand in hand with my duty. Without assuming for these humble endeavors any special merit or influence, it is certain that a peaceful policy has in point of fact been maintained up to the present date by the seceded states, including South Carolina, from whose authorities I was not justified in asking a formal pledge after being informed by Ex-President Tyler that none such would be given by President Buchanan. It will be gratifying to the General Assembly to reflect that this policy may have been adopted or pursued in deference to their intercession. It may not be improper to say that as far as my opportunities have enabled me to judge, the people and authorities of the Southern Confederacy are resolved inflexibly and with unparralleled unanimity to meet all the consequences of the step they have taken.''

In the meantime, commissioners had been appointed by several of the southern states for the purpose of inducing Virginia to pass an ordinance of secession and unite herself with the destinies of the Southern Confederacy; and the commissioners from Mississippi, Georgia, and South Carolina had asked permission to be heard orally before the convention.

Accordingly, on the 18th February the Honorable Fulton Anderson, commissioner from the state of Mississippi was heard; and on the same day Honorable H. L. Bening, from the state of Georgia made known the wishes of that state and in concluding his remarks, he presented to the convention a copy of an ordinance of the state of Georgia to dissolve the union between that state and the United States.

On the 19th February the convention gave audience to Honorable John S. Preston, commissioner from the state of South Carolina, and in his eloquent address he urged upon Virginia to give her powerful aid to the cause of her southern sisters.

On the 4th of March following President Lincoln was inaugurated to succeed President Buchanan, and the public feeling was more and more excited and agitated.

The convention still paused, and, notwithstanding the failure of reconciliation or adjustment, under the resolutions of the General Assembly, it still determined to make another effort to prevent a rupture of the union. On the 8 of April 1861 a resolution was adopted in the following terms:

"Whereas, in the opinion of this convention the uncertainty which prevails in the public mind as to the policy which the Federal executive intends to pursue towards the succeeded states is extremely injurious to the industrial and commercial interests of the country — tends to keep up an excitement which is unfavorable to the adjustment of pending difficulties, and threatens a disturbance of the public peace; therefore,

"Resolved, That a committee of three delegates be appointed by this convention to wait upon the president of the United States, present to him this preamble and resolution and respectfully ask of him to communicate to this convention the policy which the Federal executive intends to pursue in regard to the Confederate States."

Under this resolution a committee, composed of William Ballard Preston of Montgomery county, Alexander H. H. Stuart of Augusta, and George W. Randolph of the city of Richmond, was unanimously chosen.

The report of this committee states briefly its action:

"The committee appointed on the 8th instant by this convention, with direction to wait upon the president of the United States and present to him the preamble and resolution adopted on that day, report that, in the fulfillment of our duty, we left the city of Richmond on the morning of the 9th instant for Washington city; we were, however, prevented by injuries sustained by the railroad, from a violent protracted storm, from reaching Washington until 11 o'clock on Friday, the 12th instant. At 1 o'clock on that day, we called on the president, and informed him that we had been appionted a committee by the convention of Virginia, then in session, to make a communication to him from that body, and request him to designate an hour at which it would be aggreeable to him to receive us. We accordingly attended him at that hour, presented him the resolution of the convention, and explained to him our mission. He then read to us a paper, which he stated he had just prepared as the answer to the commission from the convention, declaring that he had seen in the newspapers the proceedings of the convention and the character of our mission.

We herewith communicate the president's reply to the preamble and resolution of the convention.

"Wm. B. Preston,
"Alex'r H. H. Stuart
"George W. Randolph."

The reply of the president is to be found in Document No. 17, Journal of the convention. In this paper the president referred to his inaugural address as the best expression he could give of his purposes, repeating, "The power confided to me will be used to hold, occupy and possess the property and places belonging to the government, and to collect the duties and imposts; but beyond what is necessary for these objects there will be no invasion — no using of force against or among the people anywhere."

"But if, as now appears to be true, in pursuit of a purpose to drive the United States authorities from these places, an unprovoked assault has been made upon Fort Sumter, I shall hold myself at liberty to repossess, if I can, like places which had been seized before the government was devolved upon me. And in any event I shall to the extent of my ability repel force by force."

In a short time after this reply the president issued his proclamation, calling forth a force of seventy-five thousand men to suppress the insurrection and repel the invasion supposed to be intended by the Confederate States.

142

An extract will show its tenor and purport:

"Whereas the laws of the United States have been for some time, and now are opposed, and the execution thereof obstructed in the states of South Carolina, Georgia, Alabama, Florida, Mississippi, Louisiana and Texas, by combinations too powerful to be suppressed by the ordinary course of judicial proceedings or by the powers vested in the marshals by law: now, therefore, I, Abraham Lincoln, president of the United States, in virtue of the power in me vested by the constitution and laws, have thought fit to call forth, and hereby do call forth, the militia of the several states of the Union to the aggregate number of seventy-five thousand, in order to suppress said combinations and to cause the laws to be duly executed."

This proclamation was generally regarded as an indication of an intention, under the pretext of suppressing insurrections and repelling invasions of waging war upon the Confederate States; and when a requisition was made upon the governor of Virginia for her quota of militia under the proclamation, the governor issued a proclamation declaring that Virginia would under no circumstances supply troops to aid in any manner in any assault upon the southern states.

The government of the Confederate States had been organized — many of the people in Virginia were urgent for the passage of a secession ordinance — the public mind was agitated and kept up to fever heat by the requisitions for troops, and the war-like preparations everywhere making — volunteers were tendering their services, and every indictation of an outbreak was imminent.

At the commencement of the convention a large majority of the members were conservative, and in favor of preserving the Union, if possible, yet great changes had taken place. After sitting for some days with closed doors, on 17 April 1861, the convention adopted an ordinance to repeal the ratification of the constitution of the United States and resume all the rights and powers granted under said constitution.

This ordinance declared: Now, therefore, we, the people of Virginia, do declare and ordain that the ordinance adopted by the people of this state in convention on the 25th day of June, in the year of our Lord one thousand seven hundred and eighty-eight, whereby the constitution of the United States of America was ratified, and all acts of the general assembly of this state ratifying or adopting amendments to said constitution, are hereby repealed and abrogated; that the union between the state of Virginia and the other states under the constitution aforesaid is hereby dissolved, and that the state of Virginia is in the full possession and exercise of all the rights of sovereignty which belong and appertain to a free and independent state. And they do further declare that said constitution of the United States is no longer binding on any citizens of this state.

This ordinance authorized the question to be submitted to the people on the 4th Thursday of the following May, to ascertain whether the action of the convention would be ratified.[1]

After the passage of the ordinance, the convention appointed John Tyler, William Ballard Preston, S. McD. Moore, James P. Holcombe, James C. Bruce, and Lewis E. Harvie, commissioners on the part of Virginia to confer with Alexander H. Stephens, commissioner of the Confederate States, for a temporary union of Virginia with said Confederate States.

These commissioners entered into a temporary agreement by which the whole military force and military operations, offensive and defensive, of the state, in the impending conflict with the United States, were placed under the president of the Confederate States, as if the state were actually a member of said Confederacy.

2d. They agreed that the state, after the consummation of the union with the Confederate government, should turn over to said government all the public property, naval stores, and munitions of war; &c., she may then be in possession of, acquired from the United States, on the same terms, and in like manner, as the other States of said Confederacy have done in like cases. And

3d. The expenditures of money incurred by Virginia, before the union under the provisional government shall be consummated, were to be met and provided for by the Confederate States.

This agreement was entered into in the city of Richmond, on 24 April 1861, the whole being subject to the approval and ratification of the proper authorities of both governments respectively.

On the 25th of April, 1861, the convention passed an ordinance ratifying and confirming the convention entered into between the commissioner of the Confederate States and the commissioners of the state of Virginia. Ord. Conv., No. 2, p. 5.

On the same day an ordinance was passed for the conditional adoption of the constitution of the provisional government of the Confederate States of America; provided that this ordinance shall cease to have any legal operation or effect, if the people of this Commonwealth, upon the vote directed to be taken on the ordinance of secession, passed by this convention on the 17th of April, 1861, shall reject the same. Ord. Conv. No. 3, p. 6.

It is stated in the papers of the day, immediately after the election, that the majority in favor of ratifying the secession ordinance was about one hundred and thirty thousand votes.

On 1 May 1861, an ordinance was adopted to release the officers, civil and military, and the citizens generally of the state of Virginia from all obligation to support the constitution of the late Confederacy known as the United States of America, which ordained that the said oaths and the said constitution are inoperative and void and of no effect. Ord. No. 41, p. 33, Acts, 1861.[2]

And then, on 19 June 1861, an ordinance was passed adopting the Constitution of the Confederate States of America on 11 March 1861, and proclaimed it to be binding upon the people of the Commonwealth, but with the distinct understanding on her part that she expressly reserves to herself the right, through a convention representing her people in their sovereign character, to repeal and annul this ordinance and to resume all the powers hereby granted to the Confederate government whenever they shall in her judgment have been perverted to her injury or oppression. Ordinance Convention 1861, c. 56, p. 51.

About the same time a proclamation was issued by the president of the United States, in which it is declared that "in pursuance of an act of congress, approved July 13, 1861, the inhabitants of Georgia, South Carolina, Virginia, &c., except the inhabitants of that part of the state of Virginia lying west of the Alleghany mountains and of such other parts hereinbefore named as they may maintain a loyal adhesion to the Union and the constitution, or may be from time to time occupied and controlled by forces of the United States (engaged in the dispersion of said insurgents) are in a state of insurrecton against the United States, and that all commercial intercourse between the same and the inhabitants thereof, with the exceptions aforesaid, and the citizens of other states and other parts of the United States, is lawful and will remain unlawful until such insurrection shall cease or has been suppressed." (U.S. Stat. at Large, vol. 12, p. 1262.)

Thus the state of Virginia, by its own acts, through its organized convention, under the authority of its legally constituted organs, was declared to be no longer a component part of the United States. And it was proclaimed by the president of the United States to be in a state of insurrection, and all commercial intercourse between its citizens and those of the other states was interdicted.

But it had to contend, moreover, with a formidable opposition on the part of citizens within its limits who remained loyal to the United States.

Proceedings To Restore The State Government

As soon as the ordinance of secession was passed, most of the members of the convention from the counties in the northwest and west of the state beyond the Alleghany mountains, who had been opposed to its adoption, retired from the convention, and though the vote in that body had been 81 for, to 51 against it, they resolved to oppose the action of so large a majority by every means in their power. Meetings were called in several counties, denouncing the secession movement; and a large meeting was held at Clarksburg, in Harrison county, of a like character, inviting the people in each and all the counties composing northwestern Virginia, to appoint not less than five delegates each, to meet in convention at Wheeling on the 13th of May following, to determine what action should be taken.

The people of these counties were by no means unanimous in their opposition to the secession movement. In some counties there were majorities in favor of the action of the state convention, and in others there were large minorities of the same sentiment, and if the vote could then have been fairly taken, it is at least doubtful what would have been the result. The call for the convention to be held at Wheeling was not even addressed to the people of the counties outside of the disaffected district. The people of the residue of the state were neither invited nor expected.

There were no elections regularly held for delegates to this convention; they were generally appointed by meetings, rarely composing a majority of the voting population of a county — sometimes by a few men signing a paper requesting gentlemen to act as representatives, and some members occupied seats without even this formality.[3]

On the 13th of May, before the question had been submitted to the people for the ratification of the ordinance of secession, this convention at Wheeling assembled. It was composed of the members of the convention thus selected, and of a large crowd of the citizens of Wheeling and of Ohio counties. The committee on credentials reported duly accredited delegates from twenty-six counties, there being then one hundred and forty counties and three cities entitled to representation; and these counties and cities were then holding another convention in comforty to the constitution and laws to which these northwestern counties had elected delegates, and in which they were still entitled to representation. The convention thus composed, however, was organized by the appointment of John W. Moss, of Wood County, as its president. It appointed a committee (of one member from each county) represented on state and federal relations; and in its report, this committee declared it to be the deliberate judgment of the convention, that the ordinance of secession, by which the repeal of the ratification of the constitution of the United States was attempted, was unconstitutional, null and void; that the schedule attached to that ordinance, prohibiting the election of members of the house of representatives of the congress of the United States, at the election on the fourth Thursday of May, then current, was a manifest usurpation of power, to which they, as freemen of Virginia, ought not to and would not submit; that the ordinance of the convention at Richmond, ratifying and approving the agreement between the commissioners of the Confederate States, upon the same principle and footing as if the Commonwealth were a member of said Confederacy, and the acts and conduct of the executive officers of the state, in pursuance of said agreement, were plain and palpable violations of the constitution of the state, and utterly subversive of the rights and liberties of the people; that they earnestly recommend the citizens of the state to vindicate their rights by voting against the ordinance of secession; and that they urged upon them to vote for members of Congress of the United States in their several districts, in the exercise of their rights under the constitutions of the United States and of Virginia; that they recommend them to vote for such persons for members of the house of delegates, as entertained sentiments in harmony with those before expressed; that it was the imperative duty of the citizens to maintain the constitution of the state, and the laws made in pursuance of the same; and, among other things, recommended the appointment on the 4th day of June, 1861, of delegates to a general convention, to meet on the 11th day of the same month, to devise such measures as the safety and welfare of the people they represented should demand, each county to appoint a number of representatives to the convention equal to double the number to which it was entitled in the house of delegates; and that the senators and delegates to be elected at the general election on the fourth Thursday of May following, should be entitled to seats in the convention as members.'' This report was adopted with almost unanimity, and the convention adjourned *sine die.*

In accordance with this recommendation at the election on the fourth Thursday in May, the people of the counties of the northwest voted for members of the Federal congress in the three districts west of the Alleghany mountains.

At the election on the fourth of June, delegates were elected to the convention which was to assemble on the 11th of the same month. The convention met at Washington Hall,[4] in the city of Wheeling. The committee on credentials reported delegates from thirty-one counties, including the senators and members of the house of delegates, and this number was subsequently increased to thirty-five counties, the convention being composed of seventy-seven members. Arthur I. Boreman, of Wood County, was its president, and G. L. Cranmer of Ohio County its secretary. The officers and members were sworn to support the Constitution of the United States and the laws made in pursuance thereof as the supreme law of the land, anything in the ordinance of the convention which assembled in Richmond on the 13th of February, 1861, to the contrary notwithstanding — the constitution of Virginia being completely ignored.[5]

A committee of thirteen members was appointed to prepare and report business. On the 13th of June, two days after the organization of the convention, this committee recommended the adoption of a declaration, to be, in fact, a declaration of independence from the state government at Richmond, demanding the reorganization of the government, and declaring the offices of all the departments of the state — legislative, executive, and judicial — to be vacated. On the 17th of the month this declaration received the unanimous vote of the convention, and though made by a convention composed of thirty-six out of one hundred forty counties, was announced as a declaration of the people of Virginia.[6] It is as follows:

"A DECLARATION OF THE PEOPLE OF VIRGINIA.

"The true purpose of all governments is to promote the welfare and provide for the protection and security of the governed, and when any form or organization of government proves inadequate for or subversive of this purpose, it is the right, it is the duty of the latter to alter or abolish it. The bill of rights of Virginia, framed in 1776, reaffirmed in 1830, and again in 1851, expressly reserves this right to a majority of her people. The act of the general assembly calling the convention which assembled at Richmond in February has, without the previously expressed consent of such majority, was therefore a usurpation, and the convention thus called has not only abused the powers nominally entrusted to it, but, with the connivance and active aid of the executive, has usurped and exercised other powers, to the manifest injury of the people, which if permitted will inevitably subject them to a military despotism.

"The convention, by its pretended ordinances, has required the people of Virginia to separate from and wage war against the government of the United States, and against the citizens of neighboring states with whom they have heretofore maintained friendly, social and business relations.

"It has attempted to transfer the allegiance of the people to an illegal confederacy of rebellious states, and required their submission to its pretended edicts and decrees.

"It has attempted to place the whole military force and military operations of the Commonwealth, under the control and direction of such confederacy, for offensive as well as defensive purposes.

"It has, in conjunction with the state executive, instituted, wherever their usurped power extends, a reign of terror, intended to suppress the free expressions of the will of the people, making elections a mockery and a fraud.

"The same combination, even before the passage of the pretended ordinance of secession, instituted war, by the seizure and appropriation of the property of the federal government, and by organizing and mobilizing armies, with the avowed purpose of capturing or destroying the capital of the Union.

"They have attempted to bring the allegiance of the people of the United States into direct conflict with this subordinate allegiance to the state, thereby making obedience to their pretended ordinances treason against the former.

"We, therefore, the delegates here assembled in convention, to devise such measures, and take such action, as the safety and welfare of the loyal citizens of Virginia may demand, having maturely considered the premises, and viewing with great concern the deplorable condition to which this once happy Commonwealth must be reduced, unless some regular adequate remedy is speedily adopted, and appealing to the Supreme Ruler of the Universe for the rectitude of our intentions, do hereby, in the name and on behalf of the good people of Virginia, solemnly declare, that the preservation of their dearest rights and liberties, and their security in person and property, imperatively demand the reorganization of the government of the Commonwealth, and that all acts of said convention and executive tending to separate this Commonwealth from the United States, or to levy and carry on war against them, are without authority and void, and that the offices of all who adhere to the said convention and exeuctive, whether legislative, executive or judicial, are vacated."[7]

In conformity with this declaration, the convention, on 19 June 1861, passed an ordinance for the reorganization of the state government. This ordinance gave to the lieutenant governor, Attorney General, and council to consist of five members, that consult with and advise the governor respecting such matters pertaining to his official duties as he shall submit for consideration, and to aid in the execution of his official duties.

It declared that the General Assembly elected on 23 May 1861, and those elected to fill vacancies who shall qualify, by taking the oath prescribed by the convention, shall constitute the legislature of the state and assemble at Wheeling on the first of July succeeding.

It required all officers, elected or appointed, to take an oath to support the Constitution of the United States, and the laws made in pursuance thereof, as the supreme law of the land, and anything in the constitution and laws of the state, or in the ordinances of the convention which assembled at Richmond on 13 February 1861, to the contrary notwithstanding.

It moreover required them to uphold and defend the government of Virginia as indicated and restored by the convention which assembled at Wheeling on 11 June 1861.

The offices of all officers failing or refusing to take the oath were declared vacant, and the vacancy was required to be filled.

On the following day, June the 20th, in conformity to the ordinance, Francis H. Pierpont, of the county of Marion, was elected governor, and Daniel Polsley, of the county of Mason, Lieutenant governor; and a few days afterwards, James S. Wheat was chosen attorney-general; Peter G. Van Winkley, Daniel Lamb, William Lazier, William A. Harrison, and J. T. Paxton were selected the members of the executive council.

Thus the constitution of the state, which required the first three of three officers to be elected by the people for a term of four years, was set aside without abrogation or amendment, and a council was established which the constitution did not authorize, and the officers of the existing government were not allowed time to comply with the ordinance prescribing the oaths to be taken, a failure to take the reorganization of the state government was partially effected.[8]

By an ordinance passed on 21 June 1861, the legislature was required, as soon as organized, to elect an auditor of public accounts, a treasurer, and a secretary of the Commonwealth.

The convention then adjourned to reassemble on the first Tuesday in August.

The first general assembly of the restored government met at Wheeling on the first day of July, 1861. The session was held at the custom-house, where the governor had already established his office, and where the other officers of the government were subsequently located.

On the 9th of July, in conformity with the ordinance of the 21st of June, the legislature elected L. A. Hagans, secretary Commonwealth, Samuel Crane, auditor of public accounts, and Campbell Tarr, treasurer. On the same day they elected John S. Carlile and Waitman T. Willey senators to represent the state of Virginia in the United States States.

These senators, and the representatives who were chosen at the election in May, for the three districts of the northwest, repaired to Washington, and were admitted to seats in the respective houses as senators and representatives from the state of Virginia.

And in a short time, by the proclamation of the new governor, elections were held, and judges were elected by the people for the several circuits, to supply vacancies created by the participation of the incumbents in the rebellion, or from their failure to take the oaths prescribed by the convention.

According to their adjournment, the convention reassembled on the 6th of August, and on the ninth of the month passed an ordinance declaring null and void the proceedings of the Richmond convention of 1861.

The ordinance is as follows:

"The people of Virginia, by their delegates assembled in convention at Wheeling, do ordain as follows:

"All ordinances, acts, orders, resolutions, and other proceedings of the convention which assembled at Richmond on the 13th day of February last, being without the authority of the people of Virginia, constitutionally given, and in derogation of their rights, are hereby declared be illegal, inoperative, null and void, and without force or effect."

In like manner, all acts and proceedings of the General Assembly, convened at Richmond at its various sessions, were

150

declared to illegal and void, as being passed by members illegally elected, and not qualified according to the ordinances of the convention at Wheeling, which required a prescribed oath to be taken, which they had failed to take. In consequence of which failure vacancies had been produced, which had been supplied by other elections to the legislature at the city of Wheeling. — Ordinance of Convention, passed on the 20th of August, 1861.

Proceedings for the Formation of the State of West Virginia.

The convention then passed, on the same day — 20 August 1861 — an ordinance to provide for the formation of a new state out of a portion of the territory of Virginia, by which it was ordained that a new state, to be called the state of Kanawha: Wyoming, Raleigh, Fayette, Nicholas, Webster, Randolph, Tucker, Preston, Monongalia, Marion, Taylor, Barbour, Upshur, Harrison, Lewis, Braxton, Clay, Kanawha, Boone, Wayne, Cabell, Putnam, Mason, Jackson, Roane, Calhoun, Wirt, Gilmer, Ritchie, Wood, Pleasants, Tyler, Doddridge, Wetzel, Marshall, Ohio, Brooke and Hancock. At the time of voting on the querstion of forming this state out of Virginia, the voters were authorized to vote for delegates to a convention to form a constitution for the government of the proposed state. This convention was authorized to include within the proposed state the counties of Greenbrier and Pocahontas, or Jefferson, or either of them, and also such other counties as lie contiguous to the counties named above, if the said counties, or either of them, by a majority of the votes given, shall declare their wish to form part of the proposed state, and shall elect delegates to the said convention.

The governor was required, on or before this 15 November 1861, to ascertain and proclaim the result of the vote, and if a majority of the votes given by the counties named should be in favor of the formation of a new state, he was to convene the convention in the city of Wheeling on 26 November 1861. The ratification or rejection to the qualified voters on the fourth Thursday in December following.

It was also made the duty of the governor to lay before the General Assembly, at its next meeting, for its consent, according to the Constitution of the United States, the result of the vote, if it was found that a majority was in favor of the new state, and also in favor of the constitution proposed.

It was provided that the new state should take upon itself a just proportion of the public debt of the Commonwealth of Virginia, prior to the 1st day of January, 1861, to be ascertained by charging to it all state expenditures within its limits, and a just proportion of the ordinary expenses of the state government, since any part of it was contracted; and deducting therefrom the moneys paid into the treasury of the Commonwealth from the counties included within the new state during the same period.

When the consent of the General Assembly to the formation of the new state should be obtained, it should forward the same to the congress of the United States, together with the constitution, and

151

request that the new state be admitted into the Federal Union.

The convention then, on the 21st of August, adjourned, and unless called by the president or the governor by the first Thursday in January, 1862, it was to remain adjourned, *sine die*.

Under the ordinance the vote was taken in August, and resulted in favor of the formation of a new state. There was not twenty thousand votes cast, thousands of the voters being disfranchised by the oath required, thousands being in both the Union and Confederate armies, others intimidated by the presence of Union or Confederate troops, and other refugees from desolate homes. The vote stood eighteen thousand four hundred and eight for the new state, and seven hundred and eighty-one against it. The state could then cast, upon a fair and full vote, seventy-five thousand votes.

At the same time delegates were elected to the convention to form a constitution for the new state, and all the counties then embraced in the state, except the counties of Jefferson, Berkeley, Webster and Monroe, were represented. The body convened in Wheeling, in the Federal court-room in the custom house, on the 26th of November, 1861. And after having framed a constitution, which was directed to be submitted to the people on the 3rd of April, it adjourned on the 18th of February, 1862.

This constitution changed the name of the new state, and instead of the state of Kanawha, the name which the former convention had given it, the new constitution christened it the state of West Virginia.

On the day prescribed, the vote was taken on the adoption of the constitution, and resulted in its favor by a vote of eighteen thousand eight hundred and sixty-two in favor, and five hundred and fourteen against it. At this time the actual population of the forty-eight counties embraced in the state was three hundred and thirty-four thousand nine hundred and twenty-one whites, and twelve thousand seven hundred and seventy-one colored persons. The poulation of the whole state of Virginia then being one million five hundred and ninety-six thousand and seventy-nine.

The legislature of the reorganized government assembled at Wheeling in extra session, on the 6th day of May, 1862, and by an act passed on the 13th of the same month, gave its consent, as the legislature of Virginia, to the formation and erection of a new state within the jurisdiction of Virginia.

Thus, the people within the limits of the new state had reorganized themselves into a separate and independent state, without the consent of a population of more than a million and a half of their fellow citizens, and then elected a legislature from one-third of the counties of the old state give the consent, not of the people of Virginia, but of themselves to the separation. The constitution of the United States providing that "no new state shall be formed or erected within the jurisdiction of any other state; nor any state be formed by the junction of two or more states, or parts of states, without the consent of the legislatures of the state concerned, as well as of the congress." And this was done under the influence of bayonet pressure, compelling voters to vote or not, as was necessary to effect the object.[9]

To show the spirit which actuated this restored government of Virginia, and its disposition to despoil the state it professed to represent, it will be sufficient to refer to another act, passed on the 13th of February, 1862, by the legislature at Wheeling, entitled "an act providing for taking the sense of the voters of the counties of Accomack and Northampton whether or not they will be annexed to Maryland." Comment is unnecesary.[10]

The act which passed on the 13th of May, giving the consent of the legislature of Virginia the formation of the new state, required that the act, together with a certified original of the new constitution for that state, should be transmitted by the execution to the senators and representatives to the state of Virginia, with a request to use their endeavors to obtain the consent of congress to the admission of the state of West Virginia into the Union.

The memorial of the legislature, enclosing the act and constitution, was presented to the senate of the United States on the 29th of May, 1862, and on the 10th of July following, a bill for admitting the state into the Union was passed by the senate of the United States, but the house of representatives not acting on the bill immediately, a joint resultion was passed by the legislature on the 9th of December in the following words:

"Resolved, That feeling the greatest anxiety and interest in the successful issue of the movement for a new state in West Virginia, we earnestly request the house of representatives of the United States to take up and pass, without alteration or amendment, the bill which passed the senate of the United States on the 10th day of July last."

This resolution was passed, nominally, by the legislature of the state of Virginia, not of West Virginia, and professed to feel the greatest anxiety and interest in dismembering the Commonwealth and transferring one third of its territory to another state.[11]

On the 12th of December joint resolutions were also adopted, by the same legislature, requesting that Hon. John S. Carlile to resign his seat in the senate of the United States, in which the following paragraph appears:

"And whereas the Hon. John S. Carlile having failed not only to sustain the legitimate efforts of the Federal government to suppress the insurrection, but having opposed by his votes in the senate, measures absolutely necessary to the reservation of the Union, and the enforcement of the laws, and having also by his speeches and votes in the senate opposed the bill for the admission of West Virginia into the Union: Therefore,

"Resolved by the General Assembly, That inasmuch as he has neither regarded the instructions aforesaid, nor the known will of the loyal people of the state, he is hereby respectfully requested to resign his seat."

On the 31st of December an act was passed by the congress giving its assent to the admission of the state into the Union, requiring an amendment to be made the constitution of the new state as a condition precedent to its admission.

The seventh section of the eleventh article of the constitution, as adopted by the convention, provided "That no slave shall be

153

brought, or free person of colour be permitted to come into this state for permanent residence.''

The act of congress cited that ''It being represented to congress that since the convention, of the 26th of November, 1861, that framed and proposed the constitution for the said state of West Virginia, the people thereof have expressed a wish to change the seventh section of the eleventh article of said constitution by striking out the same and inserting the following in its place, viz: 'The children of slaves born within the limits of this state after the 4th day of July, 1863, shall be free; and all slaves within the said state who shall at the time aforesaid be under the age of ten years shall be free when they arrive at the age of twenty-one years; and shall slaves over ten and under twenty-one years shall be free when they arrive at the age of twenty-five years; and no slave shall be permitted to come into the state for permanent residence therein.' ''

The preamble to the act of congress, besides this provision, recited the previous action of the convention, the vote of the people, and the assent of the legislature, specified the counties included within the boundaries of the new state, (not including therein, however, the counties of Berkeley and Jefferson,) and declared that the constitution was republican in form, and thereupon enacted ''That the state of West Virginia be and is hereby declared to be one of the United States of America, and admitted to the Union on an equal footing with the original states in all respects whatever, and until the next general census shall be entitled to three members in the house of representatives of the United States.''

The act further provided, ''that whenever the people of West Virginia, through their said convention, and by a vote to be taken at an election to be held within the limits of the said state, at such time as the convention may provide, make and ratify the change aforesaid, and properly certify the same, under the hand of the president of the convention, it shall be lawful for the president of the United States to issue his proclamation stating the fact, and thereupon this act shall take effect and be in force on and after sixty days from the date of said proclamation.''

In consequence of this action of congress, the convention reassembled on the 12th day of February, 1863, made the change required on the 17th of the same month, referred the question to the people for ratification or rejection the vote to be taken on the 26th of March following, and adopted an address urging the voters to accept the proposed amendment.

The vote was taken at the appointed time, and the constitution, as amended, was ratified by about seventeen thousand majority, on a very small vote. The result was certified by the president of the convention to the president of the United States, and, in compliance with the act of congress, his proclamation was issued on the 19th of April following, declaring that at the expiration of sixty days thereafter, the new state of West Virginia would constitute a component part of the United States.

The convention, prior to its adjournment in February, 1863, provided, that if a majority of the votes cast at the election in March, should be in favor of the adoption of the amended constitution, then an election should be held on the 4th Thursday of May, to choose members of both branches of the general assembly, a governor and other state officers, judges of the supreme court of appeals, judges of the circuit courts, and county officers. Under this election, Arthur I. Boreman was elected governor; Samuel Crane, auditor; Campbell Tarr, treasurer; J. Edgar Boyers, secretary of State; A. Bolton Calwell, attorney-general; Ralph L. Berkshire, William A. Harrison and James II. Brown, judges of the court of appeals.

Circuit judges were also elected in all circuits but two, which circuits were in the occupation of the contending armies; and county officers were chosen in nearly all of the counties, and the new state, on the 20th of June, 1863, became one of the states of the American Union.

Proceedings For Admitting Berkeley and Jefferson Into West Virginia

At this time the constitution of the new state, in enumerating the counties which shall be included in and form a part of the state of West Virginia, does not name the counties of Berkeley and Jefferson, but it provides in the second section of the article the first, that "if a majority of the votes cast at the election or elections held, as provided in the schedule hereof, in the district composed of the counties of Pendleton, Hardy, Hampshire and Morgan, shall be in favor of the adoption of this constitution, the said four counties shall be included in and form a part of the state of West Virginia; and if the same shall be so included, and a majority of the votes cast at the election or elections held, as provided in the schedule hereof, in the district composed of the counties of Pendleton, Hardy, Hampshire and Morgan, shall be in favor of the adoption of this constitution, the said four counties shall be included in and form a part of the state of West Virginia; and if the same shall be so included, and a majority of the votes cast at the said election or elections, in the district composed of the counties of Berkeley, Jefferson and Frederick, shall be in favor of the adoption of this constitution then the three last mentioned counties shall also be included in and form part of the state of West Virginia.

The schedule of the constitution fixed, as the day for the vote on the constitution, the first Thursday of April, 1863. It is a well known fact that there was no election held in either of the three last counties on that day. But the schedule further provided, "that if from any cause the said election be not held in and for any of the said counties, at the time named, the same may be held at such subsequent time or times, as the commissioners hereby appointed may approve, if so done as not to delay the submission of the result to the legislature for its action." And it is equally well known that no such vote was taken before the meeting of the succeeding legislature.

But the act of the restored government of the 31st January, 1863, giving the consent of the state of Virginia to the county of Berkeley being admitted into and becoming part of the state of West Virginia, contained a clause, that "if the governor of this state shall be of opinion that the said polls cannot be safely and properly opened and held in the said county of Berkeley, on the fourth Thursday of May next, he may by proclamation postpone the same, and appoint in the same proclamation, or by one to be thereafter issued, another day for opening and holding the same." — Acts 1862-3, c 54, p. 42. And by the act of the 4th of February, 1863, "giving consent to the admission of certain counties in the new state of West Virginia, of Jefferson was one, it is provided, that 'in the event the state of the country will not permit, or from any cause said election for annexation cannot be fairly held on the day aforesaid, it shall be the duty of the governor of this commonwealth, as soon as such election can be safely and fairly held, and a full and free expression of the opinion of the people had thereon, to issue his proclamation ordering such election for the purpose aforesaid, and certify the result as aforesaid.' "

The fact is equally well known and admitted, that at the time fixed for opening the polls, the state of the country, in the counties of Berkeley and Jefferson, rendered it impracticable to open the polls, and the voters had no notice of the intention to hold an election, and they did not and could not attend by reason of the Civil War, and there was no opportunity for any expression of the opinion of the people; and it well known, that at that time a very great majority of the voters of said counties were opposed to such annexation. (Argument of B. R. Curtis, Esq., for Virginia, in suit of Virginia vs. West Virginia.)

In the county of Berkeley there were nine election precincts, and in the county of Jefferson there were eight precincts, and as far as has been ascertained, votes were polled at only two of these precincts, to wit: at Shepherdstown and Harper's Ferry, in the county of Jefferson; both precincts on the remote Potomac line of the county, and the election was held under the superintendence of commissioners of election, disqualifed under the laws of Virginia from holding said offices. No commissioners were appointed for the other precincts, or if appointed were not notified of their appointment, and polls were not opened. And at these two precincts less than one hundred votes were polled, in an aggregate legitimate vote of Jefferson County of upwards of 1,700 votes and of the small number polled, many were fraudulent and illegal votes, and the election was held at a time when the county was intersected by the strictest and most vigilant military lines, that often confined the citizens for weeks to their own premises, from which, under no pretext, however urgent, they were permitted to pass. The law required a fair vote to be taken in the district, composed of the counties of Fredrick, Berkeley and Jefferson, to ascertain whether a majority of the people of this district would vote for its annexation to the new state. Each county has a right to participate in the vote, and each of them is populous and enlightened, and the vote they might poll very heavy. It has never been pretended that any vote was held in the county of Frederick.

Notwithstanding all these facts, Francis H. Pierpont, the so-called governor of the Commonwealth of Virginia, certified under the seal of the state of the governor of West Virginia, that a very large majority of the votes cast at the election was in favor of the counties of Berkeley and Jefferson becoming annexed to the new state.

And thereupon the legislature of West Virginia, on the 5th of August, 1863, passed an act admitting the county of Berkeley into, and making the same part of West Virginia. In this act it is recited, that "whereas Francis H. Pierpont, governor of the Commonwealth of Virginia, did, on the 22d day of July, in the present year, after reciting that polls were opened in the said county on Thursday, the 28th day of May, 1863, certify under his hand, and the lesser seal of the said Commonwealth, that, from the returns on file in the executive department, a very large majority of the votes cast at the said election were in favor of the said county of Berkeley becoming part of the state of West Virginia: therefore, the said county is admitted, &c. And in the same manner, the same legislature, on the 2d of November, 1863, passed another act, admitting the county of Jefferson into, and making the same part of, the state of West Virginia, reciting, in the same way, that Governor Pierpont had, on the 14th of September, 1863, certified that the said county of Jefferson, on Thursday, the 28th day of May, 1863, on the question of annexing the said county to the new state, had, by a very large majority of the votes cast, voted in favor of the annexation.

It is to be noted here that when Congress admitted the new state of West Virginia into the Union prescribed its boundaries, the counties of Berkeley and Jefferson were not included in the enumeration of the counties composing of the state, and the assent of Congress is required as much to the annexation of territory to any state as to its formation into a state.

This was the status of West Virginia when it was admitted into the Union.

The Government of
Virginia At Alexandria

As soon as it was ascertained that the new state would be organized under the president's proclamation, and before the inauguration of Governor Boreman, the new governor of that state, whose inauguration took place on the 20th of June, 1863, Governor Pierpont, the governor of dismembered Virginia, removed the seat of governor from the city of Wheeling to the city of Alexandria, and the legislature which had previously assembled in Wheeling, met on the first Monday, 7th December, 1863, in the city of Alexandria.

Among the first acts passed by this legislature, was one to provide for the election of delegates by the people to a convention, to assemble in the city of Alexandria on the 13th of February, 1864, to alter and amend the constitution of the state of Virginia. — Acts (Alexandria) 1863-4, c. 2, p. 4.

The delegates were to be elected from all the counties and districts of the Commonwealth, on the 21st January, 1864, and to be equal in number to the representation in both branches of the General Assembly from said counties and districts. But the people, with the exception of a few counties, took no part in the election, and there were no polls opened in nine-tenths of the counties then composing the state, after West Virginia had been severed from it.

The convention, nevertheless, consisting of delegates from an inappreciable number of counties, assembled on the day appointed, and on the 14th of March, 1864, adopted the bill of rights, without alteration, as it was adopted by the convention of 1850-51. And on the 7th of the following April, the constitution was adopted, which is to be found in Acts 1864-5, (Alexandria,) from p. 1 to 26, and Acts 1866-7, p. 757 to 771. This constitution, which was to be the organic law for the state, was neither voted upon by the representatives of the people, nor submitted to the people afterwards for ratification or adoption.

Nevertheless, there is one fact that ought to be noted:

The convention did not recognize the acts of the governor in transferring the counties of Berkeley and Jefferson as valid, and the constitution, framed by it, provides that in the apportionment of representation in the house of delegates, these counties shall each elect two delegates; and in the formation of senatorial districts, they constituted the 34th district, and were attached to the 13th judicial circuit.

Annexation of Berkeley and Jefferson.

Subsequently, after the Alexandria government had been removed to Richmond, and began to receive some life from the invigorating influence of the old counties, which had been restored by the power of the United States government to their position as a component part of the state, the legislature began to remonstrate, for the first time, against the enormity of the dismemberment of the state, and particularly against the annexation of these two counties to the state of West Virginia against the wishes of the people, both of these counties and the residue of the state. This legislature — the first that assembled after the close of the war — was recognized by Congress as the lawful government of the state.

A joint resolution was adopted on the 28th of February, 1866 (Acts 1865-6, No. 7, p. 433), declaring "that the people of Virginia deeply lament the dismemberment of the old state, and are sincerely desirous to establish and perpetuate the re-union of the states of Virginia and West Virginia; and that they do confidently appeal to their brethren of West Virginia to concur with them in the adoption of suitable measures of co-operation in the restoration of the ancient Commonwealth of Virginia, and all her people, and up to her former boundaries."

How different the feeling of the loyal representatives of Virginia, in "deeply lamenting the dismemberment of the state," from that other feeling of the sham legislature, who express "the greatest anxiety and interest in its dismemberment."

The resolutions also provided for the appointment commissioners "to treat with the authorities of West Virginia, on the subject of the restoration of the state to its ancient jurisdiction and boundaries,'' for a proper adjustment of the public debt between the two states, and for a fair division of the public property.

And to carry out these objects, the General Assembly, on the 2d of March, 1866, by joint vote, appointed William Martin, John Janney and Alexander H. Stuart, to be the commissioners.

The commissioners were not able to accomplish anything, it was too late to expect it; feelings had been engendered by the conflict, and interests created, which could not be reconciled. The state of West Virginia, as we have shown, had been declared by Congress to be one of the United States of America, and been admitted into the Union on an equal footing with the original states, in all respects whatever and a restoration of the people of that state, under such circumstances, was simply impossible.

But Congress had not yet given its assent to the annexation of the counties of Berkeley and Jefferson to West Virginia, and an effort was made on the part of the legislature to prevent this further wrong from being perpetrated.

On the 6th of December, 1865, Acts 1865-6, c. 84, p. 194, the General Assembly has passed an act, reciting, ''that the conditions prescribed in the several acts of the General Assembly of the restored government of Virginia, intended to give consent to the transfer from this state to the state of West Virginia, of jursidiction over the counties of Jefferson and Berkeley, have not been complied with; and the consent of Congress, as required by the constitution of the United States, not having been obtained to such transfer, the General Assembly declared that the proceedings therebefore had on this subject are simply inchoate, and said consent may properly be withdrawn; and the General Assembly regarding the contemplated disintgegration of the Commonwealth, even if within its constitutional competency, as liable to objections of the gravest character,'' therefore enacted ''that all consent, in any manner heretofore given, or intended to be given, by the General Assembly of Virginia, to the transfer from its jurisdiction to the jurisdiction of the state of West Virginia, of any of the counties mentioned in any of its acts, shall be and the same is hereby withdrawn; and all acts, ordinances and resolutions, heretofore passed, purporting to give such consent, are hereby repealed.''

The legislature, moreover, during the same session, on the 1st of March, 1866 (Acts 1865-6, c. 85, p. 195,) passed another act, in these words:

''Whereas, notwithstanding the passage, during the present session of the General Assembly, of an act repealing all laws giving consent to the annexation of the counties of Jefferson and Berekely to the state of West Virginia, it appears that said state is making an effort to obtain the consent of the Congress of the United States to said annexation; and whereas, in the judgment of the General Assembly, such action on the part of Congress would be wholly nugatory now that the consent of Virginia has been withdrawn; and whereas the state of West Virginia is exercising jurisdiction over said counties; and whereas it may be the Congress of the United States will, after the adjournment of this legislature, give its consent to their annexation to West virginia, thereby making it necessary, before the legislature shall again convene, for this Commonwealth to have its rights to jurisdiction over said counties determined by the proper legal tribunals: therefore, it shall be the duty of the attorney-general of this Commonwealth, under the direction of the governor, in case the consent of Congress should be given to such annexation, at once to institute such legal proceedings as may be proper, either at law or in equity, and to adopt and carry out all other measures as may be necessary on the part of this Commonwealth to secure, as soon as possible, a decision, by the appropriate legal tribunals, of any and all questions arising out of the attempt to annex said counties of Jefferson and Berkeley, or either of them, to the state of West Virginia, or of said state to exercise jurisdiction over them. And the governor is hereby authorized and directed to employ, and associate with the attorney-general, in conducting said proceedings, Reverdy Johnson, and such other competent counsel as he may be agreed upon, together with all other necessary expenses attending the same, out of the appropriating, thereinafter made. And the governor is hereby authorized and requested, at the earliest day practicable after the refusal of Congress to give such consent, or after a decision by the appropriate legal tribunal, in favor of this Commonwealth, to proceed to have said counties fully organized in respect to all their functions, both judicial and political.''

These acts not only accomplished nothing, but seemed to stimulate Congress to prompt and efficient action; for, notwithstanding the consent of the state to the annexation of these counties had been withdrawn and annulled, and in the teeth of these appeals to the people of West Virginia to co-operate in the restoration of the Commonwealth to her former boundaries, Congress, in a few days after the action of the legislature, took up the subject, and, though Virginia was not represented in either branch of the national legislature, West Virginia was, adopted, on the 10th of March, 1866, the following joint resolution:

"Resolved, That Congress hereby recognizes the transfer of the counties of Berkeley and Jefferson, from the state of Virginia to West Virginia, and consents thereto.''

Under the resolutions of the General Assembly of the 1st of March, 1866, the legal proceedings contemplated were instituted by the attorney-general of the state in the supreme court of the United States in 1867, the case being the Commonwealth of Virginia vs. the State of West Virginia, the Commonwealth claiming jurisdiction over the counties of Berkeley and Jefferson. Upon full argument, the court was equally divided, and of course the claim of Virginia was not sustained. In 1871, the supreme court was reconstructed, and two new judgies were appointed. The case came up again for reconsideration. To the bill of the Commonwealth, setting forth the facts, a demurrer was filed by the counsel of West Virginia, and the main argument was upon the demurrer. The state was represented by Attorney-General James C. Taylor, B. R. Curtis, and Andrew Hunter, and the state of West Virginia by Messrs. B. Stanton, Charles J. Faulkner, and Reverdy Johnson. The argument was able and full, but the decision of the court sustained the demurrer and dismissed the bill. See Wallace's Supreme Court Reports, case of Virginia vs. West Virginia, p. 51.

Thus the counties of Berkeley and Jefferson were annexed to West Virginia, and are now incorporated within her boundaries and under her jurisdiction. And this was the conclusion of events, by which was consummated, under the flimsy gauze of law and legal proceedings, a shameless violation of fundamental laws, state and Federal — a contempt of right, equity, decency and honor, against the dictates of justice, propriety and truth — and a noble old Commonwealth, that deserved high consideration for her uniform generosity and unequalled patriotism in the better days of the republic, was, by such means, unblushingly despoiled.

Continuation of the Alexandria Government.

In order to preserve a connected view of the annexation of these counties of West Virginia we have been compelled to anticipate a little, the chronological sequence of events which resulted in the close of the Civil War, and the resumption of the seat of government at Richmond, by the Restored Government which had been located at Alexandria.

After the adoption of the constitution by the convention at Alexandria, as before stated, that body, on the 4th of April, 1864, adopted an ordinance, "providing for the establishment of the Restored Government" in which it is provided that it shall be the duty of the governor to issue his proclamation, declaring all of the offices therein vacant, civil and military, accompanied by writs of election to supply the vacancy, and all officers elected under this ordinance as required to enter upon their duties immediately upon election and qualification.

On the 3rd of March, 1865, a joint resolution was adopted by the legislature authorizing the governor to change the seat of government of the state of Virginia from the city of Alexandria to the city of Norfolk, or any other convenient place in the state, whenever in his opinion the interest of the state would be promoted by such removal: Provided, however, That nothing in his resolution shall be so construed as to authorize the location or continuation of the seat of government at any other place than the city of Richmond, when the said city of Richmond can be safely occupied as the seat of government of the state.

Several amendments to the constitution adopted by the Alexandria convention were proposed and approved. — See Acts, (Alexandria,) Extra Session, c. 1, p. 3; Acts 1865-6, c. 86, p. 197; and an ordinance to alter and amend the third article of the constitution, passed 24th February, 1866. Space will not allow us to dilate upon these acts.

The state of Virginia had transferred all her resources to the Confederate government, and acted throughout the whole war as the main-spring for its machinery and operations. Her fields and cities had been the theatre of a terrible conflict — were devastated and laid waste; her people were exhausted; her finances were

161

almost hopelessly crippled; and she was powerless for further resistance. The Confederate States had been carrying on the war with a force and energy rarely equalled by an infant nation, and that, too, with inadequate means and inadequate armies, and without a navy to keep open its ports. They had met and encountered, with varying results sometimes of triumphant victory, and then of gloomy defeat — all the power and immense military and financial resources of the government of the United States, and had sustained themselves vigorously for four years. But at length the grand army of the Confederacy, which had fought so nobly in so many desperate conflicts in the state, and had made such an invasion into the heart of the northern states, and around the very capital of the Union, and had so long and so gallantly defended Richmond, the capital of the state and of the confederacy, with its great leader, Robert E. Lee, without hope of reinforcement, and with augmenting forces to contend against, sufficient to overpower and crush it, capitulated on the 9th day of April, 1865. From that moment it was manifest to the merest tyro that the war had been brought to a close beyond the power of resuscitation.

Government At Richmond Prior To Secession Ordinance

While these different governments, representing Virginia, were severally acting the parts herein detailed, the government, as it existed prior to the secession ordinance, continued at Richmond, with the various departments, executive, legislative and judicial in full operation. Its acts have been declared to be illegal and rebellious, but from the stand-point from which it acted, no government ever evinced a purer patriotism or displayed greater loyalty to Virginia, and from its energy and zeal deserved greater success. We cannot pause to recount those acts, they must be sought in the laws which were published, and in the executive and legislative journals, and reports of the decision of the supreme court, and in the extended and truthful narrations of the historian. At the expiration of Governor Letcher's terms, by a vote of the people of the counties within the state, exclusive of West Virginia, Governor William Smith, who had once before been the honored governor of the state was again chosen govenor, and continued as the governor *de facto*, and exercising all the functions of the executive until the close of the war. All the other departments within their respective spheres were recognized by the people as the officers of their choice, and full obedience was unhesitatingly given to their acts and orders, without murmur or dissent.

After the evacuation of Richmond, Governor Smith designed carrying on the government of the state at Lynchburg or Danville, and therefore issued an executive order directing the several heads of departments to remove the archives of the government, containing at least the official acts of these departments during the war, to the city of Lynchburg. This order, on the night of 3rd of April, 1865, they proceeded to execute, and many of the records of the executive department, and of the auditor and treasurer, were removed by the route of the James river and Kanawha canal, as far as the county of Buckingham, but finding it impossible to proceed, in consequence of the destruction of the canal and the impracticability of obtaining transportation, they were conveyed and deposited in the courthouse of that county; and when Gen. Lee capitulated in Appomattox county, on the ninth of the month, these records were all taken possession of by the Federal army, and were transmitted to the war department at Washington, and have been to this day refused to be delivered to the state of Virginia.

No people ever sustained greater losses by the termination of a war than the people of Virginia. At one blow their entire slave population was emancipated, their vlaue utterly lost, and their accustomed labor instantly stopped — their circulating medium, state and Confederate, was rendered worthless — their bank stocks, deposits, savings institutions, state and municipal stocks, reduced to a minimum value — no Federal money in circulation — houses, barns, fences, mills, given to conflagrations — forests, to a great extent, cut down and burned — lands impoverished, and having no money value — and they themselves were entirely powerless to purchase, and, for the want of buyers, equally powerless to sell.

Under such circumstances, from the day of the surrender of Gen. Lee, there ws no organized opposition to the government of the United States in the state of Virginia. The troops called into the field by the state and the Confederacy, returned to their homes, and the people of Virginia, as far as they were permitted, and attended to their usual occupations, with saddened hearts and gloomy thoughts, bearing their utter destitution with a bravery only equalled by their gallantry in the field.

Alexandria Governor Transferred To Richmond

On the 9th of May, 1865, President Andrew Johnson issued the executive orders of which the following are extracts:

"Ordered, First, that all acts and proceedings of the political, military and civil organizations which have been in a state of insurrection and rebellion within the state of Virginia, against the authority and laws of the United States, and of which Jefferson Davis, John Letcher and William Smith were late the respective chiefs, are declared null and void. All persons who shall exercise, claim, pretend or attempt to exercise any political, military or civil power, authority, jurisdiction or right, by, through our under Jefferson Davis, late of the city of Richmond, and his confederates, or under John Letcher or William Smith, or civil commission or authority issued by them or either of them, since the 17th day of April, 1861, shall be deemed and taken as in rebellion against the United States, and shall be dealt with accordingly."

"That to carry into effect the guarantee by the Federal constitution of a republican form of government and afford the advantage and security of domestic laws, as well as to complete the reestablishment of the authority and laws of the United States, and the full and complete restoration of peace within the limits aforesaid, Francis H. Pierpoint, governor of the state of Virginia, will be aided by the Federal government, so far as may be necessary, in the lawful measures which he may take for the extension and administration of the state government through the geographic limits of said state." — U.S. Stat. at Large, vol. 13, p. 775.

The time had, therefore arrived, for the government at Alexandria to proclaim itself the recognized government of the state, and accordingly Governor Pierpoint, with his executive officers, removed the seat of government from Alexandria to Richmond, and took possession of the governor's house and the capitol, which such of the state archives as had been preserved.

We find the first entry made in the executive journal, after his removal, dated the 23rd of May, 1865, is as follows:

"His excellency the governor, in pursuance of the authority in him vested by the laws of the Commonwealth, and upon due informaton of the suppression of insurrection and domestic violence within the limits of this Commonwealth, ordered that the seat of government be restored to and re-established at the city of Richmond, from and after this date, and issued his proclamation accordingly.

FRANCIS H. PIERPOINT"

Thus the restored government of the Commonwealth of Virginia, was recognized by the United States, and backed by its armies and power, the executive elected by an insignificant portion of its population, assumed the authority of the state.

But among the worst features of these eventful times in its subsequent effects, was the establishment by the Federal government of a freedman's bureau, which undertook to administer broadcast charity to the newly emancipated slaves, inducing them to abandon labor necessary for their own future support, and for the support of the whole agricultural community, and to look to a precarious charity (which could not continue) for daily sustenance.

But the agents employed by this bureau seemed to take a savage delight in instilling into the willing minds of their wards and pupils, a hatred of their former best interests. Moreover, by disfranchising a majority of the whites, and enfranchising all the colored mass, and giving them the power to vote for any officer and to hold any and all the offices, it was intended to humiliate and degrade the former masters, and give the power of the government to their ignorant and experienced laborers. Luckily, this last purpose they failed to accomplish, but to this day the effects of their thorough organization is seen and felt; and it is only sufficient for the white man to originate any measure, however advantageous it may be to both races, to ensure for it an uncompromising opposition from the colored population, and to obtain their undivided antagonistic vote; and this is variably done, no matter who are candidates for office, however exalted in virtue, wisdom and experience: and done, too, against those whom they are dependent, and from whom they receive, with few exceptions, nothing but unvaried kindness.

It was supposed that as the war had terminated and the restored government of Virginia had been recognized by the United

States as the legitimate and constitutional government of the state — and it had been proclaimed that the United States would sustain that government — that Virginia would once more resume her old position and standing in the Union. And after the president's proclamation of the 2nd of April, 1866, there could not be any ground for apprehension of a different course. That proclamation declared that "Whereas standing armies, military occupation, martial law, military tribunals, and the suspension of the writ of *habeas corpus*, are, in time of peace, dangerous to public liberty, incompatible with the individual rights of the citizen, contrary to the genius and spirit of our free institutions and exhaustive of the national resources, and ought not therefore to be sanctioned or allowed, except in cases of actual necessity, for repelling invasion or suppressing insurrection or rebellion, &c.: therefore I, Andrew Johnson, president, &c., do hereby proclaim and declare that the insurrection which heretofore existed in the states of Georgia, South Carolina, Virginia, North Carolina, Tennessee, Alabama, Louisiana, Arkansas, Mississippi and Florida, is at an end, and is henceforth to be so regarded."

Virginia Military District, No. 1

Notwithstanding all this, an act was passed by congress on the 2nd of March, 1867, to provide for the more efficient government of the rebel states. — U.S. Stat., vol. 14, p. 428.

It appears, however, that during the administration of Governor Pierpoint, as shown by the records of the war department at Washington, upon information furnished by the adjutant-general of the United States, the following commanding generals had established headquarters at Richmond, with a supervisory power over the state government, to keep not only the state in subjection but to act as a watch over Governor Pierpoint — the governor who President Johnson, in his proclamation of the 9th of May, 1865,[12] declared "will be aided by the Federal government, so far as may be necessary in the lawful measures which he may take for the extension and administration of the state government throughout the geographical limits of the state" to-wit:

Major-General Godfrey Weitzel, United States volunteers, from April 3rd, 1865, to April 13th, 1865.

Major-General E. O. C. Ord, United States volunteers, commanding department of Virginia, April 13th to June 14th, 1865.

Major-General II. W. Halleck, U.S. army, commanding military division of the James, April 22nd, 1865, to June 27th, 1865.

Major-General Alfred II Terry, United States volunteers, June 14th, 1865, to August 16th, 1866.

Major-General John M. Schofield, United States volunteers, August 16, 1866, to June 2nd, 1868, except during the month from September 26th, to October 26th, 1866, when Major-General Henry S. Burton, United States army, held command during his temporary absence.

Major-General George Stoneman, from June 2nd, 1868, to April 2nd, 1860.

Brevet Major-General Alexander S. Webb, from April 2nd, 1869, to April 20th, 1869.

Major-General Edward R. S. Canby, from April 29th, 1869, to January 28th, 1870.

Therefore Governor Pierpoint was subject to the orders of military generals from the evacuation of Richmond. on the 3rd of April, 1865, to the expiration of his official connectin with the government. And then, by appointment of General Schofield, on the 6th of April, 1868, Henry H. Wells became the nominal governor of the state. The executive journal of the next day is signed, "H. H. Wells, Governor."

Hearne note: The remainder of Mr. Munford's synopsis is omitted, inasmuch as Governor Pierpont's tenure having been terminated by the military district commander, and Mr. Wells thereupon was appointed.

-----

[1]By joint resolutions of the General Assembly, of the 24th of March, 1873, the governor was requested "to make application to the state department of the Federal government for the return of the original draft of the ordinance of secession adopted by the Virginia convention in April, 1861, now on file in that department, in order that it may be preserved in the Virginia state library as part of the official history of the state." — Acts 1872-3, c. 218, p. 196.

[2]*Hearne note.* This convention acted on the assumption that their purported "ordinance of secession" was in fact *de jure* and that the convention of delegates of the people had the lawful power to make and provide for the enforcement of its ordinances without regard to any contrary provisions of the then existing constitution of the Commonwealth. The foregoing actions were taken before the convention released state officers from their oath of loyalty to the United States.

[3]*Hearne note.* The convention promptly expelled all delegates who had expressed the will of their constituents by voting against secession, many of whom felt their lives endangered.

[4]*Hearne note.* In a few days the convention moved to the Federal Custom House to hold its meetings.

[5]*Hearne note.* See my answer to this in another chapter of this appendix entitled "The Molding of Mythology . . . ", Section captioned "Many delegates held irregular credentials . . . "

[6]*Hearne note.* It was the contention of those who voted for the Declaration that the "majority" should be determined on the basis of those who supported the Union, and it was their view that the Wheeling Convention did in fact represent Union supporters in the eastern counties as well as those from the west; and there were delegates from Alexandria and Fairfax represented in Wheeling. Had the Confederacy won The War, the result would have been otherwise . . . Observe that this declaration was based on Section 3 of the Virginia Bill of Rights, and provided the basis for the reorganization of the state government as provided for an ordinance of the convention a few days later. That reorganization

served to keep the Commonwealth in the Union without change, except that the state would simply be under new management and continue under the Constitution and laws of the United States. There was no reference to the establishment of a new state.

[7]*Hearne musing.* The Virginia Bill of Rights, adopted in June of 1776, was the basis for the "Declaration of Independence" of the Fourth of July of that year. Virginia was one of the first of the colonies to "secede" from (revolt against) the Crown, and the Bill of Rights gave power to the people. Had the Crown won the War for Independence, it may well have resulted in hanging of all signers of the Declaration, as mused by Dr. Benjamin Franklin. Which raises this question: Is it wise or prudent for a state (i.e., the true sense of the word "state," which includes absolute sovereignty) to provide a means for its own destruction? The Constitution of the United States has no such provision — not even in the first ten amendments — which are commonly called the "Bill of Rights," and President Lincoln offered his opinion that no state should provide for its own destruction.

[8]*Hearne note.* The ordinances of the Wheeling convention which first assembled in June, 1861, were upheld as valid by the United States Supreme Court in Virginia v. West Virginia, 78 U.S. (11 Wall. 39) an abstract of which is set forth in this appendix preceding.

[9]*Hearne note.* "Bayonet rule" prevailed in counties held by the Confederacy as well as in counties held by Union forces.

[10]*Hearne note.* I do not condone nor do I understand the reasons for these acts of the legislature of the Restored government; and I suppose they were knee-jerk reactions caused by the passions stirred up by the heat of The War, just as the *de facto* Richmond legislature had termed Mr. Pierpont and other western Virginians as "evil disposed" citizens. (See note 6 of the Saga).

[11]*Hearne note.* For the past two decades the sentiment in Western Virginia had been for separate statehood, and this feeling had accelerated until it came to a boiling point which urged this opportunity to be a separate state. Mr. Munford, as well as all delegates who had voted for secession on 17 April of 1861 must have known that if the Confederacy lost The War that separation would be inevitable. It was a risk that the secessionists must have been prepared for.

[12]*Hearne note.* Mr. Munford credited Governor Pierpont with having the best interests of the people of Virginia at heart, contrary to the policies of the Radical Republicans who then controlled congress. But to err is human, and Mr. Munford failed to distinguish a "proclamation" as from an executive order, signed by the president on May 9, 1865.

Chapter XX — Appendix
Sketch of the Formation of West Virginia From the Territory of Virginia
By John Marshall Hagans

(Being a prefix of Volume I of the Reports of Cases in the Supreme Court of Appeals of West Virginia, published in 1866)

Biographical sketch of Mr. Hagans, from West Virginia Heritage Encyclopedia, Main Volume 10, pages 2086-87. Born 1838 in Brandonville, Preston County, (W.) Va. Attended the old Monongalia Academy, then began the study of law in the office of Waitman T. Willey. About a year later he entered Harvard University before being admitted to the Bar in 1859. Elected prosecuting attorney of Monongalia County in 1862 and twice thereafter; and appointed Reporter for the Supreme Court of Appeals in 1864 and served until 1873. Thereafter Mayor of Morgantown; Republican presidential elector, and elected to Congress in 1873; and to the House of Delegates in 1879 and in 1887. In 1888 elected judge of the circuit court for Monongalia, Harrison and Marion Counties. His wife, Sara B., was the daughter of Senator Waitman T. Willey, who had attended the Richmond Convention which had adopted The Ordinance of Secession of April 17, 1861. They had three children. Mr. Hagans graduated from this life in the year 1900.

Mr. Hagans' Sketch As Here In Presented Begins With The Inauguration Of President Lincoln

The inaugural address, whilst of a tone and character that did not threaten or would, still announced the doctrine, that nothing had yet taken place, according to the constitution, which was sufficient to tie the hands of the Executive or deter him from retaking the forts and arsenals and repossessing the property belonging to the government in the States where secession had been instituted.

This address was received and interpreted by the people of Virginia and the convention, according to the prevailing opinions of parties on the questions then being agitated. The extremists argued and asseted that it was equivalent to a declaration of hostilities, and by the superior vehemence which characterizes revolutionists, together with a resort to the sophistry of public commotions, they drew to them many who were filled with alarm at the aspect of affairs and found a temporary relief in the shadow of violent spirits.

The pressure of events brought from the committee on Federal relations, a partial majority report on the 9th of March. It claimed that Virginia being more interested in the continuance of peace than other Southern States, and having instituted measures to obtain guarantees of a proper self-respect, impelled her to demand of all parties a suspension of all action tending to produce collision forces, whilst she was making efforts for an amicable adjustment. The sovereignty was declared to rest in the States; slavery was held to be a vital element of southern socialism, and any interference either by States or the Federal government was offensive and dangerous; the formation of sectional or georgraphical parties was contrary to the principles on which the government rested and tended to its overthrown. The fourth resolution declared that the territories of the Union were equally the property of all the States, and that if the institutions of States conflicted therein, a fair partition should be made and each assigned to its respective limits. The fifth resolution was vital in its significance. It alleged that the sites of forts and arsenals belonging to the Federal government within the limits of the States of the Union, had been acquired by it, and jurisdiction ceded by the States, as trusts for the common purposes during the continuance of the Union. Whilst a State remained in the Union, the legitimate use of such forts and arsenals was to protect the country from foreign fores and to suppress domestic insurrection; but to use them to intimidate a State or constrain its free action was a perversion, and that they were not intended to be used against the States in whose limits they were found, in the event of the civil war. Whilst irritating questions were pending between the States, to accumulate an unusual amount of troops and munitions of war, within any of the States, and was unwise, impolitic, and offensive.

The sixth and seventh called for delay and suggested some remedies that would forward the peaceable adjustment of pending complications.

The eighth conceded the right of the people of the States for just causes to withdraw from their association under the federative head and to erect new governments; and that the people of Virginia would never consent that the Federal power should be exercised for the purpose of subjecting the people of such States to the Federal authority.

The ninth recognized the exercise of the right by the gulf States and its disclaimer by the Federal authorities; and the tenth asserted that the people of Virginia desired to confer upon the national government the powers necessary to enable it to deal with all questions arising from the action of these States, in a peaceable manner, and to recognize their independence and make such treaties with

169

them as might be proper.

The eleventh proposed that certain amendments should be submitted to the people of all the States for their ratification, and if a satisfactory response was not elicited, then Virginia would resume her powers granted under the constitution of the United States and throw herself upon her reserved rights; that a resonable time would be allowed for this course, but during the interim nothing but pacific measures should be adopted, and no attempt should be made to reinforce the forts or to recapture any within the limits of a seceded State; nor should there be any payment of impost upon commerce to the Federal authorities, nor any measures be resorted to, justly calculated to provoke hostile collision.

The thirteenth declared that any action of the Federal government tending to produce collision of forces, pending negotiations, would be aggressive and injurious to the interests and offensive to the honor of the Commonwealth; and that any such action by the Confederate States would be regarded as hurtful and unfriendly, and as leaving Virginia free to determine her future policy.

The fourteenth and last suggested a conference of the border slave States, and requested the proper authorities to appoint commissioners to meet at Frankfort, Kentucky, on the last Monday in May ensuing.

The report of the committee was a signal for a general onset between the parties. One of the most animated and spirited debates which modern times has witnessed, immediately began. It was characterized by a warmth and ability which the great interests of the occasion demanded and the high order of intellect engaged brought forth. The vehemence and rancor of the secession cabal, was met by the sturdy determination and lofty eloquence of the unionists, in defense of all that was honorable and revered in the history of their country. Every influence that could be exerted by the factionists, was brought to bear in the argument. State pride, that fatal deity of the Virginian, was urged with all the eloquence of the most accomplished orators. On the part of the unionists, the traditions and the glory of the past, and the magnitude of a mighty future, were portrayed with a zeal and faithfulness which the proudest intellects of any age never excelled. The most gifted minds of the times poured the rich treasures of their maturity into the agitated flood of patriotic duty. After elaborate discussion a vote was had on the 4th of April. Both parties desired it, for the purpose of ascertaining the progress of accretion and defection. The resolutions were voted on separately, and were amended or stricken out, on a basis generally favorable to the Union cause. But the great test vote was on the sixth, for which a substitute was offered providing that an ordinance of secession from the Federal Union should be submitted to the people of Virginia at the annual election in May following. This propsition with a most signal rebuke, by a vote of forty-five for and eighty-nine against it. The spirits of the Union members rose triumphant with the result, which evinced such a decided majority against direct secession, however much diversity of sentiment might exist on questions of adjustment involving neutrality or non-coercion. Prior to this time, a few days, a scheme had been concocted by the secessionists, designed to accomplish in the most revolutionary manner, what they feared could not be done through the convention in its present temper. A circular was issued signed by six members of the convention, two members of the House of Delegates and the clerk, and extensively distributed throughout the State. It called upon the parties to whom it was addressed, to present themselves in Richmond on the 16th day of April, to consult with the friends of the southern rights as to the course Virginia should pursue in the present emergency; and to send from each county a full delegation of true reliable men. The object of this, viewed in the light of subsequent events, as to the time of meeting and other circumstances, can not be misunderstood. It was one link in the chain of combinations which had brought about such a disordered state of public affairs, and was designed to effect secession with or without even the semblance of the forms of law, which many would have attached to such action by the regular convention.

After the vote on the report of the committee, a new system of tactics was inaugurated. No longer was it a discussion in which giant minds wrestled for the supremacy. The voice of reason and the impassioned appeals to the conscience, were soon interrupted by the low mutterings of those disordant passions ever heard when physical force, having been overcome by the sublime powers of moral causes, raises its ghastly tones to animate the fury of its might. Terms of obloquy and reproach were applied to those who still resisted the secession mania; they were scornfully denominated "submissionsts." The galleries and lobbies of the hall were filled with a wild, excited throng, hounded on by negro traders of Virginia and bands of negro hunters from South Carolina. They frowned and hissed when patriots below were pouring out upon the altar of their country the most magnificent tributes from their noble hearts and enlightened consciences. When they left the hall it was to be insultingly met at the door and on the streets, by epithets of ignomiary and reproach. Another part of the infernal devices, was, the employment of bands of music, which traversed the streets collecting a motely crowd of lewed fellows and desperate characters, who tore down from the marked places and public squares the flag of the republic, and hoisted in its stead the palmetto and Confederate emblems. These same characters roamed the streets at night from place to place, and called out the public men from the South, sojourning the city, and applauded the most extreme sentiments with the wildest echoes. It was part of their duty also, to intimidate the Union members of the convention, especially those from the northwestern part of the State; and these on arising from their beds in the morning would discover in close proximity to their windows, ropes with suggestive nooses at their ends, pending from an adjoining tree or lamp post. But still they remained firm, proudly conscious of the integrity of their position, rejoicing in the knowledge that they were in the best of earthly causes — supporting a good government; they stood like the eternal hills, secure in their foundations. The policy adopted by the conspirators produced its effects on the people. That portion of society which takes but

171

little interest in public affairs in ordinary times, is the element from which factionists draw the largest agency in furthering their purposes. They are ready to distinguish between ordinary and extraordinary periods in the passing events; and when they discover violent measures controlling the hour, either from timidity or ignorance, they hasten to join themselves with those who are usurping the reins of power, or who occupy the largest share of public attention. This class also became attached to the party of the conspirators and thus swelled to the proportions of respectability, they deemed the hour for action had arrived. A prominent actor in the scenes in Virginia, was dispatched to Charleston, South Carolina, to announce that everything was in readiness in Virginia for the inauguration of the final act of the drama. He told the Carolinans that they must strike the blow, and "in an hour, by Shrewsbury clock, his State would be with them." This was a welcome announcement of the Southern leaders. For months the public mind had been frenzied by anticipations. Society had experience some of those upheavals which precede revolutions, and go far towards resolving it to its original elements. War had been the theme of conversation in all circles, and all who had dared lift a voice against the universal rage, had been silenced without mercy. Armies had been equipped and disciplined, and in the gush of their enthusiasm the young soldiers were crying to be led to the field. Public expectation was at the highest point and was clamoring for gratification. The chiefs however, were awaiting the auspicious moment, when the greatest moral force could be set in motion to and their schemes. This promise then, from the "Mother of States," which to the people, would give sanction to the enterprise and success if it were within the range of possibility, was the signal for the boasts and efforts of thirty years to culminate in the first direct assault of active warfare and the opening of hostilities. The fruits of this advice was the firing on the walls of Fort Sumpter, [sic] in Charleston harbor, the echoes from which were returned by the mountains of a continent, and only ceased when the national honor was baptized in the blood of a million of citizens.

During the progress of the bombardment of Fort Sumpter, [sic] the excitement in Richmond and in the convention was intense. Bonfires and illuminations blazed high in the streets and public squares; the national flag was torn from its place over the dome of the capitol and trampled under the feet of an infuriated mob. Stores and public places were closed and the populace sought the streets to give vent to their feelings. Strangers rushed to the city from all parts of the State and helped to sell the throngs. Many who had come in advance of the call before mentioned, to meet on the 16th of April, assembled together in a large hall and sat with closed doors. No ingress could be obtained to the sessions of this mysterious body. To add to the alarm of the times the convention went in secret session, and all further knowledge as to its operations, to the Union people at least, was at an end. But the scenes witnessed within the walls of that room, as detailed by members, have no parallel in the annals of ancient or modern times. The Union men began to appreciate their position only, when they saw those who had been their active co-laborers bowing before the storm, and yielding to the pressure of events. In vain did they appeal, exhort, entreat them to remain firm in the adhension to the national bond. On the morning of the 17th, Mr. Wise, the member from Princess Anne, rose in his seat and drawing a large Virginia horse pistol from his bosom, laid it before him, proceeded to harangue the body in the most violent and enunciatory manner; he concluded by taking his watch from his pocket and with glaring eyes and bated breath declared that events were now transpiring which caused a hush to come over his soul; at such an hour, he said, Harper's Ferry and its armory were in the possession of Virginia soldiers, at another period the Federal navy yard and property at Norfolk were seized by troops of the State. It was then that the Union members saw the object of the other assemblage which had sat with closed doors from its beginning, and whose concealed hand seizing the reins of government, had left them the form without the power to resist.

It was true, as he has spoken; the volunteer companies which had been organized after the raid by John Brown, in the Shenandoah Valley had, under orders from some mysterious power, assembled to the number of two thousand or more, and moved on Harper's Ferry with the design of seizing the armory and arsenals at that point belonging to the Federal government; the small garrison of marines after destroying the most valuable property, fired the buildings and fled in precipitate haste.

On the 17th of April, after much confusion and excited discussion, the convention came to a vote on an ordinance of secession from the Federal Union. The vote stood eighty-one for and fifty-one against it. It was entitled "an ordinance to repeal the ratification of the constitution of the United States of America, by the State of Virginia, and to resume all their rights and powers granted under such constitution." It set forth that, the people of Virginia in their ratification of the constitution, on the 25th of June, 1788, had declared that the powers granted under it were derived from the people of the United States, and might be resumed whenever it should be perverted to their injury and oppression, and the Federal government had perverted said powers, not only to the injury of the people of Virginia, but to the oppression of the Southern slaveholding States; therefore the people of Virginia, declared and ordained that the ordinance of ratification and all acts of the General Assembly, ratifying or adopting amendments to the constitution, were repealed and abrogated; and that the union between Virginia and the other States under it was thereby dissolved; that the State was in full possession, and exercised all the rights of sovereignty which belong and appertain to a free and independent State, and that the constitution was no longer binding on any citizen thereof; that the ordinance was to take effect when ratified by a majority of the votes cast at a poll to be taken on the fourth Thursday in May following, in pursuance of the schedule thereafter to be enacted. The schedule was passed on the 24th of the same month, and provided the manner of holding the polls, — "For Ratification," and "For Rejection," — giving citizens absent from their counties in the military service of the State the right to vote in their camps, providing for returns and a proclamation of the result by the Governor, and suspending and prohibiting the election for members of Congress of the United States at the coming annual election in May. On the 25th, the convention passed an ordinance ratifying a convention, which had been entered into by the military committee previously appointed by it, and certain commissioners of the Confederate government, for a temporary union with that government, pending the adoption by it of a permanent constitution. The agreements of the convention were that until Virginia should become a member of the Confederate government, the whole military force and military operations, offensive and defensive, of the Commonwealth, in the impending conflict with the United States, should be under the chief control and direction of the president of the Confederate States; and that upon the adoption of a permanent constitution by the Confederate States, and Virginia becoming a member of the same, she would "turn over" thereto "all public property, naval stores and munitions of war she had then in possession, acquired from the United States."

This ordinance was a clear assumption of power, and was a transfer of the people, without their assent or request, to a foreign and hostile government. On the 26th, an ordinance was adopted ratifying "the constitution of the provisional government of the Confederate States of America"; it was, however, not to be effective, unless the secession ordinance was ratified by the people. The convention passed, on the same day, an ordinance amending the State constitution, by striking from it the provisions which exempted slave property under twelve years of age from taxation and caused a valuation of three hundred dollars only to be placed on all over that age; this latter ordinance will be hereafter more extensively noticed. Afterwards, on the 1st of May, an ordinance was adopted, releasing all officers of the State from the obligations of their oath to support the constitution of the United States. The convention soon thereafter adjourned to meet again on the return of the vote by the people in the secession ordinance.

Immediately after the passage of the fatal ordinance, the convention began to diminish in numbers. The delegates from the northwestern part of the State, from the counties which now compose the State of West Virginia, finding themselves in a hopeless minority, quietly, and in some instances secretly, took their departure for their native mountains, where their humble yet more faithful constituents, received them with open arms and anxious minds.

A slight review of the geographical position of that part of the State which has since been erected into a separate organization, together with a sketch of the character, habits and history of the people, may be necessary to enable a just estimate to be formed of the causes that impelled them to take the bold and defiant attitude which resulted in that organization. By a glance at the map of what was then known as Northwestern Virginia, it will be seen that the country is wholly separated by lofty ranges of the Alleghanies which run entirely through its center, from the remainder of the

State. This range of mountains, is not a single upheaval rising from out of the bosom of a vast plain according to the popular conception of mountains, but is a succession of parallel ridges, varying from twelve to twenty-five hundred feet in height, separated from each other at their base, by small valleys from the fourth of a mile to two miles in width. From the most westerly range to the eastern slope bordering on the Shenandoah Valley, is about fifty miles. The western slope to the Ohio River presents a country of singularly wild and beautiful appearance. It is drained to the north by the Monongahela and Cheat Rivers, which rise far in the mountain fastnesses of the interior, and pursuing their course of crooked and tortuous channels over rocky beds and between shelving precipices, join their waters a few miles north of the Pennsylvania line. To the west the country is drained by the Little Kanawha River, emptying into the Ohio River at Parkersburg. The southwestern part of the State is watered by the Great Kanawha and its tributaries. The head waters of this latter river rise in the mountains of North Carolina, and running nearly north for a hundred miles, it bears gradually to the west an equal distance and pours its waters into the Ohio River about fifty miles above the Kentucky line. Its principal tributaries are the Elk and Gauley Rivers, which take their heads from the opposite watershed to the Monongahela and Cheat Rivers, and running parallel with each other in a southwesterly direction empty into it, the former at Charleston, and the latter about thirty miles above. These rivers have their various creeks and tributaries which divide the country into continuous broken and irregular sections of hills and undulations. The Monongahela, Cheat, Elk, Gauley and Little Kanawha, all take their rise in a tract of country not over twenty miles square, the two former forcing their way through the mountains to the north and joining their waters with the Allegheny at Pittsburgh, from the LaBelle Rivere of the early French settlers; the latter after draining a section of country for 150 miles in an opposite direction, find their way to the same stream, the Little Kanawha two hundred and the other three hundred miles lower down.

The climate in the valleys, is of that peculiarly mild and agreeable character which is found in the heart of the temperate zone. Where the soil is cultivated a yield is unfolded which rivals the increase of western prairies. The hillsides spontaneously produce a growth of herbage and wild grass unexcelled for grazing purposes, while far upon the mountain heights amid giant oaks, lofty poplars and wide spreading maples, a luxuriant vegetation covers the face of a nature with mossy intermixture of wild flowers, exhaling a thousand sweets. In the more populated sections, along the Ohio and Pennsylvania borders, the country presents a delightful view to the traveler. Large farms stretch along the little valleys and spread their outstretching fields to the uplands, smiling in the morning sun or receiving the tinges of the dying day, girt by noble forest trees which have been spared as monuments, to mark the glory of primeval solitudes. Farther in the interior, nearer the heads of the streams, a more primitive aspect is to be met. The sharp ring of the woodman's axe and the keen crack of the rifle, are the music that enchant the silence. Here and there, openings have been made by adventurous pioneers, which serve to guide the traveler on his way, or should he be benighted, no more hospitable hearth in the land will bid him welcome, than that of the honest host of the West Virginia cabin.

At the time of these events, the people of this part of the State were the representatives of no particular class, nationality or religion. No settlements had been made in West Augusta as it was known then, at the period of the Revolution, which were worthy of the name. It was an unbroken wilderness which had but seldom been penetrated by the foot of civilized men. Shortly after that, however, some of the bolder spirits of the eastern part of the State began gradually to seal the Alleghanies and disturb the silence by the sounds accompanying the path of civilization. The district of Monongalia was formed out of the county of West Augusta, about the year 1770 and subsequence additions were made in 1779. After the Revolution the spirit of the emigration began to set towards the wilderness west of the mountains. The first settlers were followed, in a generation afterwards, by a class of people whose style of life let them abandon the older counties of the east, where their pecuniary affairs had become involved with the more expensive habits of those localities. Possessing still some remnants of fortunes which enabled them to live in quite an independent manner in a country where there was but little opportunity to gratify the passions and but little disposition to mere display, they became large land holders, and with the few slaves brought with them, relics of the past, they tilled the soul sufficiently to supply their needs, and spent their time in hunting and the chase.

The land titles became much involved in litigious dispute, by a conflict between patentees from the Commonwealth, and the descendants of grantees from the sovereigns of Great Britain who in colonial times gave away tracts sufficient for a Dukedom, to courtiers and favorites. This subject became a frightful magnitude, and was one of the many causes which deterred emigration to this section of the State. Portions of the emigration during the early part of the present century, came from the eastern counties of Pennsylvania, some from Maryland, and a limited number from New Jersey. In later years a part of the rush of emigration which hurried to the great west, paused and looked favorably at the country, but inquiry into the internal economy of the State usually accelerated the speed of the emigrant in his western flight.

A general spirit of inquiry, however, was awakening among the people. With envious eyes they held the progress of States on their borders, whilst they were compelled to advance in the paths known to man in the most primitive times, or emigrate to distrant Commonwealths. So much indeed, had this spirit taken hold of the people, that, believing the policy of the eastern portion of the state to be inimical to the interests of the west, and the customs and habits of the former so dissimilar to the latter, they had no more than one occasion endeavored to obtained a separate State organization west of the Allegehanies.

Many causes had conspired to produce this state of feeling.

The convention of 1850-51 had provided a system of taxation that bore heavily on the west. The constitution prohibited taxation upon slaves under twelve years of age, and placed an equal valuation of three hundred dollars on all over that age. Thus the white laborer and farmer of west was required to pay a revenue to the state upon all the chattels he possessed, whilst the eastern planter whose wealth consisted principally of slaves, was exempted from bearing his fair and equitable porportion of the burdens of government, by reason of his ownership in that particular species of property, which, had it been even to the inclination or taste of the western man to hold or enjoy, would have been, from the character of the country an the adverse influences of climate and surroundings, wholly to his disprofit. This disporportion, or unjust discrimination, was the fruitful theme of the western politician on the hustings; and he was the successful contestant, who succeeded in convincing the constituency of his eternal hostility to the principal, and of his ability to further the means of relief.

There was also another grievance which was the subject of great complaint by the west. It was the basis of representation fixed by the constitution, whereby the slave wealth of the east was represented in the legislative branch of the State government, and brought to bear against the exercise of the elective franchise by the whites of the west. The appointment of delegates to the lower house of the General Assembly, and the creation of the senatoral districts were founded upon his system of "mixed basis," as it was denominated, by the convention of 1850-51. It gave an unequal proportion of representatives to the east, through their preponderance of wealth, principally in slaves. It enfranchised property and inhabitants in the east, and inhabitants only in the west.

This mixed basis was fastened irrevocably upon the people by a provision that, no amendments, should be made thereto until the year 1865, when the General Assembly was to submit to the people the question of "suffrage basis," that is, representation according to the number of voters in the Commonwealth; or mixed basis, representation according to the number of white inhabitants contained, and the amount of all state taxes paid in the several counties of the Commonwealth, deducting therefrom all taxes paid on licenses and law process and capitation tax on free negroes, allowing one delegate for every seventy-sixth part of the inhabitants, and one delegate for every seventy-sixth part taxes. The effect of this measure was to give to the cast a power in the law-making branch of the government, to which its wealth alone, and not its numbers, entitled it. It was repugnant to the spirit of the age and anti-democratic in its tendency. It gave to property an influence which all republics founded on the rights of personal liberty, have hitherto given to the person. The circumstances of the hour were such that the people could not reject the constitution embracing even such provisions. In many particulars it was essentially better than the one under which the people were then living. It abolished the landed qualification of voters, remodeled the judiciary system of the State, and provided for the election of Governor and many other officers by the people, and defined more distinctly the line of

177

demareation between the legislative, executive and judicial branches of the government. Prior to this time there was scarcely an officer from the most insignificant, either in executive or judicial stations, elected by the people, indeed, the only exception was in selecting members of the General Assembly.

The constitution was adopted, receiving large majorities therefore in the eastern portions of the State, but many western counties voted heavily against it, preferring rather, the absence of many privileges, than the surrender of so vital a principal as the unrestricted and independent exercise of personal franchise.

There was still another source of discontent upon the part of the west, which called forth loud and protracted complaint, and was perhaps, an evil of greater magnitude than any other which it was compelled to endure. This was the unequal distribution of the public funds in constructing works of internal improvement. From participating in the benefits of the various lines of traffic and travel inaugurated by, and under the auspices and patronage of the State, the west was practically debarred. A magnificent system of improvements in railroads and canals, was entered upon and completed in the east, by large donations from the public treasury. Charters with liberal provisions were readily granted by the General Assembly to the eastern section, whilst the west vainly endeavored, in many instances, to get the bare privilege of constructing works by aid of individual enterprise alone. Large loans were made by the General Assembly, and heavy subscriptions were taken by the State for the east, whilst the west received but a mere pittance, though annually swelling the exchequer with many hundreds of thousands of dollars. Indeed the delegate from a western county, when he returned to his constituency and informed them of his having secured an appropriation of a few thousand dollars to aid in the construction of a mud pike, thought himself entitled to the civic wreath, and on the high way to popular favor and esteem; although in thus procuring a miserable bounty for his section, he had to combine with eastern members, and vote magnificent sums to cherished schemes of eastern aggrandizement.

These things had been a matter of great irritation to the people of the west. The public temper was in no amiable mood; the bearing of the east towards the west was always of an affected, supercilious superiority, and had been carried so far that they had in contemptuous derision denominated the citizens of the latter as, "the peasantry of the west." Smarting under these accumulated grievances, it is not difficult to account for the storm of opposition that swelled up from the people, when their faithful deputies to the Richmond convention, returned one by one in rapid succession to their several counties, bearing in their pale, disconsolate countenances the marks of the terrible struggle through which they had passed. When too, they listened to their stories of fraud and violence and heard in detail the means by which it was designed to transfer them to the horrid embrace of a government founded upon an institution which had for three generations ground them beneath its iron heel, all the remembrances of their past wrongs rose like a torrent of their mountains long pent-up and overleaping every obstruction, brust forth in one prolonged shout of defiance.

As yet it was not understood in what manner the Federal government would aid loyal citizens in States or parts of States assuming to act under secession; still the determination of this people was to resist the secession movement of Virgina, against the whole power of the Confederate States; and failing in this, they would gather up the wrecks of their fortunes and their household goods, abandoning every other interest, and seek distant homes in the wilds of the far west, away from the hated influence of their life-long foe. Loyalty to the government of their fathers was deeply implanted in their breasts, and they turned toward the old flag with a glowing pride in its memories, instinctively divining that beneath its folds libert dwelt in conscious strength and repose.

They early gave an indication of the state of their feelings upon the questions which began to agitate the country after the election in November, 1860. The first meeting that was held to express the sentiments of the people, took place in Preston County, on the 12th day of November, 1860. Men of all parties participated in the proceedings. The partisans of the two democratic candidates, who had waged a furious warfare but one short week previously met in honest and earnest council to give expression to their views upon the result of the late election, and the questions that were rapidly assuming a dangerous tendency thereunder. The supporters of the Bell and Everett ticket joined in the deliberations, and the few but independent and active adherents of the successful part added their voice. After little delay and no discussion, so unanimous were men of all parties, that they passed a series of resolutions strongly opposing secession, and declaring that any attempt upon the part of the State to secede, would meet with the unqualified disapprobation of the people of the county. A meeting was held in Harrison County on the 24th of November, under like circumstances, which declared that, the people would first exhaust all constitutional remedies for redress before they would resort to any violent measures; that the ballot box was the only medium known to the constitution for a redress of grievances, and to it alone would they appeal; that it was the duty of all citizens to uphold and support the lawfully constituted authorities. An assemblage of people at the courthouse of Monongalia County on the 26th of November, in which the acknowledged leaders of all parties took part, unanimously resolved that, the election of the candidates of the republican party, did not justify secession and that the Union of the States was the best guarantee for the present and future welfare of the people.

The people of Taylor County, at their courthouse, on the 3rd of December following, resolved that they were opposed to taking any steps looking to a dissolution of the Union for existing causes. A large meeting of citizens in Wheeling, on the 14th of the same month, passed resolutions of like import and significance. Indeed, throughout the western counties, such meetings were generally held, and subsequent events proved that they were not the ordinary concomitants of political or partisan machinery, but they were the expressions of a people with whom fealty, in a republican govern-

179

ment, meant an acquiescence in the will of the majority, when that will was ascertained in the mode prescribed by the organic law, and on the maintenance of which principle the whole structure was founded.

When, therefore, it became no longer a matter of doubt, that the convention had passed an ordinance of secession, and the people were forced to choose their position; when actual hostilities had commenced, and words of deprecation and resolution declaratory of sentiments were no longer available, there came over the people that feeling which a generation experiences but once, and few centuries have ever seen repeated. It was that grand upheaval of all that is good and evil in mankind, so strangely intermingled that none can tell where one begins and the other ends, as the radiant beams of a setting sun falling athwart a passing angry cloud illumines the whole in indefinable magnificence. Men looked in each other's faces for confidence and direction, and found only those indications which were the mirror of their own breasts. But high over all and written on every countenance was the spirit of determined resistance to the action of the convention.

It was then that a series of meetings commenced, which has had no parallel in history, except the almost continual sessions of the citizen assemblies during the early part of the French Revolution; and this too, in a sparsely settled country, where facilities for convening were of the most primitive character. The earliest and first of these meetings was held at Morgantown, on the night of the 17th of April, 1861, the day the ordinance of secession passed. The temper of the people was not to be mistaken; the most violent sentiments of the orators were the most vehemently applauded. The meeting solemnly resolved that, the time had come when every friend of the Union should rally to the support of the flag of his country and maintain it under the most adverse and trying circumstances; that the people of Monongalia, without distinction of party, entered their solemn protest against the secession of Virginia; that they were attached to the Federal Union as the ark of their political safety and would cling to it despite the efforts of traitors to precipitate them into the gulf of secession; that secession as practically exemplified in the so-called Southern Confederacy, was unmitigated treason against the constitution and the government of the United States, and its leading actors were traitors and liable to be treated as such; that the idea of seceding from the general government, and being attached to the Southern Confederacy, was repulsive to every feeling and instinct of patriotism, and that the meeting was unalterably opposed to such a measure; and that, Western Virginia had patiently submitted to and borne up under the oppressive policy of Eastern Virginia for the last half century, as shown in her denying equal representation and refusing to bear an equal share of taxation, (on her slave property); that now the measure of eastern oppression was full, and that, if, as was claimed by the east, secession was the only remedy offered by it for all the wrongs of the west, the day was near at hand when the west would rise in the majesty of its strength and repudiating its oppressors, would dissolve all its civil and political connection with the east, and remain firmly under the stars and stripes.

A resolution of thanks to the members of the convention from the county, for their firmness, was passed; also that in the event of the passage of the ordinance of secession, (which it appears was not certainly known to have passed, although so reported) the delegates be requested to propose a division of the State.

The citizens of Taylor County were equally emphatic in their denunciation of secession. On the 13th of April, they resolved in a meeting at the courthouse, after declaring in a preamble, that Western Virginia had no interest in common with a government established for the sole purpose of protecting and propagating African slavery, that, they did not recognize the right of, nor any present cause for, any State, on its own motion, to secede from the Union; nor any cause to justify revolution; that the government of the United States ought to be maintained and all constitutional laws enforced; and that, if the eastern portion of the State should secede from or revolutionize the General Governent, they were in favor of establishing an independent State government for the western portion of the State, in which they could regulate their own internal affairs according to their own interests.

Actuated by a similar desire and in pursuance of a like spirit, the people of Wetzel County held a meeting, on the 22nd of April, and resolved that secession was no remedy for the evils which environed the country; that they pledged themselves to oppose any act of secession which would sever them from the Federal Government; that they appealed to their fellow-citizens to uphold the national banner; and that strong as were the ties that bound them to Virginia, yet nevertheless, should the convention, by an ordinance of secession (in consequence of the convention being in secret session it was not definitely known that it had passed) force them into a connection with the Gulf States, as citizens of Western Virginia, they would deem it a duty to themselves and posterity, to adopt such means and use such measures as should result in a division of the State.

As yet no definite steps had been taken to secure such a result by a combined movement. But the remedy was soon brought forward by the decided action of a large meeting of people at Clarksburg, in Harrison County. This meeting was held on the 22nd of April, under the auspices of the Hon. John S. Carlisle, the late delegate from that county to the convention. It was attended by about twelve hundred people. After reciting in a long preamble; declaring the means that had been resorted to by the secessionists to transfer the State from its allegiance to the Federal Government to the so-called Confederate States, without the consent of the people, as wholly unjustifiable, and as having seized, without the authority of those in whose name they professed to act, the property of the Federal Government within the limits of the State, and hereby inaugurated war, the meeting recommended to the people in each and all of the counties composing Northwestern Virginia to appoint not less than five delegates of their wisest, best and discretest men, to meet in convention at Wheeling on the 13th day of May following, to consult and determine upon such action as the people of Northwestern Virginia should take in the present fearful emergency.

This, in the exigency and under the pressure of events by which the people were surrounded, was a bold and startling measure. No aggressive movements had yet been attempted in this section of the Union, nor indeed was there anywhere any invasion of the territory of the Southern States by the Federal Government. About this time or shortly after a few companies of troops under the control of the secessionists took possession of Grafton, on the Baltimore and Ohio railroad, the key to Northwestern Virginia, for the purpose of preventing the military of the Federal Government from passing east to the defense of Washington, and overawing the inhabitants. In this latter, however, no success was attained. Following the recommendation of the Clarksburg meeting, delegates were appointed in all the northwestern counties. In some, home guard companies were formed and organized by the election of officers, who drilled the men in military tactics. All of the meetings declared unequivocally against the ordinance of secession. some of them went so far that they declared that in no event would they submit to secession, but would resist it to the last extremity.

The condition of the people of the northwest at this time was truly remarkable. In consequence of the violent denunciations of those who were regarded as secessionists, they wisely maintained silence, and hence nothing was heard but loud and defiant shouts of opposition to the scheme of secession. It is safe to say that a large majority of the magistracy and office-holders generally, either from conscientious scruples in relation to their oaths of office, which included that of fealty to the constitution of the State as well as of the United States, or from inclination and sentiment, favored the secession movement. Others again refused to perform the duties of their offices by reason of the commotions of the times and the general uncertainty that pervaded all classes. No one could furnish a solution to the great problem in process of demonstration. The tenure of property became a matter of great doubt; none felt secure in the enjoyment of civil rights. Distrust was everywhere. Questions to which this generation, or indeed any past generation of American citizens, were strangers, had arisen and were to be determined; how or in what manner none could answer. Duty to the State required that the citizens should follow its fortunes and fight its battles, if not inconsistent with other and higher duties. But this was not an hour for speculation nor refining distinctions; as the past has proven, doubtful questions go down like the reed before the angry blast, in the presence of that physical force ever the arbiter in civil commotions. Where the officers of the militia were loyal to the Union cause they called out their commands and endeavored to discipline them.

It had been whispered about, first in an undertone, and then the rumor grew and swelled into a terrible reality, that there was no law. Then sprang up that class of men who for years had been, from various causes, but nominal citizens in every community; men who sought retirement from the public gaze, and who had endeavored to screen themselves by the debris of some by-gone wreck. They were now among the foremost in promoting the general confusion incident to the apparent disruption of society. Bands of armed men traversed the country, bearing at their head the national banner, shouting death to all opposers. All persons who refused, after being notified by a committee, to plant the stars and stripes before their dwelling, were held to be enemies to the Union, and were required by the force of public opinion, expressed in no unqualified terms and frequently in no undemonstrative manner, to take the oath of allegiance to the constitution of the United States. The people ceased to follow their usual avocations; the farmers left their plows in the furrows, the mechanics their anvils and benches, not knowing who would reap the fruits of their harvest or labors. They assembled at the usual points of public manifestations, armed with their trusty rifles, and here and there a musket of antique pattern was to be seen in the hands of the descendant of a revolutionary sire.

During the excitement produced by the John Brown raid of a few years previous, several hundred stand of muskets and equipments, had been sent by Governor Wise to some of the counties in this section, for the purpose of arming the militia against invasion; there was also at the courthouses of most of the counties, quite a number of arms which had been used by volunteer companies organized under the law, and equipped by the State. These were immediately seized and distributed among the people. The whole country presented the appearance of a vast military camp, acting under no common head and acknowledging no superior power except that of superior force. Yet among the Union people, so actuated were they by a common impulse, no serious difficulties occurred. At every cross road groups of excited men were to be seen, whose firmly set mouths and determined countenances indicated the fixedness of their resolves. They were the hitherto quiet, even-tempered yeomanry of this agricultural country, whose lives had been spent in the peaceful pursuits of husbandry, now rousing themselves to the call of patriotism, with the sole inquiry, "have we a country?" The roads were picketed in every direction, and all passers were requested to give satisfactory information of their identity and errands; and the luckless traveler whose explanations were not such, was turned back in his course or only permitted to proceed under guard.

It was, indeed, a perilous hour; and it is not, perhaps, saying too much to aver that, no other people but Americans could have thus passed through every shade of anarchy with so great violence and so little bloodshed; as no instances of death by violence, have ever been authenticated. And it is, likewise, a valuable instance to the philosophic statesmen, of the superior dignity of human nature when fostered by the genial and ennobling influences of republican institutions.

Lest however, all the enthusiasm evoked by the nature of the crisis, should exceed the bounds of that holy patriotism in the name of which men may, nay ought, to purify an atmosphere pestilent with the odor of treason and tyranny, by acts unjustifiable in ordinary times, but the non-performance of which becomes criminal at others, the really earnest and firm men of the community, who

183

felt the full force of the tremendous issues involved, enrolled themselves into companies of home guards. This step produced something of order in the immense fragments of elementary power in the country. Any attempts at lawlessness were promptly suppressed; the maliciously disposed, or those who gave evidence of Ismaelitish tendencies, and of which every community has its representatives, were taught to know that the cause for which this people had risen, was the cause of order and law, in opposition to insurrection and rebellion; that the faithful maintenance of law was the life, breath, soul and immortality of a republic.

While this was the condition of affairs on the border and in what might be termed Northwestern Virginia proper, farther in the interior of what is now the State of West Virginia, the status was not so favorable to the Union cause. There parties were more equally balanced and consequently the contest became one of strategy as well as actual conflict. In many of the counties the secessionists had small majorities and claimed to act through the legal authority of the State government. Intimidation, therefore, became the order of the day, and when this failed, persecution sought to do what arguments and threats failed to accomplish. Being so situated that troops from the east soon found their way into them, the Union people were forced to remain quiet or betake themselves to the mountains to escape the operations of a fierce military despotism which seemed to crush out everything in its path. But whilst the spirit of the unionists was awed, it was not crushed, and many councils were held far in the recesses of the mountains, attended by a sturdy band of patriots who held their trusty rifles in their hands, whilst they deliberated and resolved. Many are the incidents related of such councils in the deep wood, whilst the wary comrades stood sentinel to warn of the approach of the foe; incidents and scenes which exceed in dramatic interest the fanciful sketches of the novelist, and possess all the charm and daring of a stern reality. It was at such meetings, in a number of instances, when hunted by the military and surrounded by the espionage of watchful and unrelenting civilians, that the national flag was carefully unfoled and kissed by the faithful patriots, who then swore with uplifted hands to never yield in its support and to die in its defense. Through the influence of such spirits, delegates were also appointed from their several counties, to the convention at Wheeling, to be held on the 13th of May.

To the meeting of that convention all looked forward with hope. That was thought to be the rallying point from which all succeeding movements would take their origin. No objections could be taken to the holding of such a convention either by the State or the Federal Government, as it was only called for the purpose of determining what course the people of the North-west should pursue; still it is quite probable that had it been in the power of the State troops, already assembled in some force, to have prevented it, no such body had ever met in Wheeling or elsewhere. In fact, the undertaking was a perilous one. No Federal troops had penetrated into Virginia, or indeed, crossed the Ohio River. A regiment of Union troops was hastily forming on Wheeling Island, under Col.

B. F. Kelley, an ardent and active unionist of the time, but it was so freshly organized as to be almost unavilable for the purposes of military defense, or protection. Yet the morning of the thirteenth of May beheld the city swarming with an excited multitude of its own inhabitants, and the delegates to the convention. All were enthusiastic and eager for the beginning of the work, yet none were fully assured of the direction matters would take. By arrangement the delegates met at Washington Hall at eleven o'clock A.M. The large building was filled to overflowing with an eager throng, whose anxious countenances depicted the depth of their feelings. it was a remarkable spectacle; the faces of the delegates were not familiar to those who had attended political meetings for several years previous. They were a new set of men whom the people had thrust forward in the peril of the emergency, whose recommendations were, an entire sympathy with the masses in the struggle before them, and a hearty confidence in their fidelity. They were plain, unassuming men too, but as plain men always do, they possessed those traits of character which make honesty the accompaniment of simplicity. Above all, they were filled with a noble spirit caught from their constituents, an undying attachment to the government of their fathers, and a holy hope of relief from the task-masters of the east. It was a spirit grand in its conception, glorious in its development, and sublime in its execution. It was the fierce youth of the freshly lighted faces of pure and righteous revolution. The meeting was called to order by Chester D. Hubbard, of Ohio County, on whose motion William B. Zinn, of Preston County, was called to preside. George R. Latham, of Taylor County, was appointed temporary secretary. Before proceeding further in the business for which they had assembled, a venerable prelate, the Rev. Peter T. Laishley, of Monongalia County, himself a delegate, invoked the aid of Deity, on the deliberations of the body; a pious act of faith not without its usefulness in estimating the character of the delegates and the rectitude of their motives.

A committee on permanent organization and representation was appointed. In the afternoon session, John W. Moss, of Wood County, was reported for permanent president, and a long list of vice-presidents: Colonel Wagner, of Mason, Marshal M. Dent, of Monongalia, and G. L. Cranmer, of Ohio County, were appointed as secretaries.

The president on being escorted to the chair, addressed the convention. After thanking it for the honor conferred he remarked that the object of the body was to consider the unhappy condition of the country, and particularly to deliberate calmly upon the position Northwestern Virginia should assume in the momentous history of the country. He further said that the destiny of thousands was involved in the result of their action, and therefore it should be characterized by the solemnity befitting the occasion and by the harmony and conciliation so necessary to any movement inaugurated by the convention.

The clergymen of the city were requested, by motion, to open each day's session with religious exercises. Two doorkeepers and a sergeant-at-arms were appointed. The committee on credientials reported duly accredited delegates from twenty-six counties, as follows: Hancock, Brooke, Ohio, Marion, Monongalia, Preston, Wood, Lewis, Ritchie, Harrison, Upshur, Gilmer, Wirt, Jackson, Mason, Wetzel, Pleasants, Barbour, Hampshire, Berkeley, Doddridge, Tyler, Taylor, Roane, Frederick and Marshall. They also reported a resolution, that, the vote of the convention upon any question, when demanded by twenty-five members, should be taken by giving to each county the aggregate vote cast by it respectively at the last presidential eleciton; and that the vote was to be cast by the chairman of the county delegations. Other questions were to be voted on per capita.

A committee, consisting of one member from each county represented, was appointed on State and Federal relations. The following persons composed it: C. Tarr, Brooke County; W. T. Willey, Monongalia; John S. Carlisle, Harrison; J. J. Jackson, Wood; Charles Hooton, Preston; Dan'l Lamb, Ohio; Geo. McC. Porter, Hancock; Jos. Macker, Mason; D. D. Johnson, Tyler; James Scott, Jackson; G. W. Bier, Wetzel; R. C. Holliday, Marshall; A. S. Withers, Lewis; E. T. Trahorn, Wirt; F. H. Pierpoint, Marion; S. Dayton, Barbour; G. S. Senseney, Frederick; J. S. Burdett, Taylor; A. R. Mcquilkin, Berkeley; S. Cochran, Pleasants; J. E. Stump, Roane; S. Martin, Gilmer; Asbury B. Rohrbough, Upshur; O. D. Downey, Hampshire; Mr. Foley, Ritchie.

The body now fairly began its work and on the second day resolutions were poured upon the committee. A very excited controversy sprang up on the plan to be adopted for immediate action. There were those who came to the convention, with the recollections of wrongs and insults burning in their memories; men of high resolves and unquenchable zeal, and who under the stimulus of a great excitement, were bold to rashness in their objects. This class of men came to vote for an immediate and unqualified division of the State, however violent or evolutionary it might appear. Some delegations, indeed, came to the city with a banner flying at their head, endorsed, "New Virginia, now or never." This party had a powerful leader in the Hon. John S. Carlisle, who smarting from the injustice and contumely that he had experiences in the convention at Richmond, raised his deep resonant voice to the highest pitch of revolutionary fervor. His plan was to immediately adopt a constitution and form a government for the counties represented, and proceeded to fill the offices by temporary appointment. This was a popular idea with the mass of the convention, and it became almost perilous to oppose it; those who ventured to do so, subjected themselves for the time to the liability of having imputations cast upon their loyalty. But there was a minority, respectable, both as to members and intelligence, who felt and saw the irreparable mischief that would follow in the train of such a course. This party found a leadership in the Hon. W. T. Willey, of Monongalia, whose more equable temperament enable him to discern the true point of distinction between spasmodic disruption and authorized resistance. It was argued that the proceeding urged by the majority

186

was wholly unwarranted by the call that had led to this assemblage; that the delegates had not been appointed with this view nor empowered to act with such extreme vigor; that this was but an informal meeting of the people, not legally convened and could not bind the people to acquiescence either in law or reason, or by any known rule or precedent; that no vote had yet been taken by the people on the ordinance of secession, and hence the State of Virgina had a government under the constitution of the United States, at Richmond; that the Federal Government would not recognize a State created thus, because it was not after the mode prescribed in the constitution of the United States.

The whole of the second day was consumed in acrimonious debate. The partisans of both views maintained their ground with unrelenting hostility. A crisis was rapidly approaching, when a motion to adjourn was carried. Great dissatisfaction prevailed on all sides, and it appeared as though the contending parties were about to separate without arriving at any conclusion, from which good results would flow. There was that lack of harmony which is so essential to the accomplishment of great designs, when men have a common object in view, but are widely dissonant as the manner of effecting it. On the third day the debate was continued, but in a better spirit; the voice of better counselors was beginning to prevail, and all felt the imperative necessity of some action and that it should be, so far as the same was possible, harmonious in its character. Late at night the committee reported through its chairman, Mr. Tarr. The report was a skillful blending of all opinions. It set forth that, it was the deliberate judgment of the convention, that the ordinance of secession, by which the repeal of the ratification of the constitution of the United States was attempted, was unconstitutional null and void; that the schedule attached to that ordinance, prohibiting the election of members of the House of Representatives of the Congress of the Unites States, at the election of the fourth Wednesday [sic] of May, then current, was a manifest usurpation of power, to which they as freemen of Virginia, ought not to, and would not submit; that the ordinance of the convention at Richmond, ratifying and approving the agreement between the commissioners of the Confederate states and Virginia, whereby the whole military power and operations, offensive and defensive, of the State were placed under the control and direction of the president of the Confederate States, upon the same principle and footing as if the Commonwealth were a member of said Confederacy, and the acts and conduct of the executive officers of the state in pursuance of said agreement, were plain and palpable violations of the constitution of the state, and utterly subversive of the rights and liberties of the people; that they earnestly recommended the citizens of the State to vindicate their rights by voting against the ordinance of secession; and that they urged upon them to vote for members of Congress of the United States in their several districts, in the exercise of their rights under the constitutions of the United States and of Virginia; that they also recommended them to vote for such persons for members of the House of Delegates, as entertained sentiments agreeing with those before expressed; that it

187

was the imperative duty of the citizens to maintain the constitution of the State and the laws made inpursuance of the same, and all officers acting thereunder, that, in the language of Washington, expressed in his letter to the president of Congress, on the 17th of September, 1789: "In all our deliberations on this subject, we keep steadily in view that which appears to us the greatest interest to every true American, the consolidation of our Union, in which is involved our property, felicity, safety and perhaps our national existence." Therefore they would maintain and defend the constitution of the United States and the laws made in pursuance thereof, and all officers acting thereunder the lawful discharge of their duties; that in view of the geographical, social, commercial and industrial interest of North-western Virginia, the convention was constrained to give expression to the opinion of its constituents, in declaring that in assuming to change the relation of Virginia to the Federal Government, the convention at Richmond acted not only unwisely and unconstitutionally, but adopted a policy utterly ruinous to all the material interests of this portion of the State, by severing all the social ties, and drying up all the channels of trade and prosperity; that in the event of the ordinance of secession being ratified by the people, the counties there represented, and all others disposed to cooperate, were recommended to appoint, on the 4th day of June, 1861, delegates to a general convention, to meet on the 11th day of the same month, at such place as should be designated by a committee to be afterwards appointed by the convention, to devise such measures as the safety and welfare of the people they represented should demand; each county to appoint a number of representatives to the convention, equal to double the number to which it was entitled in the next House of Delegates; and the senators and delegates to be elected at the general election on the fourth Thursday of May following, to the next General Assembly of Virginia, should be entitled to seats in the convention as members; that it being a conceded political axiom that government is founded on the consent of the governed and instituted for their good, and that the course of the ruling power of the State was utterly subversive and destructive of the interests of North-western Virginia, that the people of the same could rightfully and successfully appeal to the proper authorities of Virginia, to permit them to peacefully and lawfully separate from the residue of the State, and form a government that would give effect to their wishes, views and interests; that the public authorities be assured, that the people of the north-west would exert themselves to preserve the peace, which they felt satisfied they could do until an opportunity was afforded to ascertain if the difficulties could not receive a peaceful solution; and expressed a hope that no Confederate troops would be introduced among them, as the same would be calculated to produce civil war; that a central committee of five be appointed with powers to carry out the object of the convention and to assemble the body at any time it might think necessary; and that such counties represented, and all others disposed to cooperate, would appoint a committee of five to attend to all things necessary to be done and to correspond with the central committee. After but little discussion, the report was adopted by the body; but two voices in the vast throng being dissentient. The central committee was appointed as follows: John S. Carlisle, James S. Wheat, Chester D. Hubbard, Francis H. Pierpoint, Campbell Tarr, George R. Latham, Andrew Wilson, S. H. Woodward and James W. Paxton. A vote of thanks was tendered to the citizens of Wheeling for their hospitality; also the president and other officers of the body. Several eloquent speeches were made. A prayer was then offered, invoking the blessings of Heaven upon the labors of meeting. The "Star Spangled Banner" was sung by the united voices of over a thousand people, three cheers were given for the Union, and amid a blaze of enthusiasm, the convention adjourned *sine die*.

Thus closed the session of as earnest and fearless body of patriots as ever assembled in this or any other country in any age. The convention was composed of about five hundred in number, representing every shade and degree of former political opinions, yet not one word of their former associations was brought forward to disturb the equilibrium or excite the jealousy of any particular party. Over all were spread those great clouds of lowering danger and portentous gloom, which caused all minor differences to dissipate before the general instincts of self-preservation.

After this event, matters progressed with more regularity; and the superiority of combined action over vague and ill-concerted movements, however much spirit they might possess, or stern enthusiasm might be evoked, was made manifest by the well-timed public demonstrations and systematic convocations, brought about by the potent agency of the county committees.

A large meeting of citizens was held in Berkeley County, on the 13th of May, which it is proper to notice, from the fact of that county lying at the foot of the valley of the Shenandoah from which issued such numerous bands of secessionists who overran the country. The preamble is a master-piece of statement remarkable for the genuine patriotism in every line, and the truthfulness of the charges alleged against the secessionists, whilst it furnishes a complete vindication for the cause of which they committed themselves in their resolutions. They warn their brethren of the States, that if their course be persisted in the division of the State was inevitable; they declared that they knew of no oppression by the Federal Government; that they owed no allegiance to any section of the country, but to a United Republic of Free States; and that they would cast their votes against the ordinance of secession.

From the close of the convention till the election which took place on the 23rd of the same month, the country was in a feverish excitement. In the north-west the feeling against secession became an absolute passion. Nothing could withstand the tremendous weight of public sentiment so unequivocally placed in the balances against it.

The central committee appointed by the convention, issued an address to the people of the north-west, replete with argument and glowing with patriotism. The address urged them to prepare themselves for a firm and decided stand against the efforts of the secessionists to destroy the unity of government through which alone their liberties could be transmitted to posterity. To do so, was the only means of saving themselves from the horrors of civil war. The people of the north-west should not permit themselves to be dragged into a rebellion inaugurated by ambitious men for the purpose of destroying a government formed by their patriotic fathers, and which had secured to them all the liberties consistent with the nature of man; whilst it had sheltered them for more than three quarters of a century in sunshine and storm, and conferred upon them a title more honored, respected and revered than that of king or potentate — the title of an American citizen. Free men who would remain free must prove themselves worthy to be free, and strike the first blow.

Secession was not a deed accomplished in the broad glare of a noon day sun, but a deed of darkness, which was performed in secret conclave, in contempt of the people, by reckless spirits who were determined to enslave them. It was bankruptcy, ruin and civil war, ending in military despotism. Prior to the adoption of secession all was peace and prosperity, since then all was confusion, business was paralyzed, State, corporation and individual credit were prostrated and civil war was upon them.

Who would stand the brunt of this war? not those who inaugurated it; they woudl remain at a respectable distance from danger, and fill the lucrative offices, whilst those whose heart were for the Union, would be called upon to uphold the honor of Virginia at a mere pittance per day, and undergo all the hardships of war. Was this the only way that devotion to the honor of the Commonwealth could be manifested? A far better evidence would be exhibited by repudiating the tyrannical rule of the secession convention. The people would resist this tyranny, and would stand by the liberties secured by the Revolutionary fathers, and the authors of the constitution. As yet no resistance had been offered to the quartering of troops in the country, and to the taking of the young men, who in times of profound peace had attached themselves to volunteer companies, to fill armies to aid in a rebellion; but stunned by the magnitude of the crime, the people had already sent up the cry of "resistance to tyrants is obedience to God." The people were urged to send representatives to the convention to assemble on the 11th of June, which was to organize action. They were requested to remember the words of the president of the Montgomery convention, Howell Cobb, who had declared that the people of the Gulf States need have no apprehensions, as the theatre of war would be along the borders of the Ohio River and in Virginia. They were also cited to the remark of the Hon. Daniel Webster, in 1851, that, the inhabitants of that portion of Virginia between the Alleghany Mountains and the Ohio and Kentucky borders, could not hope to remain a part of Virginia one month after Virginia had ceased to be a part of the United States.

On the 23rd, election day, much excitement prevailed, but no serious breaches of the peace occurred throughout the north-west. The people voted for members of the House of Representatives of the Federal Congress, in the three districts, west of the Alleghanies.

In twenty-five counties embracing a part of what is now West Virginia, there was a majority of over twenty-four thousand votes against secession. In many of these counties, the vote was larger than that polled in 1860 for president; in some of them the vote was as great as twenty-two against secession, to one for it. In the twenty-five other counties the majority was about sixteen thousand against secession. Out of about forty-four thousand votes in the counties of the north-west, forty thousand were cast against the fatal ordinance. Shortly after the election an advance was made by the Union forces from the west simultaneously along the lines of the Baltimore and Ohio Railroad from Wheeling, and along the North-western Virginia Railroad from Parkersburg. This put the rebel forces at Grafton to flight; from whence they fell back to Phillippi in Barbour County, where they were surprised and barely escaped capture by the loss of their camp equipage, munitions of war, arms and other property. They retreated to Rich Mountain and Laurel Mountain, from whence they were subsequently driven by the skillful and brave lieutenants of General George B. Mc-Clellan, then in command of the Department of the Ohio. This last movement completely dislodged the secessionists from the north-west, and they never gained a foothold therein during the sec-ceeding struggle, but were compelled to be content with annoying the inhabitants by predatory bands of horse thieves and raiding free booters.

Such was the unanimity of the people of the subject of seces-sion as disclosed by the returns of the election, that all opposition to the prevailing sentiment at once ceased, and but one voice was heard throughout the north-west. Great interest was manifested in the coming election for delegates to the convention of the 11th of June. The county committees appointed persons to hold the elec-tion at the various precincts on the 4th of June. There was a full vote in many of the counties, and delegations of the best men were returned.

The delegates met at Washington Hall, in Wheeling, on the 11th of June, 1861. The committee on credentials reported delegates from thirty-one counties, including senators and members of the House of Delegates. This number was subsequently augmented to thirty-five counties, producing an aggregate of seventy-seven members. Arthur I. Boreman, of Wood County, was unanimously chosen president of the convention; C. L. Cranmer, of Ohio County, was elected secretary. Other officers were also ap-pointed. The committee recommended a form for the oath of the president, which was adopted. It required him to swear to support the constitution of the United States, and the laws made in pur-suance thereof, as the supreme law of the land, anything in the or-dinances of the convention which assembled in Richmond on the 13th of February, 1861, to the contrary notwithstanding. The report further provided that all members of the convention should take a similar oath, to be administered by the president. The presi-dent took the oath upon assuming the chair; it being administered by a justice of the peace; after which, the members took the oath, as they were called forward by delegations.

The body being duly organized many interesting questions arose as to the objects to be attained and the mode of arriving at substantial results. There were in this, as in the May convention, many men whose primary and sole hope lay in the immediate formation of a government for the counties represented, wholly independent of the organism of the old State, and in total disregard of the officers then performing its functions. They claimed that the conduct of the executive authorities, acting under the ordinance of secession, was not warranted by the constitution of the United States, and that it was, therefore, revolutionary in its character, and as such was open to resistance that had for its basis a submission to that constitution; and hence was justifiable. It was held, however, by the majority, many of whom had entertained similar sentiments in May, but in whom the revolutionary heat had subsided into a steady glow of legalized opposition, that whilst the ordinance of secession was in itself a nullity, still the position of the people of the State was not changed toward the Federal Government; that whilst in a monarchy, the throne could only be declared vacant by a greater or less degree of violence according to circumstances, where the monarch had abdicated or violated his contract with the people, which was his oath to preserve their liberties, that in a republic where the rulers were mere functionaries when those rulers usurped the liberties of the people or abdicated of their own motion, those unalterable principles which had received the endorsation of the founders of the Americna Government, came forward to their relief, and declared that as the people were sovereign, when government failed to fulfill the purposes for which it was created, the temporary authority delegated to the rulers, reverted to them with the stamp of peaceful legitimacy, and as of right. This doctrine had a precedent in the case of the change of succession consequent upon the flight of James the Second, when the estates of the realm declared that the reigning monarch had violated his contract with the people by various acts of tyranny, so far as the same can be analogous to a republican form of government.

The question was not a new one, but the application of the principle was, for the first time, to be attempted in American politics. The ordinance of secession was mere phraseology, which effect no change in the relation of the people of Virginia of the Federal Government. The constitution of the United States is the supreme law of the land. It was adopted by the people of the United States in their sovereign capacity, and can only be changed or amended by the same power which created it.No provisionis made for wholly annulling it. To change or amend it requires the assent of three-fourths of the States acting through their legislatures, or conventions specially called for the purpose, as shall be determined by Congress. When therefore, any State, or combination of parties, seeks to change or amend the constitution in any other mode than that prescribed by the instrument itself, the movement is clearly contrary to the organic law and as such is revolutionary. How much more so does it become when the whole is sought to be annulled and destroyed? it is the "supreme law" of the land, and the people of each and every State can appeal to every branch of its legitimate departments for protection against any power that seeks to disturb its action or thwart its laws in their midst, though that power should be their own State government. And in the maintenance of the principle and for the purposes of its establishment, a minority may make such appeals, with all the force of, and perhaps oftener with more justice than, the majority.

To follow this course, was soon disclosed to be the intention of the majority of the convention. Before proceeding to make an appeal to the Federal Government, they resolved formally to declare in justification, the motives which impelled them to adopt such policy. The committee which was appointed to prepare and report business to the body consisted of thirteen members: — Carlisle, of Harrison; Lamb, of Ohio; Pierpoint of Marion; Hagans, of Preston; Van Winkle, of Wood; Berskire, of Monongalia; Polsley, of Mason; Boreman, of Wood; Caldwell, of Marshall; Frost, of Jackson; Porter, of Hancock; Farnsworth, of Upshur; and Copley, of Wayne.

On the 13th of June, but two days after the session began, they reported a declaration, which will be found to contain such a statement of grievances as will compare with any known precedents. But it can be maintained that, whilst the matters alleged were sufficient justification for revolutionary acts, still the anomalous condition of affairs and the structure of the government are a vindication of the policy on abstract principles. No government existed in Virginia recognized by the constitution of the United States; therefore it was the duty of the people to erect one. It was an absolute duty not confined alone to the impositions of responsibility resting on civilized men, but impelled by the discharge of a high patriotic trust, in the interest of constitutional government. The declaration is in the following language:

"A Declaration of the People of Virginia, represented in Convention, at the city of Wheeling, Thursday, June 13, 1861.

"The true purpose of all government is to promote the welfare and provide for the protecton and security of the governed; and when any form or organization of government proves inadequate for, or subversive of this purpose, it is the right, it is the duty of the latter, to alter or abolish it. The Bill of Rights of Virginia, framed in 1776, reaffirmed in 1830, and again in 1851, expressly reserves this right to a majority of her people. The act of the General Assembly, calling the convention which assembled at Richmond in February last, without the previously expressed consent of such majority, was therefore a usurpation; and the convention thus called has not only abused the powers nominally intrusted to it, but, with the connivance and active aid of the Executive, has usurped and exercised other powers, to the manifest injury of the people, which, if permitted, will inevitably subject them to a military despotism.

"The convention, by its pretended ordinances, has required

193

the people of Virginia to separate from and wage war against the government of the United States, and against the citizens of neighboring States, with whom they have heretofore maintained friendly, social and business relations.

"It has attempted to subvert the Union founded by Washington and his co-patriots, in the former days of the Republic, which has conferred unexampled prosperity upon every class of citizens, and upon every section of the country.

"It has attempted to transfer the allegiance of the people to an illegal confederacy of rebellious States, and required their submission to its pretended edicts and decrees.

"It has attempted to place the whole military force and military operations of the Commonwealth under the control and direction of such confederacy, for offensive as well as defensive purposes.

"It has, in conjunction with the State Executive, instituted, wherever their usurped power extends, a reign of terror intended to suppress the free expression of the will of the people, making elections a mockery and a fraud.

"The same combination, even before the passage of the pretended ordinance of secession, instituted war by the seizure and appropriation of the property of the Federal Government, and by organizing and mobilizing armies, with the avowed purpose of capturing or destroying the capital of the Union.

"They have attempted to bring the allegiance of the people of the United States into direct conflict with their subordinate allegiance of the State, thereby making obedience to their pretended ordinance treason against the former.

"We, therefore, the delegates here assembled in convention to devise such measures and take such action as the safety and welfare of the loyal citizens of Virginia may demand, having maturely considered the premises, and viewing with great concern the deplorable condition to which this once happy Commonwealth must be reduced unless some regular adequate remedy is speedily adopted, and appealing to the Supreme Ruler of the universe for the rectitude of our intentions, do hereby, in the name and on behalf of the good people of Virginia, solemnly declare that the preservation of their dearest rights and liberties, and their security in person and property, imperatively demand the reorganization of the government of the Commonwealth, and that all acts of said convention and Executive, tending to separate this Commonwealth from the United States, or to levy and carry on war against them, are without authority and void; and that the offices of all who adhere to the said convention and Executive, whether legislative, executive, or judicial, are vacated."

It received the unanimous vote of the convention on the seventeenth following.

The convention then proceeded to reorganize the government of Virginia. The committee reported an ordinance on the fourteenth, which received the unanimous sanction of the body on the nineteenth, after a few verbal amendments. To show that the convention was actuated by a spirit of candor, and entertained a true regard for the dignity of the undertaking in which they were engaged, as well also the magnanimity of their enlightened patriotism, it is proper to state that an amendment offered to the effect that, no person who had voted for the ordinance of secession should be eligible to hold any office, during the existence of hostilities by the seceding States against the Federal Governor, was voted down by a majority of five to one. The whole document is as follows:

An ordinance for the reorganization of the State government passed June 19, 1861.

"The people of the State of Virginia, by their delegates assembled in convention at Wheeling, do ordain as follows:

"1. A Governor, Lieutenant Governor and Attorney General for the State of Virginia shall be appointed by this convention, to discharge the duties and exercise the powers which pertain to their respective offices by the existing laws of the State, and to continue in office for six months, or until their successors be elected and qualified; and the General Assembly is required to provide by law for an election as in their judgment such an election can be properly held.

"2. A council, to consist of five members, shall be appointed by this convention, to consult with and advice the Governor especting such matters pertaining to his official duties as he shall submit for consideration, and to aid in the execution of his official orders. Their term of office shall expire at the same time as that of the Governor.

"3. The delegates elected to the General Assembly on the 23rd of May last, and the senators entitled under existing laws to seats in the next General Assembly, together with such delegates and senators as may be duly elected under the ordinances of this convention, or existing laws to fill vacancies, who shall qualify themselves by taking the oath or affirmation hereinafter set forth, shall consitute the legislature of the State, to discharge the duties and exercise the powers pertaining to the General Assembly. They shall hold their offices from the passage of this ordinance until the end of the terms for which they were respectively elected. They shall assemble in the city of Wheeling, on the 1st day of July next, and proceed to organize themselves as prescribed by existing laws, in their respective branches. A majority in each branch of the members qualified as aforesaid shall constitute a quorum to do business. A majority of the members of each branch thus qualified, voting affirmatively, shall be competent to pass any act specified in the twenty-fourth section of the fourth article of the constitution of the State.

"4. The Governor, Lieutenant Governor, Attorney General, members of the legislature, and all officers now in the service of the State, or of any county, city or town thereof, or hereafter to be elected or appointed for such service, including the judges and clerks of the several courts, sheriffs, commissioners of the revenues, justices of the peace, officers of the city and municipal corporations, and officers of militia, and officers and privates of volunteer companies of the State, not mustered into the service of the United States, shall each take the following oath or affirmation before proceeding in the discharge of their several duties:

" 'I solemnly swear (or affirm) that I will support the constitution of the United States, and the laws made in pursuance thereof, as the supreme law of the land, anything in the constitution and laws of the State of Virginia, or in the ordinances of the convention which assembled at Richmond on the 13th of February, 1861, to the contrary notwithstanding; and that I will uphold and defend the government of Virginia as vindicated and restored by the convention assembled at Wheeling on the 11th day of June, 1861.'

"If any elective officer, who is required by the preceding section to take such oath or affirmation, fail or refuse so to do, it shall be the duty of the Governor, upon satisfactory evidence of the fact, to issue his writ declaring the office to be vacant, and providing for a special election to fill such vacancy, at some convenient and early day to be designated in said writ; of which due publication shall be made for the information of the persons entitled to vote at such electons; and such writ may be directed, at the discretion of the Governor, to the sheriff or sheriffs of the proper county or counties, or to a special commissioner or commissioners to be named by the Governor for the purpose. If the officer who fails or refuses to take such oath or affirmation be appointed by the Governor he shall fill the vacancy without writ; but if such officer is appointed otherwise than by the Governor or by election, the writ shall be issued by the Governor, directed to the appointing power, requiring it to fill the vacancy."

On the following day, June twentieth, the convention went into an election for officers as provided by the first clause of the ordinance. Francis H. Pierpoint, of Marion, was unanimously elected Governor of Virginia; Daniel Polsley, of Mason, was elected Lieutenant Governor, without opposition. A few days afterward, James S. Wheat, of Ohio, was chosen Attorney General. Peter G. Van Winkle, of Wood, Daniel Lamb, of Ohio, William Lazier, of Monongalia, William A. Harrison, of Harrison, and J. T. Paxton, of Ohio, were selected as members of the Governor's council, under the second clause of the ordinance.

It will be observed that no changes were made in the form of the government, and none essentially varying its administration. It was mere reorganization or restoration.

Upon the election of the Governor, he was waited upon by a committee who informed him of the fact, and escorted him to the hall of the convention, where he took the prescribed oath before a justice of the peace, in the presence of the convention. A resolution was adopted providing for the appointment of a committee to procure a great and a lesser seal, the seals of the Commonwealth being in the possession of the late Executive, respectively bearing on obverse and reverse the devices and mottos on the seals theretofore used by the State, with the addition on each seal of the words, "Liberty and Union." There was a peculiar propriety in this, which excites greater interest, when it is remembered that the seals of

Virginia bear the device of a slave of the plebian order, who having broken the bonds of his servitude and obtained the ascendency over his master, stands trimphantly with his foot upon the despot's prostrate form, illustrating the motto of *Sic Semper Tyrannis* circling around him. So likewise did the "Peasantry of the west," in the name of Liberty and Union.

Resolutions were passed setting forth that, foreign and domestic traitors had driven many peaceable citizens from their homes, by threats of injury and death, or no other crime had fidelity to the constitution of the fathers, and had disregarded the right of suffrage by surrounding the polls with cannons and bayonets, thereby excluding citizens from the free exercise thereof; and that they had attempted to set aside the supreme law of the land, by ordering that no election should be held for a presentation in the congress of the United States. They therefore appealed to the government of the United States, to which their highest allegiance was due, for protection against the armed invaders, and for the aid guaranateed by the constitution to secure the continuance of a republican form of government.

An ordinance was adopted relating to the receipt and disbursement of public revenue, requiring the General Assembly so soon as convened to elect an Auditor of Public Accounts, a Treasurer and Secretary of the Commonwealth, and providing the mode for the qualification of these officers and their duties. Also an ordinance to authorize the apprehension of suspicious persons in time of war.

Having reorganized the government and elected a chief executive officer and provided for the election of all other officers, civil and military, the labors of the convention were evidently drawing to a close. Nothing had been done that appeared to directly inaugurate the popular movement for the formation of a new State. In reality, however, the true theory had been adopted, and the only legitimate mode of arriving at that most desirable result, had been conceived and acted upon the convention. If the government thus restored, was acknowledged by the Federal authorities, as the only government in Virginia, then the legislative branch of it could give its assent to the formation of a new State, as provided for by the constitution of the United States. Leaving the great question to be adjusted at a subsequent day, the convention adjourned on the twentieth of June, to meet on the first Tuesday of August.

The General Assembly met, in pursuance of the ordinance of the convention, at Wheeling on the 1st day of July. The session was held at the Custom House, where the Governor had already established his office, and where the other officers of the government were subsequently located.

The House of Delegates organized by the election of a temporary clerk who enrolled the members, when it was ascertained that there were thirty-one present. A permanent clerk was elected, one of the members enrolled calling the names of delegates. A speaker was then chosen. A committee waited upon the Governor, who transmitted his message to both houses. The message was a plain statement of the history of the movement, including the action of the Richmond convention, and the subsequent acts of the late executive and other officers of the State. They were at war with the loyal people of the State and the constitutional government of the United States. After a review of the matters leading to his election, the Governor proceeded to state that he had communicated with the President of the United States, briefly reciting the circumstances with which the loyal government of Virginia was surrounded and claiming protection against invasion and domestic violence. He had received assurances from him, through the Secretary of War, that such aid as the constitution guaranteed in such caes should be promptly given.

He transmitted copies of communications received from the Secretary of the Interior, certifying officially the apportionment of representation in the thirty-eighth Congress, to which Virginia was entitled under the census of 1860. He called the attention of the General Assembly to the fact of a proclamation by the President of the United States, convening Congress, on the fourth of the month, and that the senators from Virginia were engaged in the conspiracy to overthrow the Federal Government, and recommended the election of senators to fill the vacancies caused by their defection. A considerable portion of the message was also devoted to matters demanding a change to suite the altered condition of affairs.

On the 9th of July, the houses on a joint vote, elected L. A. Hagans, of Preston, Secretary of the Commonwealth; Samuel Crane, of Randolph, Auditor of Public Accounts, and Campbell Tarr, of Brooke, Treasurer. On the same day they elected John S. Carlisle, of Harrison, and Waitman T. Willey, of Monongalia, senators to the Federal Congress.

The legislation of this session was principally of a military character. Laws were enacted for the raising and equipping of State troops, and to facilitate the organization of companies for Federal service. The salaries of public officers were fixed and a general law staying the collection of private debts was passed. The session closed on the twenty-fourth of the month.

On the election of the senators, they went to the Federal capital, where, with the representatives chosen at the May election, they were admitted to seats in the respective houses, as senators and representatives from Virginia.

The triumph of the movement was fully completed shortly afterwards by the proclamation of the Governor ordering elections for the judges of the several circuits of the west, in consequence of the posts being vacated by the participation of the incumbents in the rebellion, or from failing to take the oath prescribed by the convention. Every branch of the government was at length in full operation, with all the fictions of the law and all the positive enactments on the statue books, in full force and effect.

This position placed the loyal people of Virginia on a firm basis. They now had a government organized with every stamp of legitimacy known to modern political science.

Their government received the full sanction of the Federal authorities, by express recognition, and by being the medium of communication to the people, according to the constitution and laws. They could not be regarded as rebels, nor indeed as revolutionists, unless the doctrine of secession in its most obnoxious sense was conceded.

It was not without a just and honorable pride that they regarded the result of their labors. Aside from the consciousness of having performed a solemn duty to their country, they beheld officers of their choice residing in their midst, elevated to high and responsible trusts. Hitherto the people of the north-west had seen the offices filled and enjoyed by the east. In the whole history of the State but one Governor had ever been selected from this section, and he on one occasion barely escaped the violence of a mob at the capital. In no instance had any of the Federal offices, except representative, been given to them. But now there was found among them, men, who on being transplanted from the bar to the senate, shed a lustre upon their State, by the brilliancy of their talent, in no wise inferior to the great lights of Virginia in her halcyon days. The lawgivers and statesmen were the yeomanry, improvised by the logic of events.

There was still a question of primary importance agitating the people. They were not content with having erected for the old Commonwealth, a government in fact as well as in right. The sum of the North-western Virginian's hopes was centered in a new State of homogeneous people, west of the Alleghanies. It was felt, therefore, by the convention on reassembling on the 6th of August, that they had but one duty to perform.

The convention was augmented by the appearance of several members from the Kanawha Valley counties, which had, during the previous session, been occupied by the secession forces, under General Henry A. Wise. This latter section had, from the outbreak of hostilities, been prevented from participating in the thrilling scenes already recorded; it had been the theatre of outrage and violence through the erratic course of the General commanding. Mock courts had despoiled citizens of their property in the name of justice, and life was held on the tenure of abject acquiescence. The advance of a column of Union troops under General Cox, put the enemy to flight and restored the sentiment of the country to its opposition to the secession cause. These new members were burning with the memory of insult, contumely and wrong. They were eager to participate in the work of division. On the twentieth of the same month, the convention passed an ordinance providing for the formation of a new State out of a portion of the territory of the State of Virginia. It described the boundaries of the State so to be formed, and included the counties of Logan, Wyoming, Raleigh, Fayette, Nicholas, Webster, Randolph, Tucker, Preston, Monongalia, Marion, Taylor, Barbour, Upshur, Harrison, Lewis, Braxton, Clay, Kanawha, Boone, Wayne, Cabell, Putnam, Mason, Jackson, Roane, Calhoun, Wirt, Gilmer, Ritchie, Wood, Pleasants, Tyler, Doddridge, Wetzel, Marshall, Ohio, Brooke and Hancock; thirty-nine in all.

All qualified voters within these counties, should be entitled to vote on the question of the formation of the new State, which was to be called the State of Kanawha, at an election to be held on the fourth Thursday of October succeeding; at which time, also delegates should be elected to a convention to form a constitution for the proposed State. That convention was empowered to change the boundaries so as to include the counties of Greenbrier and Pocahontas, or either of them, and the counties of Hampshire, Hardy, Morgan, Jefferson and Berkeley, or either of them, and also all counties contiguous to the boundaries of the proposed State or to the counties just named, if the people thereof by a majority of the votes given in any of them should express a desire to be included, on the same day that the election was held in the other counties, and should elect delegates to the convention. Provision was made for the manner of conducting the election, and the officers by which it was to be held. Authority was given to voters to exercise the privilege in any part of their counties, where the usual places of voting were in possession of military forces or hostile assemblages. All officers were required to take the oath prescribed by the convention at the previous session. Returns were to be made to the Secretary of the Commonwalth at Wheeling. The Governor was required to ascertain the result and make proclamation of the same, on or before the 15th of November succeeding; and if a majority of the votes cast was in favor of the formation of a new State, he should call the delegates elected to meet in Wheeling on the 26th of November, to organize themselves into a convention. The convention was required to submit to the people within the bounadaries, for ratification or rejection, a constitution of the new State, on the fourth Thursday of December following.

The Governor was required to lay before the General Assembly at its next meeting, for its consent according to the constitution of the United States, the result of the vote, if it was found that a majority was in favor of the new State, and also in favor of the constitution proposed to the voters for their adoption.

It was provided that the new State should take upon itself a just proportion of the public debt of the Commonwealth of Virginia, prior to the 1st day of January, 1861, to be ascertained by charging to it all State expenditures within its limits, and a just proportion of the ordinary expenses of the State government, since any part of it was contracted; and deducting therefrom the moneys paid into the treasury of the Commonwealth from the counties included within the new State during the same period. All private rights and interests in lands within the proposed new State derived from the laws of Virginia prior to such separation, were to remain valid and secure under the laws of Virginia, and be determined by the laws then in force. When the consent of the General Assembly to the formationof the new State, should be obtained, it should forward the same to the Congress of the United States, together with the constitution, and request that the new State be admitted into the Federal Union.

The government of Virginia reorganized as by the convention, was to retain undiminished and unimpaired all the powers and authority with which it had been vested, until the proposed State was admitted into the Union by Congress; and nothing in the ordinance was to impair its authority in any counties not included within the new State boundaries. On the same day, the convention passed a resolution to adjourn on the following day, to stand adjourned until called by order of the President or the Governor; and if not so convened by the first Thursday in January, 1862, to then stand adjourned *sine die.*

The body closed its sessions on the 21st day of August, 1861, after an unusually harmonious session. The harmony that prevailed was the chief means of the success that followed the undertaking. All seemed inspired with a common purpose and design, and even those refractory minds which are everywhere to be met with in deliberative bodies, yielded a ready acquiescence to measures that promised so fairly to bring about results that all had in view, though not in entire concord with their peculiar dogmas. But the achievements of the convention were, indeed, of no ordinary character. That government, which in Virginia had been held in unbroken succession from the settlement of Jamestown, by English noblemen, or their republican descendents subsequent to the revolution, and which beginning, "by the Grace of God," in one man, and continued by the favor made common to all men, had been ended amid the throes of a hasty suicide, and overthrown by a government erected by the efforts of statesmen new rising from the body of the people, and which did not require the stamp of antiquity to make it legitimate, or the title by prescription to invest it with the mystery of aged and honrable dignitaries. It had supplanted a government which it declared to be at war with the vital principles of every republic, and in doing so looked neither to its venerable escutcheon, nor to the long list of illustrious names connected with its administration, who had made themselves immortal by the defense of liberal sentiments and in resisting the encroachments of tyranny. It had emasculated the functions of its executive officers, who had grasped with impious hands the jewels of the nation and sought to apply them to base uses. And yet this complete transfer of governmental functions was not revolution, but the restoration of principles to their pristone vigor and purity. Neither was it usurpation of established privileges and inherent rights, which in monarchies are indefeasible by virtue of time and founded on uncontradicted precedent, but rather the resumption of a trust falsely sustained and a reassertion of what was yielded for use and not abuse. In other forms of government the principle can only be asserted when the nation is called to witness the close of a tragedy, in America it is the prologue which has for its object the statement and disposition of relative positions, that may, happily, avert the calamity, so far as the inherent defects of humanity can be controlled by purely moral inquiry. It is useless, perhaps, to attempt to contradict the affirmative of the proposition, that all changes and reform, either in the material or moral world, have their origin or development in or by the aid of physical force, either directly or indirectly applied; or indeed that power has not, to a certain degree its absolute rights, heterodox as this latter may seem; it still cannot be denied that the American system of government presents less liability to become the object of attack by the various passions that afflict and curse governments, than any other. In a republican government, the people revolutionize, change or reform in a peaceful manner, if the cardinal points of republicanism are kept in view; in a monarchy these thins are almost universally attended by violence and bloodshed. A bad ruler is the creature of a limited season, in the former; a vicious monarch is often a death knell to the hopes of two or three generations. An appeal to the aritrament of the sword in a monarchy, ends either in the fitful glare of reddened anarchy, or the profound gloom of darkened despotism; whilst a republic, as the past few years of fearful struggle have demonstrated to positive truth, may sustain the shock of civil war in its most gigantic attitude, and emerge from the smoke of contending fields, without a privilege restricted, a franchise withdrawn, a right invaded, or a liberty impaired.

The movement for a new State now assumed a form that promised success, and the people gave a hearty support to the cause. it required but little canvassing to bring out a favorable response from those citizens who were loyal to the Federal government. They were fully alive to the importance of the new State, as a matter of protection from the east, which they had dared to battle by their adherence to the national government; and fearing that when the contest should close and Virginia was restored to her allegiance to the Union, that the same policy which in times of peace had been so unjustly exercised towards them, would be redoubled through the conscious inferiority that would haunt the memories of a traitor majority. The vote was taken on the day prescribed by the convention in August. Many of the counties in the interior were nominally in the possession of the rebels; the vote in them was necessarily small, as numbers whose hearts were in the cause were deterred by the actual or threatened presence of physical force, from participating in the election. The result however fully satisfied the expectations of the chiefs of the enterprise. The vote stood eighteen thousand four hundred and eight for the new States, and seven hundred and eighty-one against it. At this time there were nine or ten thousand soldiers in the ranks of the Union army from Western Virginia, who did not vote on the question, or at least but a small portion of them did so, and whose votes would have been united for the project; many citizens had gone south into the ranks of the rebels. These facts account for the apparent disparity of the vote on this occasion, and that given six months before on the ordinance of secession.

Delegates to the convention were sent up from all the counties now embraced in the State of West Virginia (excepting those created since its formation) except Jefferson, Berkeley, Webster and Monroe. The body convened on the 26th of November, 1861, in Wheeling, in the Federal courtroom at the Custom House. It was composed of able and enlightened men who addressed themselves to their task with a just appreciation of its consequences to themselves and posterity.

On the 14th of December, Mr. Battelle, a delegate from Ohio County, offered a series of propositions designed to be engrafted into the constitution, in relation to African slavery, that brought about great debate, which happily was sustained in a spirit of fairness and candor, not always hitherto the accompaniment of the investigation of that singularly perplexing subject. His proposition embraced a provision that slaves should not be brought into the State after the adoption of the constitution; that the legislature should have full power to make laws for the better regulation of the domestic relations of the slaves then in the State, and for the gradual removal of slavery; and that slavery or involuntary servitude except for crime should not exist after a certain period, to be designated by the convention. After a prolonged struggle the propositions were defeated by a majority of one. The convention adjourned on the 18th day of February, 1862, after having completed its labors and framed a constitution, to be submitted to the people on the 3rd day of April, 1862.

The constitution submitted comprised many radical changes in the organic law as previously adopted in Virginia. It composed the State of West Virginia out of forty-four counties, absolutely; and provided that the counties of Pendleton, Hardy, Hampshire and Morgan should also be included if a majority of the votes cast at the election on the adoption of the constitution in those counties should be in favor of that adoption; and that if these latter should be so included, then by a similar vote in the counties of Berkeley, Jefferson and Frederick, they should also be included.[1] The liberties secured to persons and the rights of property as set forth in the Virginia Bill of Rights were incorporated into the new constitution. The old system of *viva voce* voting was abrogated and that of the ballot substituted. The office of Lieutenant Governor was abolished. The old county court system, which had become in Virginia a supremely antiquated folly, was dissipated by a healthier system of judicial circuits. A still greater change in the structure of the municipal body was effected in the erection of townships for the regulating of local affairs. It was a step toward practical freedom never before permitted in Virginia. Taxation was made equal and uniform for the first time in the history of this people. A check was placed upon the system of granting the credit of the State to corporations, which had enthralled Virginia in a debt of millions. No debts were to be contracted by the State, except to meet the casual deficits, to redeem a previous liability or to defend the State in time of war. An equitable proportion of the debt of Virginia prior to January 1st, 1861, was to be assumed by the new State. The vast schemes of land piracy which had so confused the titles of real estate west of the Alelghanies, and had so retarded the settling of the country, were wholly uprooted by a provision that no further entries upon waste and unappropriated lands should be made. But the feature of the instrument that demonstrates most clearly the spirit of enlightened patriotism and enlarged sense of genuine interest in the cause of humanity, was the liberal provision for a system of free schools. All the proceeds of the public domain were appropriated to this object; giving to it everything upon which the primary basis of a State is formed. The legislature was also required to provide for the establishment of schools as soon as practicable. All the proceeds of forfeitures, confiscations and fines accruing to the State were devoted to the school fund; thus providing that the consequences of crime, should supply the source of virtue. Such parts of the common law and statutory laws of Virginia as were in force at the time the constitution went into operation and not repugnant thereto, were to remain and continue the law of West Virginia until altered or repealed by the legislature of the latter. And all offences theretofore committed against the same were to be cognizable according to the laws of Virgina.

The constitution was submitted to the people of the counties embraced within the proposed new State, on the 3rd day of April, 1862, and resulted in its adoption by a vote of eighteen thousand eight hundred and sixty two in its favor, and five hundred and fourteen against it. At the same time, some of the advanced friends of the movement held a separate poll and took an informal vote on the propositions of Mr. Battelle, and about six thousand votes were cast in favor of them. The total population of the forty-eight counties in 1860, was three hundred and thirty-four thousand, nine hundred and twenty-one whites, and twelve thousand, seven hundred and seventy-one colored.

The legislature of the reorganized government assembled on the sixth of May, following, and gave its formal assent, by the passage of a bill on the thirteenth of the same month, to the formation and erection of the State of West Virginia within the jurisdiction of the State of Virginia, according to the stipulations and provisions of the constitution of the new State. It also provided that the counties of Berkeley, Jefferson and Frederick should be included in and form a part of the State of West Virginia, whenever the voters in the same should ratify the constitution and assent thereto, at an election held for the purpose at such time and under such regulations as the commissioners named in the schedule to it, should prescribe. The act was ordered to be transmitted to the senators and representatives of Virginia in Congress, together with a copy of the constitution, with the request that they use their endeavors to obtain the consent of Congress to the admission of West Virginia into the Union.

The memorial of the legislature, together with the act granting assent to the erection of the State of West Virginia, and the constitution of the latter were presented in the senate on the 29th of May, 1862. No act was passed, however, until the December, following — approved on the 31st of the month. The act was a conditional one to have force and effect when certain provisions were complied with. The preamble recited the action of the convention, the vote of the people and the assent of the legislature; and recited the counties included within the boundaries as proposed by the constitution, inclusive of Pendleton, Hardy, Hampshire, and Morgan, and declared that the constitution was republican in form. It was therefore enacted, "That the State of West Virginia be, and is hereby, declared to be one of the United States of America, and admitted into the Union on an equal footing with the original States in all respects whatever, and until the next general census, shall be entitled to three members in the House of Representatives of the Unites States: Provided, always, that this act shall not take effect until after the proclamation of the President of the United States hereinafter provided for. It being represented to Congress that since the convention of the twenty-sixth of November, eighteen hundred and sixty-one, that framed and proposed the constitution for the said State of West Virginia, the people thereof have expressed a wish to change the seventh section of the eleventh article of said constitution by striking out the same and inserting the following in its place, viz: "The children of slaves born within the limits of this State, after the fourth day of July, eighteen hundred and sixty-three, shall be free; and that all slaves within the said State who shall at the time aforesaid, be under the age of ten years, shall be free when they arrive at the age of twenty-one years, and all slaves over ten and under twenty-one years shall be free when they arrive at the age of twenty-five years; and no slave shall be permitted to come into the State for permanent residence therein. Therefore — Sec. 2, Be it further enacted, that whenever the people of West Virginia shall, through their said convention, and by a vote to be taken at an election to be held within the limits of the said State, at such time as the convention may provide, make, and ratify the change aforesaid, and properly certify the same under the hand of the president of the convention, it shall be lawful for the President of the United States to issue his proclamation stating the fact, and thereupon this act shall take effect and be in force on and after sixty days from the date of said proclamation."

On the twelfth of February, 1863, the convention reassembled and made the change proposed in the act of Congress, and shortly afterwards finally adjourned. It adopted an address to the people of the proposed new State, reciting the several changes in the organic laws, and urging their acceptance of them. The change of the section relating to slavery became the theme of universal comment. The public mind was accustomed to regard the institution as one wholly unsuited to the character and habits of the people of this section, yet the prejudices of the past were not without their potency. To many the question of congressional dictation, as it was termed, was a dangerous acquiescence in a bad precedent. Such arguments were generally at the suggestion of those, whose faith was waning in the cause, or who were in open sympathy with the rebels of the east; few real friends of the movement were affected by them. The address of the convention to the people on this subject stated plainly the issue.

The objection most insisted on relates to the change of the seventh section of the eleventh article of the constitution. By some it is urged that the imposition of a condition by Congress on the admission of a new State into the Union is a dangerous precedent, and derogatory to those accepting it. This objection comes too late. The precedent is already the rule rather than the exception, as few States have been admitted without the acceptance of some condition prescribed by Congress. Changes of boundary, the taxation of public lands, trial by jury, the use of the English language in public proceedings, as well as the prohibition of slavery, have been the subjects of these conditions. The admission of new states by Congress is not, under the United States constitution, obligatory, but merely discretionary. The words are: 'New States *may* be admitted into the Union.' It is as true in law as in mathematics, that the greater includes the less. If Congress can constitutionally refuse its consent to the admission of a State, it may certainly prescribe terms to admission within constitutional limits.

"This objection would not probably be pressed if the alleged condition related to some other subject than slavery, or if that subject had not been for so many years an element of party strife. There is so much prejudice, both for and against it existence in any locality, that the merits of a particular case are overlooked or ignored, and the prejudices on the general subject are permitted to decide it. With the latter we shall not concern ourselves in this address, as we do not think that abstract question of the propriety of the continuance or abolition of slavery should affect the vote you are called upon to give. The true question for your decision is, whether the continuance of the slavery existing within the limits of the proposed State promises any practical benefit to its people, and if so, whether the promised benefit is sufficient to induce you to forego the many positive and decided advantages which you can not obtain unless the proposed State is erected?

"There is one class of objectors whom we do not desire to conciliate while they retain their present views, and to whom, therefore, we have nothing to say. Of those who are traitors in heart, if not yet in act, and whose sympathy with rebels in arms has overcome their consciousness of duty to their country, it is sufficient to remark that their opposition is necessarily factious, and their object the injury and not the welfare of their loyal fellow-citizens. But there are others whom we are earnestly desirous to convince that the proposed State is worth greatly more than the price that will, in any event, be paid for it; and that the effort to secure it now, is not only sanctioned but demanded by every consideration of duty to themselves and their posterity.

"The convention at its first session was nearly equally divided as to the propriety of inserting in the constitution a clause providing for gradual emancipation. There was at that time no one in or out of the convention who contended that the perpetuation of slavery, as it existed in the proposed State, would be of any practical importance. Some desired to avoid the contention the agitation the question would inevitably engender, while others thought that without the insertion of such a clause the consent of Congress would not be given. It was admitted on all hands, and cannot be denied, that causes, unconnected with the rebellion, and beyond human control, were at work, which within a very few years must extinguish slavery within the proposed State. It was not denied that in a grain growing, manufacturing and commercial community, the labor of slaves is unprofitable, except perhaps as domestic servants. It was known that in twenty-seven of the forty-eight counties there had been a decrease in their respective numbers of slaves from 1850 to 1860, and in only thirteen counties an actual increase. The numbers in the years given were 14,210 and 12,783. The decrease was 2,661, and the increase including those in the eight counties formed after 1850, was 1,234; giving a net decrease of ten per cent, or 1,427 to which should be added a number equal to the whole natural increase. Those therefore who opposed the emancipation clause, did not contend that its insertion would injuriously affect the proposed State: but, on the contrary, insisted, that the causes mentioned above would extinguish slavery more rapidly and surely than any system of gradual emancipation could, if their operation was withdrawn.

"Under these circumstances a compromise clause was agreed on, which received the unanimous vote of the convention, and was inserted in the constitution. It provided, simply, that slaves should not be brought into the State for permanent residence, and was accepted and ratified by the vote adopting the constitution in April, 1862. Thus both the convention and the people have signified their willingness, that the natural causes tending to the extinction of slavery should not be counteracted in their operation. There were slaveholders both in the convention and among the people, who voted for this compromise, and they must be allowed to be able to determine what their interests required or permit, as many among the most vociferous of the objectors who have no personal interest in slavery. That it is doomed to rapid diminution, whether aided by law or constitution, or not, must be apparent to every intelligent citizen.

"The question then presents itself for your considation, whether the great and important advantages you are sure to derive from the erection of the proposed State, shall be postponed until slavery dies the natural death to which it is hastening? This is what you are called upon to do when asked to reject the amendment proposed by Congress. Slavery cannot be perpetuated by its rejection; and, as it exists among us, it cannot be of any service in a public point of view. With or without emancipation, the proposed State, will be to all intents and purposes a free State, and its legislation and social condition will necessarily be controlled by that fact."

The vote on the constitution as amended was taken on the 26th of March, 1863, as provided for by the convention at the session in February, preceding. It resulted in its adoption by a majority of about twenty-seven thousand. The majority, had the ten thousand soldiers in the Union army from the forty-eight counties participated in the election, would have been increased about that number.[2] The result having been certified to the President of the United States, as provided for by the act of Congress, he on the 20th[3] of April, following, issued his proclamation. The convention prior to adjourning in February, 1863, provided that, if a majority of the votes cast at the election in March, should be in favor of the adoption of the amended constitution, then an election should be held on the fourth Thursday of May, following, to choose members of both branches of the legislature, a Governor and other State officers, judges of the Supreme Court of Appeals, judges of the various circuit courts, and county officers. An election was accordingly held at that period, when members of the Senate and House of Delegates were chosen in nearly all of the counties, and Hon. A. I. Boreman, of Wood County, was chosen as the first Governor of the State of West Virginia; Samuel Crane, of Randolph, Auditor; Campbell Tarr, of Brooke, Treasurer; J. Edgar Boyers, of Tyler, Secretary of State, and A. Bolton Caldwell, of Ohio, Attorney

General. Hons. Ralph L. Berkshire, of Monongalia, William A. Harrison, of Harrison, and James H. Brown, of Kanawha, were elected judges of the Supreme Court of Appeals. These officers were all chosen without opposition. Judges wre also elected in all of the circuits but two, which latter were in the disputed ground between the contending forces of the war. County officers were elected in nearly all of the counties, excepting, perhaps, those embraced in the two judicial circuits just mentioned.

When, therefore, the period of sixty days from the date of the President's proclamation had elapsed, the 20th of June 1863, the new State of West Virginia had a government, consisting of all the departments, legislative, executive and judicial, provided for by the constitution; justices of the peace and other local officers held over, under an ordinance of the convention, until their successors were elected or appointed. It was not without means either, as the General Assembly of Virginia, by an act passed February 3rd, 1863, granted all the property and the proceeds of all fines, forfeitures, confiscations and all uncollected taxes belonging to and accrued or accruing to that State within the counties embraced in the boundaries of the new State, to it. It also appropriated the sum of one hundred and fifty thousand dollars out of the treasury of the State of Virginia, by an act passed February 4th, 1863. The justice of this latter act, to the people of the new State, can not be questioned, as the whole sum had been collected from them since the reorganization of the government of Virginia.

Governor Pierpoint removed the seat of government of Virginia from Wheeling to Alexandria, prior to the inauguraiton of Governor Boreman, [sic; Mr. Hagans is wrong!]which took place on the 20th of June, 1863, in Wheeling, which had been designated by the convention as the seat of government of West Virginia, until it should be permanently located by the legislature. Both houses of the legislature assembled on the same day and began the labor of altering the laws and enacting such others as were necessary to conform to the requirements of the organic law and the condition of affairs.

Thus were the hopes of the peoples of Western Virginia confirmed by the complete realization of a long cherished desire. They felt released from a bondage no less galling, when the animus of the age is considered, than that of the ancient Israelites in Egypt. They felt too, that although the scheme had been accomplished amid the dire scenes of confusion accompanying civil commontions, yet they had proceeded upon the strong foundations of wellknown precedents, established law and incontrovertible principles. Precedents are numerous in monarchial governments, for the restoration of a head when the power in authority usurps any functions not in accordance with the original grant, with how much greater force can the right apply in a republic where the people are sovereign. The reorganized or restored government of Virginia at Wheeling being the true government of the State, *de jure* as well as *de facto,* the consent of its General Assembly to the formation of the State of West Virginia was an incident of its power as undoubtedly as the right to enact any other law. That consent and the assent of Congress was all that was necessary to complete the formation, under the constitution of the United States. If the power or authority of that instrument be denied or defied, as was attempted in the late effort at secession, then indeed is the whole question open to the suspicion of doubt as to its validity and legality. But, if secession is wrong, the question is no longer one for argument; it is truth itself. Secession has been weighed in the balances. In the language of an eminent jurist, "after having been discussed in the senate hall, the cabinet chamber and on the hustings with as much zeal and ability as perhaps any other question ever was, it has been definitely decided by the legislative and executive departments of the national government, and by most of the States also. It has also been tried at the grand assize of popular suffrage, and a true verdict rendered by the American people. And last, but not least, it has been tried and determined by the wager of battle."

To retain the freedom thus acquired, it only remains for the people of West Virginia to keep constantly in view those great cardinal points of patriotism, obedience to law, honor, courage, and devotion to liberty.

---

[1]The counties of Berkeley and Jefferson did not vote on the adoption of the constitution at the time the question was submitted to the remaining part of the State, but the General Assemby of Virginia passed an act for the former on the 31st of January, 1863, and for the latter on the 4th of February, following, providing that polls should be opened on the fourth Thursday of May, ensuing, for the purpose of taking the sense of the qualified voters of these counties on the question of including them within the boundaries of West Virginia; and if a majority of the votes cast at that election was in favor of being so included, the Governor of Virginia should certify the same under the seal of the State, to the Governor of West Virginia, and that then those counties should become a part of West Virginia, when the legislature of the latter should consent to the same. Subsequently, on the 5th of August, 1863, the legislature of West Virginia gave its consent to the admission of Berkeley, and provided for the election of county officers; similar enactment was had in the case of Jefferson County on the 2nd day of November, 1863. A question having arisen as to whether the act of Congress admitting West Virginia into the Union under the constitution adopted by the people embraced these counties, a subsequent act was passed by the thirty-ninth Congress, at its first session, legalizing the transfer of the counties by the State of Virginia to West Virginia.

[2]In the errata of the first edition of this volume it appears that the vote was taken in the various regiments of soldiers in the Federal Army, by agents sent for that purpose, to the regiments of the State enlisted under the re-organized government.

[3]In the first edition it is erroneously stated as the 19th of April. This correction is made at the instance of Mr. Hagans.

Biographical Sketch of the Author

Born in Wheeling, W. Va., September 1904, son of Julian Green Hearne and Lydia Herts Cromwell Hearne.

Education. Wheeling public schools; Linsly Institute, Wheeling; The Manlius School (R.O.T.C.), Manlius, N.Y.; Washington & Jefferson College, B.S. (political science, major) 1926; College of Law, West Virginia University, J.D. 1930; The Infantry School, Fort Benning, Ga., 1937 and 1941; Strategic Intelligence School; and other Army institutions.

First civilian career, 1930-March 1941. Practiced law in Wheeling; Active in political and civic affairs; Republican nominee for House of Delegates 1932, and for State Senate 1934; Wrote Wheeling's nonpartisan council-manager form of government 1935, organized and led citizen's organization which beat city hall in 1935 and this charter is still in force after fifty years; Became charter consultant in various other eastern cities for charater campaigns; Active in Reserve Officers Association in Wheeling and in West Virginia.

Career as a soldier. Ordered to extended active duty as an infantry reserve major in late March, 1941, and assigned to 24th United States Infantry Regiment at Fort Benning, Georgia. Participated in Louisiana and Carolina maneuvers 1941; Left Fort Benning as battalion commander and went with regiment to San Francisco and sailed overseas in April 1942. War time service in the New Hebrides, Solomons; Marianas and Ryukyu Islands; Promoted to lieutenant colonel September 1942; assumed command of the regiment on Guadalcanal in September 1943; promoted to full colonel July 14, 1944; regiment engaged in "mopping-up" in the Marianas and in the Kerama Retto (small island group twenty miles west of Okinawa); Accepted first formal surrender by a Japanese garrison in history on 22 August (local date) 1945; returned stateside Sept. 1945; Chief of West Virginia Military District 1946-1947; Legislative Laison officer for Department of the Army 1948-1952; Army Language School and other schools 1952 — school system until 1953; Army Attache, American Embassy, Wellington, New Zealand, April 1953-September 1956; Intelligence Directorate, Office Joint Chiefs of Staff from then until retirement 1 July 1960. *Combat Infantryman's Badge* and *Legion of Merit;*

and campaign stars for Solomons, Marianas and Ryukyus.

Second Civilian Career July 1960-1 July 1975. No occupation from 1 July 1960 until early 1964, while residing in Alexandria, Virginia. Became rapt in newly developed hobby of learning the history of the Restored Government of Virginia and the Pierpont administration. With the files of the *"Alexandria Gazette"* (oldest newspaper in America from its founding until present time, without interruption). Many, many choice historical notes obtained. Also Library of Congress and the Alexandria Library were invaluable sources of learning, among numerous sources in the Metropolitan area. Became editor of lawbooks and city and county charters and ordinances with Equity Publishing Company in Orford, New Hampshire from 1964-67; thereafter in Charlottesville, Virginia, until final retirement in July, 1975, on the editorial staff of the Michie Company, mainly devoted to city and county charters and codes of ordinance.

Memberships. Phi Gamma Delta, Alpha Chapter, W. & J. College; Phi Delta Phi, College of Law, West Virginia University; Honorary Scabbard and Blade, ROTC unit, West Virginia University; Reserve Officers Association of the U.S.; Retired Officers Association; American Legion; Honorary Life Member, The Woman's Club of Wheeling; Episcopalian.

Family. Married Lenora Hensley, Charleston, West Virginia, August 1947; she had just been discharged from Army Nurse Corps (with rank of captain) after having served under General MacArthur in the Pacific; she was mother to my daughter Mary Lee and my son Richard C. Mrs. Hearne graduated from this life (cancer) in January 1974, in Charlottesville. Daughter now married to Mr. Allen C. Barringer, residing in McLean, Virginia, she is mother of triplets and one daughter born later. Son Richard married Beth McConkey, they have two sons, Brian and Lee, and reside in Landenburg, Pennsylvania. He is a partner with William Groff in the business of providing forest services of all kinds, including buying timber, etc. Mrs. R. C. Hearne graduated this life in 1986.

Miscellaneous. Have traveled in each of the fifty states except Alaska; Have traveled in all Canadian provinces except Newfoundland, new Brunswick, Nova Scotia and Prince Edward Island; have been in Tia Juana, and Augua Caliente. Have traveled to Panama, Haiti, Australia, Fiji, and in Europe, as well as other places hereinbefore mentioned. Have walked on crater of Vesuvius and am an initiate in to the Blackfeet Tribe of American Indians. Threw overboard a letter in a bottle from middle of Atlantic between mouth of St. Lawrence River and shores of Ireland, and letter returned to me from Rekvick on the Island Kvaloi, Norway. Threw another letter in bottle from half-way mark from Wellington, New Zealand to Panama City, and letter returned to me from Fiji.

Music Hobby. It was a well known fact during World War II that anyone who spent at least a year on any uncivilized Pacific "rock" (island) would develop some form of insanity. Well, I spent three and a half years on various Pacific rocks and my case became acute. Now I cannot nor could not read or write chords of music, whether treble or bass, nor could I nor can I play any musical instrument. Nevertheless, on Guadalcanal after the island had been declared secure I composed both music and wrote lyrics for numerous songs, one of which, a hymn, *"God Sustain Our Arms Today"* was broadcast over the NBC radio blue network on Palm Sunday and on Easter Sunday 1944 by the Wheeling Steel Company's "Musical Steelmakers" and the "Singing Mill Men and Mill Maids" from the capitol theatre in Wheeling. It was so well received that the company had several thousand copies of the piano score printed and sent to inquirers all over the states. Then Armed Forces Radio Service picked it up and it was literally broadcast around the world . . . My first assignment after the war was West Virgnia Military District, and the spring of 1946 in West Virginia was beautiful, after the desolute Pacific Islands. *"West Virginia, My Home Sweet Home"* was then composed by me and the 1947 legislature adopted it as an official state song. All told, I have had a number of my works played by the United States Army Band, The United States Army Field Band, The United States Military Academy Band (West Point); The United States Air Force Band; West Virginia University Band; Mark Warnow's Hollywood Band, and Bill Seveci's Band in Auckland, New Zealand. The number played by the West Point Band, *"Kiwi Soldiers March,"* I gave to the New Zealand Army Fund and the U.S. Copyright I placed in the name of the C.G.S., New Zealand Army; and my wife, having been elected to the board of directors of the New Zealand Y.W.C.A., I gave that organization one of my popular number Polynesian type songs. It was on the "Hit Parade" in that country for several weeks. My latest number is to the same melody as *"God Sustain Our Arms Today,"* my World War II hymn; but I have a new lyric, and the title is *"God Bless Our Defenders,"* — and "defenders" includes all the armed services, the Coast Guard and the astronauts engaged in defense positions. So far it has no sponsor. And aside from all that, I have become an expert on doing NOTHING! . . . This is my first, and quite likely my last, published book.

Caveat: Use of the term "historian" as befitting myself. While I believe I have fully qualified myself to be referred to accurately as "a" historian, I must make clear that my specialty is strictly confined to the Restored Government of Virginia and to the Pierpont administration from June 1861 to April 1868. I do not profess any special expertise on Wheeling or West Virginia history, except during the period that the seat of government of Virginia (the entire Commonwealth, *de jure*) was located at Wheeling. I've forgotten when the Wheeling suspension bridge was completed, although at the time it was erected it was the longest suspension bridge in the world. (Nevertheless, if any one wants to buy the present suspension bridge, I'll be happy to sell all my right title and interest therein to any willing purchaser at a very reasonable price.)

Prior published works. An abridged account of the Restored Government of Virginia written by me in the early 1970s is set forth in Jim Comstock's *West Virginia Heritage Encyclopedia,* Vol. 17, beginning at page 3728, captioned "Francis Pierpont, Virginia View." (I don't know who wrote that caption, for it certainly contains much that is in conflict with the traditional Virginia "Party Line." It was submitted while I resided in Charlottesville, and the compiler of the manuscripts evidently identified me as a Virginian) . . . My first article on the subject was published in *West Virginia Law Review*, December, 1963 (The Centennial Year of West Virginia), under the title "Some Unpublicized History of West Virginia and the Restored Government of Virginia." Numerous newspaper articles by me have been publicized in Wheeling newspapers and sometimes in Alexandria (Virginia) newspapers; and *West Virginia Hillbilly* over the years has been a frequent publisher of my articles.